BENCH PRESS

BENCH PRESS

The Collision of Courts, Politics, and the Media

Edited by Keith J. Bybee

STANFORD LAW AND POLITICS
An Imprint of Stanford University Press
Stanford, California

Stanford University Press
Stanford, California

©2007 by the Board of Trustees of the Leland Stanford Junior University.
All rights reserved.

Printed in the United States of America on acid-free, archival-quality paper

Library of Congress Cataloging-in-Publication Data

Bench press : the collision of courts, politics, and the media / Edited by Keith J. Bybee.

   p. cm.

 Includes bibliographical references and index.

 ISBN 978-0-8047-5677-8 (cloth : alk. paper)

  1. Political questions and judicial power—United States. 2. Judges—Selection and appointment—United States. 3. Mass media and judicial power—United States. I. Bybee, Keith J., 1965-

KF5130.B46 2007

347.73'14—dc22

        2007007299

Designed by Bruce Lundquist
Typeset at Stanford University Press in 10/14 Minion

Contents

Acknowledgments

THE ESSAYS COLLECTED IN THIS VOLUME grew out of a conference on judicial independence held in October 2005 at the JW Marriott Hotel in Washington, D.C. The conference was called, "Bench Press: The Collision of Media, Politics, Public Pressure, and an Independent Judiciary," and was organized as a collaborative effort between Syracuse University's College of Law, Maxwell School of Citizenship and Public Affairs, and S.I. Newhouse School of Public Communications.

The Honorable Joanne Alper, in discussion with SU Chancellor Nancy Cantor and College of Law Dean Hannah Arterian, conceived of the initial idea for the "Bench Press" conference in early 2005. In a remarkably short period of time, the original conference plans were developed and implemented by a diverse, cross-disciplinary organizing committee: Dean Arterian (Law), Dean Mitchel Wallerstein (Maxwell), Dean David Rubin (Newhouse), The Honorable Joanne Alper, The Honorable Rosemary Pooler, Professor Lisa Dolak (Law), Professor Mark Obbie (Newhouse), Professor Keith Bybee (Maxwell), Nicci Brown (Institutional Advancement), and Bert Kaufman (Law and Newhouse).

In addition to featuring nearly two dozen prominent speakers from the academy, the media, the judiciary, and the bar, the "Bench Press" conference also presented new court-related data from Syracuse University's October 2005 Maxwell Poll. Professors Alasdair Roberts and Jeffrey Stonecash co-directed the Maxwell Poll and both helped translate the interests of the conference planning committee into a set of workable poll questions. Jeff provided additional assistance with organizing the poll results into readily accessible form.

The findings from the Maxwell Poll provided a unifying theme for the "Bench Press" conference and are discussed at some length in the introduction to this volume.

At Syracuse University, the organization of these essays into a book was greatly facilitated by Kelley Coleman's precise transcription and by Cheryl Ficarra's timely fiscal management. Bert Kaufman performed extraordinarily deft editorial and administrative work at a variety of critical junctures. It is no exaggeration to say that without Bert neither the "Bench Press" conference nor this edited volume would have been possible.

At Stanford University Press, Amanda Moran provided excellent advice on how to fashion a coherent interdisciplinary text. Jared Smith, Sarah Ives, Cheryl Hauser, and Judith Hibbard ably guided the manuscript through the production and copyediting process. The two anonymous reviewers of the manuscript provided a number of insightful criticisms. The contributors' efforts to respond to the reviewers' criticisms made for a better, more tightly interlinked set of arguments.

Closer to home, my wife, Jennifer Champa Bybee, and my children, Evan and Ava, all provided indispensable support. I have found that a happy editor is a productive editor. As the wellspring of my happiness, my family deserves substantial credit for moving the manuscript along.

In closing, I should note that this volume is not the only product of the 2005 "Bench Press" conference. As this manuscript goes to press in the fall of 2007, Syracuse University is launching a first-of-its-kind interdisciplinary research institute devoted to the study of issues at the intersection of law, politics, and the press. It is called the Institute for the Study of the Judiciary, Politics, and the Media at Syracuse University (IJPM). Like the "Bench Press" conference that preceded it, IJPM is a joint effort between the College of Law, Maxwell, and Newhouse. IJPM will sponsor lectures, conferences, and symposia designed to foster discussion and debate between legal scholars, sitting judges, and working journalists. IJPM will provide research grants and seed money for scholars pursuing law-oriented projects that cut across traditional academic boundaries. IJPM will also host a luncheon series for graduate students featuring prominent jurists, journalists, and academic experts. And, as the program grows, IJPM plans to establish a cross-disciplinary certificate program at the College of Law. IJPM's activities and progress can be tracked at http://jpm.syr.edu.

K.J.B.

Syracuse, 2007

BENCH PRESS

Introduction

The Two Faces of Judicial Power

Keith J. Bybee

WELL OVER TWO HUNDRED YEARS AGO, during the ratification debates over the Constitution, Alexander Hamilton argued that the "complete independence of the courts of justice is peculiarly essential" for American government. Judicial independence protects constitutional guarantees from overreaching "legislative encroachments" as well as from the "ill humors" of "designing men." Hamilton insisted that without independent judges to police the polity "all the reservations of particular rights or privileges [in the Constitution] would amount to nothing."[1]

Hamilton's view has long been the conventional one, endorsed by the American Bar Association and extolled at confirmation hearings and Constitution Day celebrations. Even so, Hamilton's view has not gone uncontested. Indeed, his claims about the glories of judicial independence were questioned in his own day. The Anti-federalist opponents of the Constitution feared the power of a politically insulated judiciary: "independent of the people, of the legislature, and of every power under heaven," judges were ultimately bound to "feel themselves independent of heaven itself."[2] Rather than guaranteeing the protection of individual rights, judicial independence threatened to create vast opportunities for judicial elites to pursue their own interests under the guise of unbiased adjudication. The only solution, according to the Anti-federalists, was to constrain judicial power by somehow rendering it accountable to the people.

Associate Professor of Political Science and Michael O. Sawyer Chair of Constitutional Law and Politics at Syracuse University's Maxwell School of Citizenship and Public Affairs

The disagreement between Hamilton and his opponents is not merely of historical interest. Recent poll results indicate that the conventional understanding of judicial independence as a prerequisite for the protection of rights is locked in close competition with a contrary understanding of judicial independence as an opportunity for judges to advance their political goals. In many respects, the public seems just as likely to celebrate the virtues of an impartial and independent judiciary as it is to believe that judicial decision making is simply the pursuit of partisan politics by other means.

What can be made of these two competing views of the judiciary? How does the mix of legal principle and political skepticism that surrounds the bench affect judicial independence and the role of courts in our democracy? Scholars have explored these questions, yet they have typically done so in isolation from the practitioners and professionals that participate in and report about the American judiciary. In a first-of-its-kind effort, this volume brings together academics and practitioners to assess questions of judicial independence and judicial legitimacy from a variety of viewpoints. The essays collected here examine the current status of the American courts from the perspective of the legal academy and political science, from the perspective of sitting judges at the federal and state level, and from the perspective of working journalists. In the pages that follow, readers will find judges reflecting on the methods of selection that put them on the bench, reporters critiquing the media in which they operate, and scholars charting large-scale changes in the ways in which the judiciary is staffed and perceived. The end result is a series of different conclusions about how and whether a consensus understanding of the American courts can be achieved.

In this introduction, I begin with a discussion of the poll results illustrating the public's conflicting understandings of judicial power. As we shall see, the poll results not only illuminate the contradictory contours of public opinion but also suggest that the public's beliefs are closely related to the way in which the media covers the courts. After my discussion of the poll results, I provide an overview of the essays that make up this volume.

The Maxwell Poll

To begin, consider the idea that judges use their independence to advance political agendas. In the fall of 2005, Syracuse University's Maxwell Poll posed a battery of court-related questions as part of a nationwide survey.[3] According to the Maxwell Poll, an astounding 82 percent of those surveyed believe that the partisan background of judges influences court decision making either some or a lot. This view is shared by very different groups. An overwhelming majority of liberals, conservatives, people who attend religious services several times a week, and people who never attend religious services all agree that partisanship does not switch off when judicial robes are put on.[4]

For many, belief in the political nature of judicial decisions translates directly into doubts about the sincerity of judicial pronouncements. A majority of poll respondents agree that even though judges always say that their decisions flow from the law and the Constitution, many judges are in fact basing their decisions on their own personal beliefs. Judges may consistently "talk law," but most Americans suspect that judges are simply "doing politics."

Given the widespread agreement that partisanship skews judicial decision making, one would expect large segments of the public to view judicial selection in political terms. The Maxwell Poll confirms this expectation. Among those surveyed, Republicans are eight times more likely than Democrats to trust the president and Senate to pick good federal judges. Moreover, three-fourths of respondents reject the idea that fewer judges should be subject to popular election. Clearly, most Americans understand judicial selection to be a political process and think it makes sense to organize judicial selection in a political way.

What are the sources of the public's political perception of the courts? For many Americans, the media seems to play a critical role. According to the Maxwell Poll, 68 percent of those surveyed agree that media coverage of the courts pays more attention to partisan affiliation than to the reasoning that judges use to justify their decisions. Indeed, the poll results suggest that the greatest consumers of media coverage are the most likely to view the courts as political actors.[5] Those respondents who watch television news every day are far more likely than those who never watch television news to see partisan factors at work in judicial decision making (a similar, albeit weaker, relationship holds when those who read a newspaper every day are compared to those who never read a newspaper).[6] Daily television news watchers are also far more likely to say that the number of judicial elections should be increased and somewhat more likely to assert that judges base their decisions on personal belief rather than on the law and the Constitution (again, the story is similar with daily newspaper readers).[7]

What of the idea that independent judges are impartial guardians of our constitutional rights? In spite of the widely shared belief that judging is influenced by politics (a belief that is coupled with the commonly held opinion that judges often merely pretend their decisions are derived from the law and the Constitution), most Americans do not think that the rule of law is simply the rule of men. Next to the finding that an overwhelming majority of Americans believe partisanship affects judicial decision making, the most lopsided majority tapped by the Maxwell Poll came in response to a question about the value of judicial independence. When asked whether judges should be shielded from outside pressure and allowed to make decisions based on their own independent reading of the law, a remarkable 73 percent of those surveyed agreed.

The majority in favor of shielding judges from politics holds straight across party lines: three-fourths or more of Democrats and Republicans agree that the courts should be independent. The same is true of self-described liberals, moderates, and conservatives. And the results are also no different when responses are broken down according to frequency of church attendance. Americans who go to church several times a week support the ideal of judicial independence in the same large numbers as Americans who never attend church at all. Similar results hold for daily television news watchers and daily newspaper readers—two groups that are otherwise inclined to see judging in political terms. In fact, even among those respondents who *disagreed* with the statement "you can generally trust public officials to do the right thing," the idea that judges should be insulated from outside pressure received a high level of support.[8]

The widely shared desire to preserve judicial independence clearly reflects a popular aspiration—and it also reflects a broad-based recognition that, whatever else might be said about the politics of judging, a wide variety of citizens rely on the courts to resolve disputes. When asked why so many conflicts end up in the courts, only a small percentage of Americans blamed politicians for failing to deal with the controversies in the first place and an even smaller percentage blamed judges for actively reaching out to decide hot-button issues.[9] Instead, almost half of those surveyed say that courts are at the center of so many conflicts because the people themselves demand that the judiciary get involved.[10] Many Americans believe, in other words, that the courts respond to the demands of the citizenry as a whole. Given this belief, judicial independence makes good sense: it is by allowing judges to make decisions without pressure from specific groups or parties that the judiciary is able to preserve the trust and interests of its broad public.

In sum, the overall picture painted by the Maxwell Poll is decidedly mixed.

On one hand, large majorities of Americans see the influence of partisanship on the judicial process. On the other hand, large majorities of Americans believe that the courts are special venues in which political pressure and partisan squabbling have no place. The Hamiltonian faith in the importance of judicial independence and impartial decision making is alive and well, but so too is the suspicion that judges are advancing political goals under the cover of legal principle.

Essays in this Volume

What, then, is the significance of the public's conflicting views? In the fall of 2005, Syracuse University organized a conference in Washington, DC, to discuss the Maxwell Poll and the issues its results raised.[11] The conference was a collaborative effort involving the College of Law, the Maxwell School of Citizenship and Public Affairs, and the S.I. Newhouse School of Public Communications. Participants were drawn from the ranks of legal scholars, political scientists, judges, and journalists. The result was a wide-ranging discussion about the state of judicial independence and the larger context in which public perception of the courts has been formed.

The collection of essays in this volume grew directly out of the conference. Part I features two essays that examine historical background and trends. In the first essay, the legal scholar Charles Gardner Geyh charts the rise of efforts to ensure public confidence in the courts by regulating the appearance of judicial impropriety. Geyh argues that the preoccupation with judicial appearance began in the early twentieth century. With image-based, media-generated impressions central to the public understanding of government affairs and with successive waves of anti-court criticism emanating from both ends of the political spectrum, regulators became increasingly concerned with ensuring that judges project the right public persona. As consequence, the Canons of Judicial Ethics, enforced in all fifty states, now require judges to avoid the appearance of impropriety in all their activities.

As well-established as the regulation of judicial appearances is today, Geyh notes that it is also under serious assault. Many claim that it is better to allow judges to speak and to act however they please. Judges will benefit, the argument goes, because their rights of free speech and free association will be liberated from the restrictive shackles of current law. The public will benefit, too. When judges say what they really think and behave as they truly wish, then the public will know exactly what kind of judges it is getting. If a specific litigant believes that a judge's past statements and acts will bias the judge's handling of a case, then the litigant can petition to have the judge disqualified. In this way, good judges will be rewarded and bad judges will be punished. Public confidence in the courts will be sustained precisely because judges will be given ample opportunity to express their political views and personal beliefs.

Although Geyh seriously doubts that any regulatory regime in which judges are encouraged to air their prejudices will actually work, he worries that such a regime is on the horizon. In the second essay of Part I, the political scientist G. Alan Tarr suggests that Geyh has good reason to be concerned, at least at the level of state courts. Tarr examines the "hyper-politization" of state judicial elections that has taken place in recent years as races for judicial seats have grown as costly and as contentious as campaigns for ordinary political office.[12] Canvassing judicial elections around the country, Tarr details the growing reliance on television advertising, the intense pressure for fund-raising, and the heightened involvement of single-issue interest groups and political parties. Tarr argues that the trend toward more aggressively political judicial elections is driven in part by the spread of two-party competition throughout the nation, and in part by the increasing involvement of state supreme courts in highly controversial issues like tort reform, abortion, and same-sex marriage. Opposing political groups recognize the importance of state court decision making and are all too willing to battle for control of the state bench.

At root, Tarr links the politicization of state judicial elections to shifts in public opinion. The argument for insulating judges from politics rests on the notion that judges ought to be made responsive to the law rather than to partisan pressure. "Implicit in this rule-of-law argument," Tarr writes, "are two key assumptions, namely, that the law provides a standard that can guide judicial decisions and that it is possible to assess judicial fidelity to law."[13] Unfortunately, the public increasingly doubts that judicial decisions flow from the law in a concrete, verifiable fashion. As public skepticism about the constraints of legal principle continues to grow, it makes more and more sense to select judges purely on the basis of political preference.

Taken together, the essays by Geyh and Tarr sound a note of alarm, warning that judicial independence and impartiality are under pressure and, perhaps, on the verge of collapse. The two essays identify powerful new political forces that threaten to change the judiciary in unprecedented and dangerous ways.

The next four essays in Part II, written by sitting judges, strike a different tone. Even as they acknowledge that many people see the judiciary as being in a state of crisis, the judges are generally confident that the integrity and stature of the judiciary can be maintained by working with existing institutions. Of course, a cynic might give little weight to such views on the grounds that sitting judges are bound to be satisfied with the status quo rules that put the judges on the bench in the first place. But this cynical conclusion is surely too quick. Although people may have a natural tendency to favor the rules under which they have succeeded, that does not mean that the reasons any given individual offers in favor of an existing practice must therefore be dismissed out of hand. As Hamilton once noted, in public debate what ultimately matters is that arguments "be open to all and may be judged of by all" regardless of what motives may be alleged.[14]

In the first essay of Part II, Harold See, a member of the Alabama Supreme Court, provides a general taxonomy of judicial selection processes in the United States. In order to evaluate the merits of each selection process, See argues that one must consider the position that the courts are expected to occupy in American government. More specifically, See argues that we should seek a judiciary that is capable of holding its ground against the encroachments of other branches. Thus, we should value judicial selection processes that create courts with enough independence to fend off the executive and the legislature, with enough popular legitimacy to have genuine power, and with enough knowledge and character not to abuse the power bestowed by legitimacy.

See finds that the popular election of judges actually looks quite good when measured against the appropriate criteria of judicial strength. Examining some of the same events and trends that Geyh and Tarr find alarming, See argues that the condemnation of judicial elections has overlooked the connections between elections and a vigorous judiciary. It is true, as critics charge, that judicial election campaigns can become expensive and contentious when competing interests have a stake in the race. But See contends that the involvement of competing interests will inject financial resources and heated disagreement into any judicial selection process. The real question, then, is not whether money and mudslinging can be expunged from judicial selection, but whether the courts are ultimately made stronger with these factors exposed by the publicity of an election or concealed by the behind-the-scenes maneuvers of an appointment. See maintains that the long-run vitality and power of the courts are well served when the public knows what is going on.

In the next essay, James E. Graves, Jr., a member of the Mississippi

Supreme Court, reflects on his experiences being appointed to the bench and running for judicial office. Graves, like See, argues that regardless of whether judges are selected by election or appointment the process will be fraught with politics. Although Graves prefers elections (in his view elections, unlike appointments, tend to avoid the problem of allowing a small minority to select judges), his recognition that politics is pervasive leads Graves to worry less about the nature of any given judicial selection process than about whether judicial candidates have made conscious choices to set aside personal views in the interests of justice. The key to judicial independence and impartiality is not how judges get onto the bench, but whether they choose the common good over individual preference once in office.

Graves argues that legal history is filled with examples of judges making the right choice, as the nine members of the Supreme Court did when they decided *Brown v. Board of Education* on the basis of "what was good for those plaintiffs, what was good for those schools, and, ultimately, what was good for our democracy."[15] Judges today can make the same choice as the justices who decided *Brown*. In fact, judges today have the additional benefit of being able to use the media to educate the public about the judiciary's appropriate role, thereby making it easier to make the right choice. Some judges may resist talking to reporters out of fear of being misrepresented in the press. But judges and reporters should be able to work together because "[t]he fact is both the media and the courts need each other."[16] The media can improve their coverage of the courts by developing relationships with judges; in turn, judges can improve the public's understanding of what courts actually do by using the media to disseminate accurate information.

In his essay, John M. Walker, Jr., Chief Judge of the United States Court of Appeals for the Second Circuit, examines the federal judicial selection process. Like Graves, Walker argues not only that judges must subordinate their judgment to impersonal legal principles and processes, but that properly constrained judicial behavior must be effectively communicated to the public. Thus, Walker, like Graves, contends that other actors must be enlisted to help judges broadcast undistorted information about how courts actually function. We need a "new partnership between a press that works hard to understand the difference between a judge's political views and the legal tools that he or she employs to decide a case, and politicians who not only recognize this difference but refrain from capitalizing on the public perception that judging is just politics by another name."[17]

Walker does not, however, believe that the good offices of sympathetic politicians and a hard-working press corps are completely sufficient to the task. Examining the confirmation hearings of Supreme Court nominees John Roberts and Samuel Alito, Walker argues that the unmediated voices of the nominees themselves play a major role in communicating the proper understanding of the judicial process. Federal court nominees have a chance to speak directly to the public and the chance should not be squandered. "One might reasonably expect," Walker writes, "that a few clear sentences from a nominee carry more weight than ten minutes of senatorial oration."[18]

In the final essay of Part II, Joanne F. Alper, a judge on the Virginia Circuit Court, surveys some of the same concerns that trouble Graves and Walker. She finds the judiciary is often "caught in the middle of a highly politicized and emotional atmosphere" advanced by a sensationalist media and self-interested politicians. Moreover, Alper claims that the politicized atmosphere persists because the citizenry remains "uninformed about the role of the judge as impartial arbiter with the responsibility of enforcing the laws."[19] For Alper, as for Graves and Walker, the basic problem is one of helping the public to recognize the true value of keeping the courts independent of politics.

Alper draws her solution from the existing process of judicial selection in her state of Virginia. Unlike almost any other state in the country, Virginia allows the state legislature to directly select state judges. The legislature is obviously a political institution and Alper identifies instances in which "raw partisan politics" have determined who will sit on the bench.[20] But, based on her own experience, Alper argues that it is highly unusual for results-oriented politicking to play a role in Virginia's judicial selections. When she went through the process, legislators did not ask about her political views or about how she would handle particular issues. Instead, the legislators were most concerned about her intellect, patience, and sense of fairness. For her own part, Alper was freed from the burdens of public campaign and did not have to worry about "fund-raising and the specter of bias that attends to any judge who must rely on the bar and other interest groups to raise money, only to have those same individuals and groups appear before him or her."[21] According to Alper, then, the crucial lesson of the Virginia process is not that the election of judges per se is to be avoided. After all, elections help confer legitimacy on judges and work to ensure that those on the bench are in touch with their communities. The lesson of the Virginia system is that public campaigns in the context of popular elections are to be avoided. Legislative elections give the people an indirect voice in the process, permit judicial candidates to state their positions, and allow for public debate of candidates' qualifications—all the while maintaining a level of dignity and professionalism that is impossible to reach in the hurly-burly of elections open to the people.

How can one adjudicate between the pessimistic analyses of the essays in Part I and the general optimism of the essays in Part II? One approach is to examine the role of the media more carefully. The essays in Part II all suggest the problems plaguing the judiciary can be alleviated by effective communication: if the public is given a more accurate picture of judicial behavior, then citizens will learn that courts are not to be pressured to achieve particular results, but rather are to be valued for their independence and impartiality. See and Alper argue that right method of judicial selection will itself broadcast the right message to the public (though See and Alper do not agree on what the right method of judicial selection is). But the concern in effective communication does not stop there. Because the public understanding of the judicial selection process is inevitably shaped by the media, one must also be concerned with the content of media coverage (in this vein, recall that the Maxwell Poll shows that large majorities of Americans blame the media for distorting the operation of the courts by overemphasizing the partisan background of judges). Thus, it is with an eye toward the media's influence that Graves and Walker call for a collaborative relationship between reporters and judges.

The essays in Part I arguably cast doubt on both the prospects for and the benefits of a collaboration between the courts and the media. Geyh and Tarr link the assault on judicial independence to larger political forces—forces that shape the context in which the media operates. From this perspective, it seems unrealistic to expect media reform to take place; even if such reform did occur, it seems unlikely to alter the basic dynamics at work.

Is the media is really doing a bad job covering the courts, as most Americans and many commentators seem to believe? If so, then how might media coverage be improved? And what sort of difference should we expect improved coverage to make? The essays in Part III, written by working journalists, offer a range of answers to these questions.

In the first essay, Mark Obbie, a seasoned legal reporter and current professor of journalism, systematically considers the kind of coverage the media gives the courts. In particular, Obbie undertakes an empirical study of news articles about Samuel Alito's Supreme Court nomination that appeared in the *New York Times* and the *Washington Post*. Obbie's goal is to determine whether the newspapers engaged in "results-oriented legal journalism," defined as "reporting on the outcome of a court case without acknowledging the legal authority that the court cited in reaching that outcome." To the extent that it exists, results-oriented legal journalism is a problem, Obbie argues, not because all judges scrupulously rule on the basis of legal principle but because the failure to mention the law at all "strips legal news of much of its meaning and likely leads citizens to the belief, fair or not, that their courts dictate policy."[22] Whether a given judge is in fact an exemplar of impartiality or a partisan hack, results-oriented legal journalism does not give readers the information necessary to make a genuinely informed evaluation. Instead, readers are simply left with the impression that judges reach whatever legal result they want.

Obbie finds that results-oriented journalism prevailed in roughly half of the *New York Times* and the *Washington Post* stories on the Alito nomination. Given the resources and importance of the two newspapers, as well as the salience of the nomination itself, the frequent failure to supply a complete record of the relevant facts and context is troubling. Even so, Obbie remains hopeful that legal reporting can be improved. He concludes with a list of recommendations, ranging from a call to hire more reporters with legal expertise to an admonition to avoid the "sad and false assumption that there is no appetite for the news about the law beyond tabloid-style 'trials of the century'."[23]

In her essay, Dahlia Lithwick, senior editor and legal correspondent for Slate.com, assesses the quality of legal reporting on the Internet. Unlike the world of newspapers examined by Obbie, Internet coverage of the courts is not dominated by a few hierarchically organized players. Primary legal resources are readily available on a number of websites, many of them run by courts themselves. Commentators feed on these easily accessible resources and then disseminate their legal analyses on hundreds of online news sites and legal blogs. The loose structure, freedom, and speed of the Internet not only make it different from print journalism but also make it different from the courts. As Lithwick writes, the "Internet looks forward, courts face backward. The Internet celebrates "edginess" and opinion, the courts reify wisdom. The Internet is informal, open and democratic, the courts operate under the most rigid of rules and hierarchical constraints."[24]

The great promise of the Internet is that it will inject its best qualities into popular discourse, significantly democratizing legal discussion and stripping away the unnecessary mystification that obscures what judges do. And

Lithwick argues that this promise is already being realized: the extraordinary online availability of case law, statutes, law review articles, and expert commentary have made it possible "to peel the oak paneling off the courthouses and show the public that this isn't just politics in black robes."

At the same time, however, the Internet also threatens to debase popular discourse, allowing "citizens to believe themselves well-informed and well-educated, even while they read hundreds, even thousands, of sources that merely reflect back their own, ferociously held views." Rather than being presented with a straightforward opportunity to learn more, the Internet-reading public finds itself awash in unmediated information, left to sort out accurate accounts from "hysterical conclusions about activist judges who fabricate the law from spun sugar and rampant ideology."[25]

What will be the ultimate impact of the Internet on public understanding of the courts? Like Obbie, Lithwick is hopeful that the story will have a happy ending. Although there is no editorial staff in place to police the Web, the public itself can alter the mix of information on the Internet by consistently choosing balance and accuracy over bias and partisan exaggeration.

The final essay in Part III, written by the veteran reporter and journalism professor Tom Goldstein, is somewhat more skeptical about the prospects for brokering a positive relationship between the courts and the news media. There are, Goldstein agrees, steps that reporters and judges can take to improve the level of mutual understanding. But Goldstein's broader point is that the estrangement between the media and the courts is sustained by many factors and, as a consequence, may never be fully overcome.

Drawing on his own experience covering the courts, Goldstein describes how we have come to live in a "culture of disclosure" that has been generally promoted by journalists and largely resisted by judges. This is not to say that judges are altogether opposed to media coverage; on the contrary, many judges are willing to work with reporters so long as the judges can be assured they will be given media coverage that is appropriately focused. Goldstein argues that this desire to dictate the terms of media coverage is rooted in a misunderstanding of how the news works. "News involves novelty, conflict, and finding out what others wish to keep secret," Goldstein writes. Journalists "feel that their goal is to keep those in power accountable, and this alone can make those in power feel uncomfortable."[26] Better news coverage means more exposure. It does not mean that journalists will faithfully transmit the image and self-understanding that a judge wishes to present.

In the end, the contributors to this volume seem to agree that the American courts are at a crossroads. On one side, there is an understanding of judges as independent and impartial guardians of the Constitution. This understanding is supported by well-established convention as well as by current public opinion. On the other side, there is a conflicting understanding of judges as partisan actors committed to political goals. This second understanding is articulated by politicians, expressed in news coverage, and endorsed by a large majority of Americans.

In the Afterword, the former *New York Times* columnist Anthony Lewis argues that the courts cannot remain at this crossroads; inevitably, one understanding of judicial power must be chosen over the other. Lewis identifies several powerful factors pushing the country toward a political view of the courts. Court dockets are crammed with "agitated issues that touch the emotions of Americans." On such issues it is easy for people "to care only about the results judges reach rather than the quality of their reasoning."[27] Moreover, the chorus calling for preferred judicial outcomes has many elected officials in its ranks. Members of Congress will endlessly debate whether a given nominee to the federal bench will decide a case in a particular direction, but they will rarely consider whether the nominee has the temperament to sort through conflicting arguments in a dispassionate, fair-minded way.

Yet even as Lewis recognizes that most Americans seize on specific legal results, he also notes that most Americans still believe in judicial independence. Lewis hopes that this belief in judicial independence will ultimately determine the direction in which the country moves. He suggests that the courts have become mired in politics because the public is unaware of the degree to which the federal courts have become infected with politics, not because the public has embraced a model of political judging. Like several of the other contributors to this volume, Lewis argues that the basic problem is one of public ignorance, not public opinion. "If Americans come to know what is at stake," Lewis concludes, "I cannot believe they will choose a system like that in China, where political officials tell judges how to decide cases. I cannot believe that we are willing to give up the independent courts that guarantee our rights."[28]

In which direction will the courts move? What role will the judges, politicians, the media, methods of judicial selection, public opinion, and larger political forces play? In the end, will an understanding of the courts as impartial guarantors of individual rights triumph over the contrary understanding of the courts as partisan actors?

In closing, I would suggest that it is not only important to reflect on the range of answers to these questions given by the essays collected here but also worth considering a response that is not found in the following chapters. As Judith Shklar once argued, contradictory perceptions of the judiciary may never be resolved into a single internally consistent understanding because we expect our courts to perform contradictory functions: we constantly ask them to be guided by general principles and to be responsive to political needs.[29] Shklar's old insight is supported by the Maxwell Poll findings and reinforced by research on popular legal consciousness performed by Patricia Ewick and Susan Silbey.[30] Drawing on a series of in-depth interviews with 430 individuals, Ewick and Silbey argue that ordinary Americans typically define, use, and understand law in conflicting ways: on one hand, law "is imagined and treated as an objective realm of disinterested action . . . operating by known and fixed rules," and, on the other hand, law "is depicted as a game, a terrain for tactical encounters through which people marshal a variety of social resources to achieve strategic goals."[31] The same people hold these contradictory conceptions at the same time. Law is popularly understood to be "both sacred and profane, God and gimmick, interested and disinterested" all at once.[32]

As a number of the authors in this volume suggest, we may be in the middle of an important struggle between competing ways of thinking about the courts, a struggle that existing institutions may or may not be able to contain. Alternatively, as the work of Shklar, Ewick, and Sibley suggest, we may be living in a period when the contradictions bound up together in one enduring perspective on the judiciary are simply becoming more plain. We should attend to all these possibilities as the debate over the status and future of judicial independence continues to unfold.

Notes

1. THE FEDERALIST NO. 78, at 466, 69 (Hamilton) (Clinton Rossiter, ed., 1961). On the Federalists generally, *see* Gordon S. Wood, THE CREATION OF THE AMERICAN REPUBLIC, 1776–1787 (1972).

2. "Essays of Brutus" in THE ANTI-FEDERALIST 183 (Herbert Storing, ed., University of Chicago Press, 1985). On the Anti-federalists generally, see CECELIA KENYON, INTRODUCTION, THE ANTI-FEDERALISTS (Cecelia Kenyon, ed., Bobbs-Merrill, 1966); and HERBERT J. STORING (with the editorial assistance of Murray Dry), WHAT THE ANTI-FEDERALISTS WERE FOR: THE POLITICAL THOUGHT OF THE OPPONENTS OF THE CONSTITUTION (University of Chicago Press, 1981).

3. Campbell Public Affairs Institute, Maxwell Poll on Civic Engagement and Inequality, at 5 (Oct. 2005) (margin of error ±5 percent), *available at* http://www. maxwell.syr.edu/campbell/Poll/CitizenshipPoll.htm. Last visited August 14, 2006.

4. Here are the percentages of each group that agree the partisan background of judges influences court decisions either some or a lot: Liberals (88 percent), Conservatives (83 percent), Frequent Church Goers (84 percent), and Church Abstainers (88 percent).

5. Partisanship also plays a role: 44 percent of Democrats—as compared to 33 percent of Republicans—believe that the partisan background of judges influences court decisions a lot; and 52 percent of Democrats—as compared to 33 percent of Republicans—say that the number of judicial elections should be increased. Yet Democrats (60 percent) and Republicans (59 percent) alike agree that judges base their decisions on personal belief rather than on the law and the Constitution. Because attention to media has consistent effects across all three questions measuring the political nature of the judicial process (see notes 6 and 7), it is reasonable to emphasize media consumption over partisanship in the text.

6. TV News: Percent of those watching local-national television news daily who believe the partisan background of judges influences court decisions a lot: 42. Percent of those that never watch local-national television who believe the partisan background of judges influences court decisions a lot: 14. Newspapers: Percent of daily newspaper readers who believe the partisan background of judges influences court decisions a lot: 41. Percent of non-newspaper readers who believe the partisan background of judges influences court decisions a lot: 34.

7. TV News: Percent of those watching local-national television news daily who believe more judges should be subject to popular election: 46. Percent of those that never watch local-national television news who believe more judges should be subject to popular election: 25. Percent of those watching local-national television news daily who believe judicial decisions are based on the judge's own personal beliefs in spite of what the judge actually says: 62. Percent of those that never watch local-national television news who believe judicial decisions are based on the judge's own personal beliefs in spite of what the judge actually says: 54. Newspapers: Percent of those daily newspaper readers who believe more judges should be subject to popular election: 42. Percent of non-newspaper readers who believe more judges should be subject to popular election: 34. Percent of daily newspaper readers who believe judicial decisions are based on the judge's own personal beliefs in spite of what the judge actually says: 57. Percent of non-newspaper readers who believe judicial decisions are based on the judge's own personal beliefs in spite of what the judge actually says: 46.

8. Liberals (77 percent), Moderates (82 percent), Conservatives (77 percent), Frequent Church Goers (78 percent), Non-church Goers (83 percent), Daily TV News Watchers (77 percent), Daily Newspaper Readers (80 percent), and "Distrusting" Respondents (73 percent).

9. People demand judicial involvement (47 percent), Elected officials fail to deal with the controversies themselves (21 percent), Activist judges (11 percent). The

political ideology of respondents does play a role here. Conservatives (19 percent) are more likely than Liberals (8 percent) to say that many conflicts end up in court because judges actively involve themselves in controversies. Given the amount of conservative rhetoric about the errant ways of "activist judges," it is not surprising to find a difference of opinion between Conservatives and Liberals on this question. Even so, it is worth noting that the most common response of both Conservatives (46 percent) and Liberals (52 percent) was to say that many conflicts end up in court because most people want to get the courts involved. Thus, in spite of the steady conservative criticism targeting judicial activism, a large plurality of conservatives nonetheless believe that crowded, controversial court dockets are the result of popular demand.

10. As these results suggest, public perceptions are by no means a prisoner of media coverage. A majority may believe that the media overemphasizes the political determinants of judicial decisionmaking, but the public can see beyond media representations. In fact, 57 percent of those surveyed think that the media coverage of the courts does not do a good job of explaining why judges make the decisions they do. The Maxwell Poll also illustrates the point that individual views are not wholly dictated by the media in another way: it seems that the more one keeps up with the courts, the more likely one is to believe that judges are influenced by politics *and* that judges should be treated as impartial arbiters. According to the poll, 93 percent of those who said they "follow news about court decisions a lot" believe that the partisan background of judges influences court decisions either some or a lot, while only 74 percent of those who said they do not follow court news believed that judges were driven by partisan influence. At the same time, 79 percent of those who follow news about court decisions a lot thought that judges should be shielded from outside pressure and allowed to make their decisions based on an independent reading of the law, while only 70 percent of those who do not follow court news shared the same view. It would appear those individuals who attend to the available court-related information, from all sources including the media, end up endorsing the media's message along with the opposite of that message.

11. "Bench Press: The Collision of Media, Politics, Public Pressure, and an Independent Judiciary," Washington, D.C. (Oct. 17, 2005).

12. Tarr, *Politicizing the Process: The New Politics of State Judicial Elections*, in this volume at 53.

13. *Id.*, 66.

14. THE FEDERALIST NO. 1, at 36 (Hamilton).

15. Brown v. Board of Education, 347 U.S. 483 (1954). James E. Graves, Jr., *Judicial Independence: The Courts and the Media* in this volume at 116.

16. Graves, *supra note* 16 at 118.

17. John M. Walker, Jr., *Politics and the Confirmation Process: Thoughts on the Roberts and Alito Hearings*, in this volume at 125.

18. *Id.* at 127.

19. Joanne F. Alper, *Selecting the Judiciary: Who Should Be the Judge?*, in this volume at 132.

20. *Id.* at 150, footnote 57.

21. *Id.* at 143.

22. Mark Obbie, *Winners and Losers*, in this volume at 159, 160.

23. *Id.* at 172.

24. Dahlia Lithwick, *The Internet and the Judiciary: We Are All Experts Now*, in this volume at 177.

25. *Id.* at 178, 181, 183.

26. Tom Goldstein, *The Distance between Judges and Journalists*, in this volume at 183, 191.

27. Anthony Lewis, *The State of Judicial Independence*, in this volume at 199.

28. Id. at 200–201.

29. JUDITH N. SHKLAR, LEGALISM: LAW, MORALS, AND POLITICAL TRIALS (1964).

30. PATRICIA EWICK & SUSAN SILBEY, THE COMMON PLACE OF LAW: STORIES FROM EVERYDAY LIFE (1998).

31. *Id.* at 28.

32. *Id.* at 223.

I CONTEXT

1 Preserving Public Confidence in the Courts in an Age of Individual Rights and Public Skepticism

Charles Gardner Geyh

A MERICAN COURTS ARE UNDER SIEGE. Again. This time it is (for the most part) angry conservatives who have accused "liberal activist" judges of usurping power by striking down abortion restrictions, outlawing public displays of the Ten Commandments, lifting prohibitions on gay marriage, and so on. A generation ago it was conservatives again, who were grousing about the excesses of the liberal Warren Court. A generation before that, it was irate liberals who accused conservative courts of usurping political power by declaring populist, progressive, and New Deal legislation unconstitutional.

There is a dance step to these periods of anti-court sentiment—periods that have come and gone at generational intervals since the nation was founded.[1] Typically, cycles begin with courts that decide one or more cases in ways that anger politically powerful segments of the public or their elected representatives. Those factions incite some combination of legislators, governors, presidents, the media, or voters to excoriate allegedly rogue judges and threaten them and their courts with a variety of retaliatory actions that may include impeachment, budget cuts, curtailment of subject matter jurisdiction,

The John F. Kimberling Chair in Law, Indiana University at Bloomington. I'd like to thank Judge Peter Bowie for his guidance as to source materials, and Mickey Weber and Holly Yoakum for their research assistance. The views expressed in this chapter are my own, and are not necessarily shared by the American Bar Association's Joint Commission to Evaluate the Model Code of Judicial Conduct, which I have served as co-reporter.

changes in methods of judicial selection, disestablishment of judicial offices, judicial discipline, court packing, or defeat at the ballot box. Court defenders then mobilize to oppose the anti-court crusade. Voters or appointing authorities select new judges whose views are likely to be compatible with those of the majority; the courts may adjust their decision making to take a less confrontational tack; court critics lose their political steam before making good on many if any of their threats; and equilibrium is restored.

A primary concern of court defenders in each of the last three cycles of anti-court sentiment (the populist-progressive period, the Warren Court era, and today) has been that virulent attacks on judges have diminished public confidence in the courts. While court defenders have denied that judges are to blame for these attacks and have resisted proposals to subject judges to greater political control, they have actively explored other ways in which public confidence in the courts might be restored and promoted.

Public confidence is a matter of perception or appearance that may be present or absent irrespective of whether public confidence is warranted in fact. Court defenders, who are convinced that judges (on the whole) have acted properly and deserve the public's trust, have thus devoted themselves to ensuring that judges *appear* to act properly too. This chapter explores the century-long campaign to regulate appearances of judicial impropriety and the consequences of that campaign—intended and not—for an impartial judiciary and public confidence in the courts.

The principle that public officials should not only behave properly but appear to behave properly has come to occupy a prominent place in contemporary American political culture. The prevailing view declares that if public officials appear to act improperly, people will lose faith in those officials and the institutions of government that they serve; and in a representative democracy, preserving the trust and confidence of the governed in the leaders and institutions that govern them is regarded as critically important, for reasons explained by the American Bar Association's Commission on the 21st Century Judiciary:

> Appearances matter because the public's perception of how the courts are performing affects the extent of its confidence in the judicial system. And public confidence in the judicial system matters a great deal. . . . First, and perhaps foremost, public confidence in our judicial system is an end in itself. A government of the people, by the people and for the people rises or falls with the will and consent of the governed. The public will not support institutions in which they have no confidence. The need for public support and confidence is all the more critical for the

judicial branch, which by virtue of its independence is less directly accountable to the electorate and, thus, perhaps more vulnerable to public suspicion.[2]

And so, when it comes to the judiciary, the American Bar Association's Model Code of Judicial Conduct (some variation of which has been adopted by virtually every state judicial system and the federal courts) declares that a judge "shall avoid impropriety and the appearance of impropriety in all the judge's activities," and adds that judges "shall act at all times in a manner that promotes public confidence in the integrity and independence of the judiciary."

This escalating preoccupation with appearances is understandable, given contemporaneous changes in the ways that the public receives information about politics and government. Television, almost by definition, reorients viewer focus toward issues of image or appearance, which has facilitated the emergence and entrenchment of manufactured news, what Daniel Boorstin coined "pseudo-events."[3] Indeed, the age of political campaigning in the modern media was inaugurated in 1960 with the first televised presidential debates between Richard Nixon and John Kennedy, where "the most important determinant" for who won the debates "seemed to be the 'style' of a candidate . . . and his personality."[4]

Moreover, the time that major television networks have been willing to commit to delivering hard news is limited. As early as 1958, Edward R. Murrow warned that the television networks had oriented themselves almost completely toward programming that entertained, and relegated "occasional informative programs" to the "intellectual ghetto on Sunday afternoons."[5] Between 1977 and 1997, entertainment and "human interest" stories in television news programs and in major newspapers increased from 15 to 43 percent of the total.[6] Inevitably, news about politics and government became correspondingly compressed. One political scientist described the consequences: "The average news story on television takes about a minute, just enough time to announce that an event has taken place and present a fact or two about it. Complex stories may have to be scratched entirely if they cannot be drastically condensed."[7] Indeed, in 1968, the average "sound bite" from presidential candidates in televised election stories was 42.3 seconds long; by 1988, it had diminished to less than 10 seconds, and by 2000 it had dwindled to 7.[8] Insofar as the news is communicated in short, image-oriented segments, the public's understanding of judges and the judiciary will, of necessity, be impressionistic; and to the extent that public opinion influences how policy makers regulate the judiciary, the public's impressions of judges become very important.

In this chapter, I begin by chronicling the emergence and eventual entrenchment of rules regulating the appearance of judicial impropriety. As regulators came to take appearances ever more seriously, they promulgated enforceable rules that prohibited judges from saying things or associating with others in ways that could create appearance problems. Paradoxically, this effort to strengthen rules regulating appearances by making them more enforceable may (to an as yet uncertain extent) have had the opposite effect, rendering them vulnerable to constitutional challenge on First Amendment grounds. The net effect has been a detectable shift away from rules prohibiting speech or association that creates appearance problems, toward rules that implicitly authorize the underlying speech or association but require judges who thereby create appearance problems to disqualify themselves from cases in which such problems would call their impartiality into question.

This development has potentially profound implications. It suggests the possibility of a new paradigm, one in which judges are welcomed into the marketplace of ideas and encouraged, not just permitted, to say what is on their minds (on the theory that more speech is always better than less), so that litigants can better inform themselves of judicial biases that may warrant disqualification. One possible consequence of relying on disqualification to protect the public from judges who vent their prejudices and thereby call their impartiality into question on a more regular basis could be to limit the available judicial workforce in unprecedented ways, by greatly expanding the universe of judges subject to disqualification. A second, and in my view a more likely consequence, will be to force a reinterpretation of disqualification rules to allow judges to hear cases despite appearance problems created by their speech and association, so as to ensure an adequate judicial workforce. In that event, what was once a system of regulation designed to minimize appearance problems will have gradually given way to a system that cultivates them.

The Appearance of Appearances

Prior to the twentieth century, the arsenal for regulating judicial conduct in England, and later America, was limited to blunt instruments. In England, apart from several obscure, little used common law mechanisms for intrajudicial removal,[9] judges were initially subject to removal by the king, or on impeachment by Parliament—competing mechanisms that, beginning in the early nineteenth century, gave way to a unified system of removal by the king on address by both houses of Parliament.[10] The U.S. Constitution established an impeachment process authorizing Congress to remove judges for "treason, bribery, and other high crimes and misdemeanors," while the states adopted impeachment mechanisms of their own.[11] In addition, over half the states provided for removal via legislative address, whereby legislatures could petition the governor for a judge's ouster[12]; some states mandated automatic removal for judges convicted of specified criminal offenses[13]; still others created mechanisms for judicial recall[14]; and, beginning in the latter half of the nineteenth century, an increasing number of judges were subject to removal in periodic elections.[15]

With enforcement efforts focused almost exclusively on actual improprieties serious enough to warrant removal (or worse), it is not especially surprising that the "appearance" of impropriety commanded little attention among early writers concerned about judicial ethics. Prior to the twentieth century, the most comprehensive code of judicial conduct was devised in the 1600s by Sir Matthew Hale, Lord Chief Justice under King Charles II, who wrote "Rules for His Judicial Guidance, Things Necessary to Be Continually Had in Remembrance."[16] His rules consisted of eighteen points: seven elaborated on the need for a judge to remain impartial[17]; five were directed at promoting just case outcomes[18]; three emphasized the need for diligence, commitment, and integrity[19]; two underscored the need for a judge's allegiance to God, king, and, country[20]; and one called on the judge to direct court personnel to avoid personal, financial, or professional entanglements in matters before the court.[21] Noticeable by its absence (at least when viewed through the lens of twenty-first century sensibilities) is any allusion to the need for avoiding the appearance of impropriety, for preserving public confidence in the judiciary, or for conducting oneself with dignity or in a manner that is above reproach.

This is not to suggest that concern for appearances was altogether absent. In 1620, for example, Sir Francis Bacon was impeached and removed on charges that he accepted gifts from litigants, despite a showing by Bacon that the gifts had not influenced his judgment (as evidenced by several instances in which he decided cases against his benefactors).[22] Accepting gifts under such circumstances may have created an appearance of corruption sufficient to justify removal, even if Bacon had not been corrupted in fact.[23] In the 1852 decision of *Dimes v. Grand Junction Canal*, Lord John Campbell concurred in a decision of the House of Lords to render voidable the ruling of a judge who had been a shareholder in the plaintiff corporation, with the observation that

"This will be a lesson to all inferior tribunals to take care not only that in their decrees they are not influenced by their personal interest, but to avoid the appearance of labouring under such an influence."[24] And at approximately the same time on the other side of the Atlantic, Massachusetts Attorney General Rufus Choate opined that a judge "must possess the perfect confidence of the community, that he bear not the sword in vain. To be honest . . . is not yet enough. He must be believed such."[25] Such infrequent, temporally scattered references, however, pale in comparison to the systematic attention directed toward the appearance of impropriety and its relationship to public confidence in the courts that began at the turn of the twentieth century.

In the cyclical attacks on courts and judges alluded to earlier, court defenders intent on preserving the independence of judges and the judiciary have invariably squared off against court critics equally intent on subjecting judges to greater popular and political control. The most protracted of these cycles occurred during the populist-progressive period at the turn of the twentieth century, when, as William Ross writes:

> [C]ountless . . . antagonists of the courts between 1890 and 1937 alleged that a "judicial oligarchy" had usurped the powers of Congress and thwarted the will of the people by interfering with the activities of labor unions and nullifying legislation that was designed to ameliorate the more baneful effects of the Industrial Revolution.[26]

Many state and federal courts of this period subjected populist and progressive reforms to exacting scrutiny, as emblemized by the U.S. Supreme Court's 1905 decision in *Lochner v. New York*,[27] which declared that state legislation fixing the maximum hours for bakers at sixty hours per week, violated the due process clause of the Fourteenth Amendment by interfering impermissibly with the freedom of owners and bakers to contract. Court defenders, such as William Howard Taft and Roscoe Pound, did not share the view that *Lochner*-era judges had usurped legislative power and opposed proposals to subject judicial decision making to greater popular control. Pound, however, was concerned by a growing public *perception* that judges and courts were behaving badly. In a seminal address to the American Bar Association (ABA) in 1906, entitled "The Causes of Popular Dissatisfaction with the Courts," Pound called attention to "the real and serious dissatisfaction with courts and lack of respect for law which exists in the United States today," and called for sweeping reform of court administration and procedure.[28] "Courts are distrusted," he declared, and attributed the development in part to "public ignorance of the real workings of the courts due to ignorant and sensational reports in the press," and to "putting courts into politics," which "has almost destroyed the traditional respect for the Bench." In 1908, American Bar Association President Jacob M. Dickinson echoed that "[j]udicial judgments are not accorded the same respect as formerly," and that "not *a* court but *the* courts are frequently and fiercely attacked."[29] The net effect, he concluded, was "to destroy confidence in the courts and to make a subservient judiciary."

The same year as Dickinson's speech, the American Bar Association adopted the Canons of Professional Ethics, its first stab at a code of conduct for lawyers.[30] Given the ongoing crisis of confidence in the courts, one might have supposed that the time would be auspicious for developing a comparable code applicable to judges. But as Charles Boston, a New York lawyer and the principal drafter of the first Code of Judicial Conduct, would later explain, it was precisely because the judiciary was under intense fire that the ABA made no such move: "[T]he agitation for recall of the judiciary and recall of judicial decisions" was such that "it was not deemed wise to add fuel to that flame by intimating through the adoption of Canons of Judicial Ethics that the judiciary were in fault."[31] In other words, the bar implicitly believed that the improprieties judges stood accused of committing in the court of public opinion were largely a matter of appearance, not reality, and that imposing a code of conduct on judges at that juncture would create the appearance that the bar regarded those alleged improprieties as actual, rather than merely perceived. The age of obsession with appearances had begun.

The bar's latitude to temporize ended twelve years later when a scandal encircling District Judge Kenesaw Mountain Landis brought the issue to a head. Judge Landis had been a semiprofessional baseball player in his youth and, in 1905, was appointed district judge for the northern district of Illinois. In 1919, several members of the Chicago White Sox baseball team were bribed to throw the World Series. In the aftermath of the so-called Black Sox scandal, baseball owners responded by establishing the position of baseball commissioner and appointed Judge Landis to the post in 1920. Judge Landis thereupon assumed the duties of baseball commissioner at a salary of $42,500, which he undertook in earnest, without relinquishing his judgeship or its $7,500 salary. Congressman Benjamin Welty of Ohio introduced an impeachment resolution in February 1921, accusing Judge Landis of "neglecting his official duties for another gainful occupation." Although the focus of the charges was on the *actual* impropriety that Judge Landis had neglected his judicial duties, he was also charged with fostering an *appearance* of impropriety: by serving both as a sitting federal judge and commissioner of baseball, Welty asserted, "the impression will prevail that gambling and other illegal acts will not be punished in the open forum as in other cases."[32] The charges were filed too late in the 66th Congress for the House Judiciary Committee to complete its investigation. In a brief report issued in March, a majority of the committee nonetheless warned:

> [S]aid act of accepting the employment aforesaid, if proved, is . . . at least inconsistent with the full and adequate performance of the duty of the . . . Honorable Kenesaw Mountain Landis, as a United States district judge, and that said act would constitute a serious impropriety on the part of said judge.[33]

The committee's minority report, however, put its finger on a problem: moonlighting did not necessarily rise to the level of a crime or misdemeanor susceptible to removal by impeachment:

> No violation of any law has been called to the attention of the committee, nor is it claimed that the judge is guilty of any act that would establish moral turpitude. One or both of these grounds would have to be established before impeachment proceedings could be maintained.[34]

At its annual meeting in 1921, the American Bar Association adopted a resolution rebuking Judge Landis in terms that emphasized the deleterious impact of his actions on the public's perception of the judiciary. The delegates declared that the judge's conduct "meets with our unqualified condemnation, as conduct unworthy of the office of judge, derogatory to the dignity of the Bench, and undermining public confidence in the independence of the judiciary."[35] Judge Landis ultimately resigned from the bench in 1922.

Impeachment may have been too extreme a remedy for an offense of the sort Judge Landis committed. His conduct was nonetheless troubling to many, gave the judiciary a black eye at a time when it could scarcely afford one, and called for some other means to address judicial misconduct. Charles Boston, arguing that "the time is now ripe" to draft a code of judicial conduct, successfully lobbied the ABA to establish a committee for that purpose.[36] That committee, chaired by Chief Justice (and former President and ABA President) William Howard Taft, issued a draft of the Canons of Judicial Ethics that was approved by the American Bar Association in 1924.

The Canons of Judicial Ethics were replete with guidance exhorting judges to avoid conduct that could create appearance problems and thereby undermine public confidence in the courts. Canon 4 declared that a judge's official conduct should be "free from . . . the appearance of impropriety." Eleven other canons cautioned judges to avoid conduct that could create "suspicion" of misbehavior or "misconceptions" of the judicial role that might "appear" or "seem" to interfere with judicial duties, or that could "create the impression" of bias.[37]

A majority of the state judiciaries subsequently adopted the Canons of Judicial Ethics, but the canons were destined for obscurity, almost by design.[38] There were no "shalls" in the canons that might serve as standards for enforcement, only "shoulds"—hortatory pronouncements "intended to be nothing more than the American Bar Association's suggestions for guidance of individual judges."[39] The canons were thus crafted to operate behind the scenes—to advise judges on how they should conduct themselves rather than to serve as a code of conduct that judges violated at the peril of formal disciplinary action. Moreover, the cycle of court-directed animus that had spawned a perceived crisis of public confidence in the courts and fueled a movement to create the canons in the first place was already on the wane by the time the canons were adopted in 1924 and would effectively end thirteen years later when a majority of the Supreme Court acquiesced to Franklin Roosevelt's New Deal agenda in the shadow of his proposed plan to pack the federal courts with New Deal sympathizers.[40] The subsequent period of relative calm ensured that judges could quietly go about their business of following the canons (or not) without political pressure to do more.

This is not to suggest that judicial concern for the "appearance of impropriety" simply dropped off the face of the earth. Throughout the middle of the twentieth century, state supreme and appellate courts sporadically alluded to a judge's ethical duty to avoid the appearance of impropriety in the context of appellate decisions that disqualified trial judges from hearing particular cases, evaluated trial judge conduct in the context of reviewing lower court orders, or sanctioned judges qua members of the bar in lawyer discipline actions.[41]

By the 1960s, however, the Canons of Judicial Ethics had become increasingly antiquated and the next wave of anti-court sentiment had arrived. Decisions of the Warren Court ordering racial desegregation, banning prayer in public schools, and expanding the constitutional protections afforded criminal defendants had led to calls for the impeachment of Earl Warren, the introduction of legislation to strip the federal courts of jurisdiction to hear school prayer cases, and a campaign pledge by presidential candidate Richard Nixon to dismantle the Warren Court and appoint "strict constructionists" to the bench. Inquiries into the conduct of two Warren Court liberals—William O. Douglas and Abe Fortas—further fanned the flame. Former ABA President Whitney North Seymour explained at the time:

> Suddenly, toward the end of the 1960's a series of events pointed up their [the Canons of Judicial Ethics'] inadequacy. In the controversies over the activities of Justices Fortas and Douglas, and in the inquiries into the qualifications of Judge Haynesworth for appointment to the Supreme Court, the inadequacies of the canons became particularly apparent. Members of Congress began to advocate legislative regulation of judicial conduct going far beyond anything then on the books. . . . In 1969, ABA President Segal wisely decided that the time had come for the bar to re-examine the old Canons of Judicial Ethics and bring them up to date.[42]

First and foremost among the perceived problems afflicting the old canons was that they had been purely advisory. The net effect, critics complained, was to make compliance optional. And so, in 1972 the ABA promulgated the "Code of Judicial Conduct," comprised of seven broadly worded canons and a series of more specific provisions underlying each, accompanied by a preamble that declared that "the canons and text establish mandatory standards unless otherwise indicated."

Regulating appearances remained an important part of the 1972 code. Like old Canon 4, new Canon 2 declared that "a judge should avoid impropriety and the appearance of impropriety in all his activities" and added in Section 2A that a judge "should conduct himself at all times in a manner that promotes public confidence in the integrity and impartiality of the judiciary." In addition, the code retained (or added) at least eight other provisions regulating appearances.[43]

Then came Watergate and the crisis of confidence in American government that it catalyzed. Within the executive and legislative branches, rules aimed at deterring conduct that could create an appearance of impropriety were dusted off and enforced with unprecedented zeal.[44] As to the judiciary, Congress enacted a federal disqualification statute, the first paragraph of which focused on appearances, declaring that a judge must disqualify himself from "any proceeding in which his impartiality might reasonably be questioned." Judicial conduct commissions—bodies typically within the state judicial branch authorized to enforce their respective codes of conduct—began to appear in the 1960s and proliferated quickly during the 1970s until by 1981, such organizations were in place in all fifty states.[45] Sanctioning a judge who created an appearance of impropriety, typically by engaging in an actual impropriety for which sanctions were simultaneously imposed, became commonplace.

In 1990, the ABA revised its Code of Judicial Conduct again. Although the preface to the 1972 code had indicated that its terms were intended to impose "mandatory standards," recurrent use of the term *should* instead of *shall* in the body of the code had led to a common "misunderstanding" that the code remained hortatory only—a misunderstanding exacerbated in several jurisdictions that did not adopt the preface.[46] To eliminate all room for doubt, the 1990 code substituted the term *shall* for *should* whenever mandatory standards were contemplated and reorganized a series of specific sections imposing explicitly obligatory standards around a series of generally worded, but nonetheless obligatory, canons. Thus, the latest iteration of Canon 2 now declared that "A judge shall avoid impropriety and the appearance of impropriety in all of the judge's activities," while section 2A added that a judge "shall act at all times in a manner that promotes public confidence in the integrity and impartiality of the judiciary." The net effect, then, of the drafters' resolve to make the 1990 code more clearly mandatory and hence enforceable was to give the appearance provisions even more bite.

Thirteen years later, the ABA revisited the code one more time at the urging of its Commission on the 21st Century Judiciary, which had studied the impact of the latest cycle of anti-court sentiment on state judiciaries. The commission emphasized the linkage between public enforcement of the Code of Judicial Conduct and restoring public confidence in courts under attack, with the observation that "If adequately publicized . . . codes of conduct can reassure the public that there are established ethical constraints on judicial conduct."[47] It then found that another look at the code was warranted sooner than might otherwise be necessary because "the last comprehensive revision of the Model Code of Judicial Conduct occurred in 1990, prior to the acceleration of events leading to a heightened level of interest in and concern over issues of judicial independence and accountability around the country."[48] The subsequently appointed Joint Commission to Evaluate the Model Code of Judicial Conduct wrestled with the code's directive that judges avoid the appearance of impropriety, but ultimately committed to retain the essential features of the clause at the urging of the Conference of Chief Justices.

The Erosion of Appearances

Regulatory commitment to ensuring that judges not only behave well but appear to behave well has grown in fits and starts since the early twentieth century, as reflected in the preceding section. More recently, however, the regulation of appearances has encountered philosophical, practical, and constitutional objections that have placed its long-term future in limbo.

Philosophical Objections

The core philosophical objection to enforcing a rule that prohibits perceived improprieties is that obsession with appearances diverts attention from actual improprieties where regulatory efforts ought to be focused. This general concern has three specific subvariations: (1) judges who have not behaved badly may be dragged through the mud by unscrupulous accusers just for appearing to behave badly, (2) preoccupation with appearances leads judges to be more concerned with how they look than how they are in fact doing their jobs, and (3) when judges are punished for appearing to act improperly, it motivates them to conceal those appearances, which frustrates the public's ability to detect problems and address them.[49]

With one partial exception, these philosophical objections have failed to capture the hearts or minds of the regulatory community, because none of them undermines the core public confidence rationale for regulating appearances. No one seriously suggests that regulators should be more concerned about apparent improprieties than actual ones. The point is simply that addressing actual improprieties alone will not be enough to preserve public confidence in the courts if the public perceives improprieties as persisting—hence the need to regulate both improprieties and their appearance.

With respect to the first specific objection, judges who have not behaved improperly in fact may well be accused of and disciplined for appearing to behave improperly, but that is the point of a rule designed to preserve public confidence in the courts by telling judges to pay attention to how the public perceives them. As to the second objection, judges will be more concerned about how they are perceived than how they act only if regulators sanction apparent misbehavior more harshly than actual misbehavior, and there is no evidence to suggest that the tail has wagged the dog in that way. And the third objection—that judges will make problems harder to detect and ameliorate if they are told to conceal the appearance of such problems—confuses the appearance of impropriety with the appearance of imperfection: Problems with the administration of justice—even serious ones—do not necessarily constitute ethical improprieties, the appearance of which would subject judges to discipline. With respect to those problems that *do* involve misconduct, the unethical judge will seek to conceal the evidence (and so the appearance) of wrongdoing, irrespective of whether the appearance of impropriety is separately proscribed.

There is, however, a subset of this third objection that cannot be so easily dismissed: What of the otherwise honorable judge, who harbors a deep-seated prejudice against a particular class of litigant, who avoids creating the appearance of prejudice by dutifully avoiding public statements or associations that would expose his bias? Here, at least, it would seem that there may be something to the concern that by directing judges to conceal apparent partiality (as a subset of apparent impropriety), it complicates regulators' ability to ferret out actual partiality—an issue that I revisit in a later section.

Practical Objections

Regardless of the philosophical merits of directing judges to avoid the appearance of impropriety, from a practical perspective, critics have argued that it is unworkable. There is no way to know what an "appearance of impropriety" is, they contend, and thus no way to enforce such a provision coherently.[50]

This concern surfaced with a vengeance when the ABA made an ill-fated attempt to import an appearances standard into the lawyer's code. The American Bar Association's 1969 Model Code of Professional Responsibility included Canon 9, which declared that "A lawyer should avoid even the appearance of professional impropriety."[51] The provision was added for reasons explained by the U.S. Court of Appeals for the Fifth Circuit, which should, by now, be quite familiar: "[S]ome conduct which is in fact ethical may appear to the layman as unethical and thereby could erode public confidence in the judicial system or the legal profession."[52] Canon 9 did not sit well or long.

The primary concern was that the provision was deemed too vague to be enforceable. The Restatement (Third) of the Law Governing Lawyers opined that it "fail[s] to give fair warning of the nature of the charges to a lawyer respondent and that subjective and idiosyncratic considerations could influence a hearing panel or reviewing court in resolving a charge based only on it."[53]

By 1975, the ABA itself conceded that the appearance standard was "too vague to be useful,"[54] and in 1983, when the ABA promulgated the Model Rules of Professional Conduct, the appearance of impropriety had disappeared. Draft commentary explained why:

> In the context of private practice, the test has no apparent limits except what a particular tribunal might regard as an impropriety. . . . [S]uch a standard is too vague and could cause judgments about the propriety of conduct to be made on instinctive, ad hoc, or ad hominem criteria.[55]

In the years since, a small number of states have retained the appearance of impropriety in vestigial form, as a basis on which to disqualify counsel in litigation, where, if the commentary is any indication, it remains a provision that lawyers love to hate.[56]

As compared to the vituperative response to the appearance of impropriety standard in the lawyer's code, criticism of its corollary in the Code of Judicial Conduct has been less sustained. Even so, the standard has had its share of critics: Justice Arthur Goldberg characterized it as "unbelievably ambiguous."[57] Judicial ethics scholar Leslie Abramson opines that "lack of specificity as to what makes a judge vulnerable to a charge of appearance of impropriety raises serious due process concerns. Leaving the rules unidentified while expecting them to be observed is bound to burden judges with uncertainty."[58] And the Association of Professional Responsibility Lawyers, whose members defend judges in disciplinary actions "question[ed] whether a standard that has been rejected as a basis for disciplining lawyers should continue to be used to discipline judges," and added that such "vague and overbroad language should be removed from the Model Code of Judicial Conduct because it presents too great a risk of subjective interpretation, placing judges at risk of disciplinary action depending upon the whim of judicial disciplinary authorities."[59]

Objections concerning the vagueness of the appearance standard have not won the day. First, the perceived need for judges to avoid the appearance of impropriety may be greater than for lawyers, so much greater that it offsets attendant vagueness concerns. Although public confidence in the system of justice may depend on all its participants—including lawyers—being above reproach, that is uniquely true of judges, whose continued credibility atop the justice system's organizational chart depends on their perceived integrity, impartiality, and independence. Second, unlike the lawyer's code, the judge's code has included an appearance of impropriety standard since its inception;

it is language that courts have interpreted with relative frequency and that judges have come to accept—which may help to explain why it has been upheld in disciplinary proceedings over objections that it should be declared void for vagueness. When, in 2004, the ABA Joint Commission proposed to modify the way in which the code regulated appearances to accommodate the vagueness concerns that some critics had raised, the proposal was greeted with a torrent of criticism. The commission "seems to have missed" the essential point that "Americans don't appreciate it when judges behave in ways that undermine the judicial system's fairness and integrity," complained a *New York Times* editorial, which dismissed vagueness concerns as "overblown."[60] The commission withdrew the proposal, and after further deliberation and vacillation, ultimately strengthened the appearance of impropriety standard at the insistence of the Conference of Chief Justices, by embedding it in an enforceable, freestanding rule.

Constitutional Objections

In the past generation, the First Amendment freedoms of speech and association have been invoked with increasing frequency to limit regulators' authority to prohibit judges from engaging in conduct that creates appearance problems.

1. Campaign Finance   In recent years, spending in judicial election campaigns has skyrocketed. Evidence of *actual* improprieties in the form of outright bribery, wherein donors offer judicial candidates campaign dollars in exchange for the candidate's assurance that she will decide particular cases in particular ways, is virtually nonexistent. But appearance problems abound: why would contributors with an obvious interest in the outcomes of the cases that judges decide give significant amounts of money to their favorite judges, if not to buy influence? Unsurprisingly, then, between 80 and 90 percent of the public believes that judges are influenced by the campaign contributions they receive.[61]

There are, however, serious First Amendment impediments to eradicating this appearance problem.[62] Proceeding from the premise that spending money on candidates for public office is a form of political expression fully protected by the First Amendment, the Supreme Court has made it clear that the government is powerless to cap campaign spending. The government may offer public financing for judicial and other campaigns, but only if candidate participation is completely voluntary—in other words, candidates retain the First Amendment right to reject public financing and solicit private contributions. And while the government may impose contribution limits on individual contributors, those contributors have the right to spend limitless amounts on independently organized campaigns for and against particular candidates.

2. Judicial Education   A limited number of universities and private organizations have gotten into the business of judicial education by hosting seminars for judges, often at luxury resorts in attractive places, and typically on subjects of interest to the corporate sponsors who underwrite the events. The more frantic critics of these "junkets for judges" claim that the corporations involved are buttering up or brainwashing judges into changing their votes on cases before them. The mainstream press, however, has fixated more on the appearance problem: when organizations host seminars for judges at weekend retreats in idyllic settings at the expense of corporations that have an interest in the outcomes of cases that those judges decide, it creates the perception that the corporate sponsors are seeking to buy influence or access.

When members of Congress introduced legislation to ban judicial participation in expense-paid seminars, however, the Judicial Conference of the United States opposed the bill on the grounds that it "raises potential constitutional issues such as imposing an undue burden on speech."[63] It bears emphasis that the Judicial Conference is comprised entirely of federal judges, headed by the chief justice; and while the conference's position may not have constituted an advisory opinion in the technical sense, it nonetheless gave Congress a pretty clear idea of how the federal courts might rule if the legislation was enacted.

3. Judicial Speech   The Code of Judicial Conduct includes myriad restrictions on judicial speech and association.[64] For the most part, these restrictions are calculated to prevent judges from saying things or associating with people that could call their fairness and impartiality into question. These proscriptions are often more concerned with the appearance of impartiality than its reality. Thus, for example, the code declares that "a judge shall not, with respect to cases, controversies or issues that are likely to come before the court, make pledges, promises, or commitments that are inconsistent with the impartial performance of the adjudicative duties of the office." The judge who violates this rule may *appear* to have closed her mind by committing (or promising) to decide a legal issue in a specified way, but in reality remains impartial as long as she is willing to reconsider her prior commitment (or renege on her earlier promise) at the point of decision; by the same token, the judge who honors the rule may *appear* to be impartial, but in reality is not if she allows unspoken commitments to prejudice her decision making.

Once again, however, the First Amendment has been construed to impose potentially significant restrictions on the state's authority to curb judicial speech. In 2002, the U.S. Supreme Court decided *Republican Party of Minnesota v. White.*[65] In *White*, the United States Supreme Court invalidated the so-called announce clause in the Minnesota Code of Judicial Conduct, which the Court construed to bar a judge from announcing "his views on any specific, nonfanciful legal question within the province of the court for which he is running." The Court ruled that the announce clause imposed a content-based restriction on judicial speech that was subject to strict constitutional scrutiny and could survive only if it was "narrowly tailored" to serve a "compelling government interest." While the Court appears to have conceded the possibility that the state had a compelling interest in preserving an open-minded and, hence, impartial judiciary, the Court did "not believe that the Minnesota Supreme Court adopted the announce clause for that purpose." Rather, concluded the Court, the *real* purpose for the clause was to "undermin[e] judicial elections" by "preventing candidates from discussing what the elections are about."

The implications of *White* remain uncertain but are potentially far-reaching. Critics of the decision who are committed to restricting what judges may say and with whom they may associate as a means to preserve judicial impartiality and its appearance have construed *White* narrowly, to mean only that states may not prevent judicial candidates from stating their views on disputed legal issues. For them, *White* does not apply to restrictions on speech outside the context of judicial campaigns and does not affect the state's authority to restrict other forms of campaign speech, such as pledges or commitments, where the nature of the state's interest in regulating the speech is more compelling or otherwise different. Whether the critics will be vindicated, however, remains unclear. The basic approach taken by the Court in *White* was to regard state-imposed restrictions on the content of judicial speech as presumptively invalid—a presumption that the state cannot overcome without a compelling justification. Whether the state's interest in preserving the appearance of impartiality is a sufficiently compelling justification to uphold other content-based restrictions on judicial speech within or without judicial campaigns remains to be seen.

In *Mississippi Commission on Judicial Performance v. Wilkerson*,[66] decided two years after *White*, the Mississippi Supreme Court offered a glimpse into the brave new world of deregulated judicial speech. In that case, a county judge wrote a letter to his local newspaper, stating that "I got sick on my stomach" after reading an article about legislation in other states "granting gay partners the same right to sue as spouses," adding that "in my opinion, gays and lesbians should be put in some type of mental institute instead of having a law like this passed for them." The Commission on Judicial Performance concluded that the judge's conduct violated two provisions of the code: Canon 2A, which directed the judge to "act at all times in a manner that promotes public confidence in the integrity and impartiality of the judiciary," and Canon 4A, which required the judge to "conduct all extra-judicial activities so that they do not cast doubt on the judge's capacity to act impartially as a judge." The Mississippi Supreme Court rejected the commission's conclusions in light of the U.S. Supreme Court's decision in *White*. Of pivotal importance to its decision was the Court's conclusion that the state had no compelling interest in preserving the appearance of impartiality under the circumstances of this case:

> No credible person could dispute that having impartial judges is a compelling state interest. But "impartiality" is not the same as the "appearance of impartiality." We find no compelling state interest in requiring a partial judge to keep quiet about his prejudice so that he or she will appear impartial.

To the contrary, the court observed, "forcing . . . judges to conceal their prejudice" would undermine "the more compelling state interest of providing an impartial court for all litigants." If enforcement of the code dissuaded judges like Wilkerson from speaking their minds, "unsuspecting gays or lesbians" would be "[u]naware of the prejudice and not know[] that they should seek recusal," which "surely would not work to provide a fair and impartial court to those litigants."

The implications of *White* and *Wilkerson*, logically extended, are potentially profound. Rules that prohibit judges from manifesting bias, making public statements on pending cases, joining discriminatory organizations, "conveying the impression" that others may influence them inappropriately, engaging in any extrajudicial speech or associations that call their impartiality into question, or campaigning like other elected officials must be reassessed. Is the state's interest in preserving appearances generally—by prohibiting judges from engaging in various forms of speech and association that could call their impartiality into question—offset by the state's interests in "outing" biased judges so that litigants can protect themselves by moving to disqualify judges who reveal their prejudices? If so, the state's interest in preserving the appearance of impartiality is debunked and the judge's First Amendment right to say what is on her mind must prevail. The net effect would be to require a shift in regulatory emphasis away from telling judges to avoid speech or associations that appear to compromise their impartiality, toward telling them that they may say what they please and associate with whom they wish, as long as they disqualify themselves from hearing cases in which their prior statements or associations might call their impartiality into question. That way, judges' First Amendment rights to speak and associate are protected, while litigants' due process right to an impartial judge is preserved.

This shift in regulatory emphasis from telling judges they may not create appearance problems, to telling them that they must disqualify themselves after they create appearance problems, is not merely speculative. To address the appearance problem that arises when judges receive campaign contributions in amounts sufficient to create the perception of influence, the ABA revised its Model Rules of Judicial Conduct in 1999, to require that judges disqualify themselves if they accept campaign contributions in excess of a specified amount.[67] As to "junkets for judges," the ABA Joint Commission to Evaluate the Model Code of Judicial Conduct rejected invitations from the *New York Times* and others to ban judicial attendance at judicial seminars outright, in favor of commentary elaborating on when attendance at such seminars may give rise to appearance problems that would necessitate their disqualification. And in 2003, in direct response to the Supreme Court's decision in *White*, the ABA repealed a Model Code provision prohibiting judicial candidates from making statements that "appear[] to commit" them with respect to issues that could come before them later as judges, and added a new provision subjecting judges who make such statements to disqualification.

The Emergence of Partial Impartiality

The preceding sections of this chapter reveal a striking paradox. On the one hand, the business of regulating appearances is booming. The history of judicial ethics in the twentieth and twenty-first centuries tells the story of the birth and ascendance of rules aimed at discouraging the appearance of impropriety, as a means to promote public confidence in the judiciary. To punctuate their escalating commitment to monitoring appearances, regulators have striven to make rules governing the appearance of judicial impropriety increasingly enforceable.

On the other hand, the business of regulating appearances is at risk of going bust. The *appearance* of impropriety is often reflected in words or associations suggestive of underlying judicial bias, partiality, or misconduct. By manifesting their commitment to discouraging the appearance of judicial impropriety in the promulgation and enforcement of rules that restrict judicial speech and association, regulators have pitted one great twentieth-century movement (promoting public confidence in government) against another (protecting individual rights). If it comes down to a confrontation from which the individual rights movement emerges triumphant—and cases like *White* and *Wilkerson* suggest that possibility—the century-long effort to make rules regulating judicial appearances tougher may, paradoxically, culminate in making them weaker.

To avoid such a confrontation, disqualification has become the new frontier in the regulation of appearances. Let judges speak, the argument goes. We are kidding ourselves if we think that judges are unencumbered by the same prejudices that burden the rest of us. By encouraging them to share their positions and predilections we can better protect ourselves from judges whose biases render them unfit to sit. Under this new paradigm, disciplinary rules would no longer be a barrier at the edge of the cliff so much as an ambulance at its base: rather than stopping appearance problems before they occur (through the promulgation of rules that restrict the speech and association of judges in problematic ways), the emerging approach is to let the appearance problem occur and mop up afterward with disqualification.

It is premature, perhaps, to speak in terms of a new disqualification regime because disqualification too is under attack. In the aftermath of *White*, activists on the political left and right have peppered judicial candidates with questionnaires soliciting their views on a range of substantive issues, implicitly or explicitly threatening them with retaliation at the ballot box if they decline to answer. From their perspective, the holding of *White* would be eviscerated if judges were enabled to share their views on issues that matter to voters, only to be told that if judges did so they would later be disabled from deciding cases raising those issues. If judges may not be subjected to discipline and thereby punished directly for expressing their views, they argue, then judges may not be punished indirectly by disqualifying them from hearing cases that raise the very issues to which their views pertain.[68]

Those who defend a disqualification regime may counter that disqualification does not prohibit judges from speaking their minds (as the provision invalidated in *White* did). Moreover, to the extent disqualification rules burden judicial speech indirectly by encouraging judges to keep silent so as to avoid subsequent disqualification, it is a burden justified by the government's interest in protecting the due process rights of litigants who are entitled not to have their cases heard by judges who are biased or appear to be so. There is an almost postapocalyptic quality to the parallel universe in which judges have a constitutional entitlement to rule on cases that they appear to have prejudged: Put yourself in the position of plaintiff in a sexual harassment suit where the presiding judge has a "right" to adjudicate your claim despite having told an audience of corporate managers from the campaign stump that "I have no patience for sexual harassment claims, which by their nature enable lower echelon employees to terrorize hard-working middle managers."

If the emerging disqualification regime survives constitutional attack, it may lead in one of two different directions. One possibility is that the new regime will work as intended. To the extent that is so, it calls to mind the old adage: be careful what you wish for. If norms shift and judges are encouraged to air their views, vent their biases, and display their allegiances as long as they disqualify themselves later from any case in which their prior statements and associations could call their impartiality into question, one can reasonably anticipate a sizable jump in the number of cases where disqualification would be necessary. The impact on the administration of justice in areas where judges are in relatively short supply, which is to say anywhere outside of major metropolitan areas, could be especially acute. Even in urban areas, the added administrative burden could be considerable, as cases are shunted this way and that to protect litigants from judges whose extrajudicial pronouncements, membership in discriminatory organizations, or political activities disqualify them from hearing cases involving gays, racial minorities, unmarried mothers, immigrants, Christian conservatives, women, and so on.

There is reason to suspect, however, that crippling levels of disqualification will not materialize, given a second possibility: that judges will simply reassess when an appearance problem sufficient to warrant disqualification arises, so as to limit the circumstances under which recusal is necessary. Judges have permitted the practical needs of judicial administration to trump the appearance problems that come from non-disqualification in a multitude of settings. Four examples will suffice.

The first, and certainly the most notorious example, is Justice Antonin Scalia's decision not to disqualify himself from participating in a case in which Vice President Dick Cheney was a party, despite the fact that Scalia had recently flown with Cheney on a government jet to a camp in Louisiana for several days of duck hunting. Justice Scalia rejected the suggestion that he should "resolve any doubts in favor of recusal" because with one justice out, "[t]he Court proceeds with eight justices, raising the possibility that, by reason of a tie vote, it will find itself unable to resolve the significant legal issue presented by the case."[69]

A second example is Justice Stephen Breyer's decision to sit in a case addressing the constitutionality of the criminal sentencing guidelines despite the fact that Breyer had, as a Senate staffer, assisted in creating the guideline system, and as a federal judge had served as a member of the Sentencing Commission. Professor Stephen Gillers, who Breyer consulted, advised that disqualification was unnecessary. Gillers reasoned that although Breyer had been a long-standing advocate for the guidelines, he had not previously spoken to the precise issue before the Court, and that if he were disqualified under such circumstances it would pose a practical bar to accomplished advocates becoming judges.[70] Professor Jeffrey Shaman concurred: "If we applied the rule strictly, we would be disqualifying a lot of judges."[71]

A third example is the so-called rule of necessity. As one encyclopedia of law summarizes the rule, "[t]he majority view is that the disqualification of judges must yield to the demands of necessity."[72] Where all available judges would be disqualified from hearing a matter, disqualification requirements are overridden, and an otherwise disqualified judge may decide the matter. Thus, judges may resolve disputes the outcomes of which will affect their own jobs or income, insofar as all judges within the jurisdiction would be similarly affected.[73]

A fourth and highly relevant example concerns disqualification on the basis of a judge's prior relationships with lawyers or parties. Available data show that rural judges are less inclined to disqualify themselves on the grounds of bias or relationships than urban judges.[74] As one commentator has explained:

> Rural court judges often know the participants in the court case and may have strong feelings about the lawyers who litigate frequently before them. Where there are no other local judges to hear the matter, a rural judge must often sit on cases where multi-court judges would defer to another judge.[75]

To some extent, a judge's familiarity with the parties and lawyers presents less of an appearance problem in a small town than an urban setting, but courts have been quite candid that their "ethical relativity" is animated at least in part by the demands of practical necessity.[76]

In short, if the paradigm changes and judges en masse begin to vent their spleens in public fora on legal issues of the day for the benefit of voters, Oprah Winfrey, or their own immortality, it could conceivably trigger an avalanche of mass recusals. If appearance problems can be avoided only at the expense of widespread disqualifications that compromise efficient judicial administration, however, the foregoing examples suggest that judges will opt instead to endure and discount appearance problems by interpreting disqualification rules in a more forgiving manner and settling for what amounts to "partial impartiality." In either case, the public's perception will be that the judiciary is peopled with jurists who strive to elaborate on their prejudices, rather than keep them in check.

Conclusion

Lillian Hellman once wrote: "Nobody outside of a baby carriage or a judge's chamber can believe in an unprejudiced point of view." With the triumph of legal realism, it is probably safe to assume that most of us would regard her observation as overstated in its application to judges—judges are people too, and as such, are subject to the same prejudices as the rest of us. But she succeeds in isolating an essential aspect of the judicial role that renders it virtually unique in the American experience. Perhaps it is impossible for judges to be unprejudiced, uncommitted, and viewpoint neutral, but unlike others, their role as fair and impartial arbiters of disputes in an adversarial system demands that they resist their predispositions to remain as open-minded as possible.

The U.S. Supreme Court has told us that judges who stand for election (who constitute over 80 percent of the total) have a right to announce their positions on issues that they will be called on later to decide. To concede that judges have a right to do it, however, is not to concede that judges are right to do it. It is superficially appealing to say, as the Mississippi Supreme Court did in *Wilkerson*, that the state has no legitimate business hiding a prejudiced judge, and that litigants can learn what they need to know to seek the judge's disqualification only if a judge is encouraged to air her prejudices. But this argument misses two essential points. First, the good judge should not cultivate or celebrate her prejudices. She should struggle to minimize them, for the benefit of a judicial role that depends on her remaining receptive to opposing points of view. To encourage a judge to enter the extrajudicial marketplace of legal ideas as a celebrity buyer or seller is to encourage her to vest herself publicly in points of view from which it will be doubly difficult to retreat later in the context of specific cases or controversies without looking spineless, stupid, or duplicitous. Second, if the paradigm shifts and the public venting of judicial spleens becomes routine, the likely result will not be mass disqualification of all judges who have called their impartiality into question. Given the continuing need for an adequate judicial workforce, the likelier result will be a reinterpretation of the disqualification rules that downplays the size of the axes judges have been grinding so as to enable them to sit, lingering appearance problems notwithstanding.

For over a generation, regulators have sought to promote public confidence in the courts through a system of enforceable rules that direct judges, under threat of discipline, to avoid the appearance of impropriety. Appearance problems, however, often manifest themselves in judicial speech or association that when targeted for disciplinary action can provoke constitutional challenges— challenges that began in the campaign arena and have since spilled over into other contexts. The approach of the American Bar Association, which promulgates the Model Code of Judicial Conduct that most jurisdictions follow, has been to stay the course. In the ABA's view, the state's interest in preserving public confidence in the integrity, independence, and impartiality of the courts justifies a range of restrictions on judicial speech and association. And so, the ABA has modified its rules to the minimum extent necessary to accommodate cases such as *White*, but has rejected calls to embrace the spirit of *White* by deregulating judicial speech and association generally, and has determined not to go there unless and until the Supreme Court says it must.

The ABA's approach is one I support (and have assisted in developing). But there is no denying the possibility that over time, the Supreme Court may force the ABA to yield, just as it forced the ABA to abandon its long-standing restrictions on lawyer advertising and solicitation in the 1970s. The ABA's emerging fallback position would appear to be that if it must permit a judge to speak and associate in ways that create appearance problems, it can at least insist that the judge disqualify himself later from any case in which his impartiality might reasonably be questioned, but as I have argued, over time, such an approach is likely to be compromised to accommodate systemic needs.

Even if the Supreme Court invalidates additional—or, for that matter, all—disciplinary rules that seek to avoid appearance problems by restricting judicial speech and association, it would be premature to predict a sea change in the way judges perceive their roles or conduct themselves. To no small extent, the current disciplinary rules codify the norms of an Anglo-American legal culture that has been centuries in the making. For centuries, judges have created physical distance between themselves and those they are called on to judge by sitting aloft on benches, dressed in black. For centuries, judges have created psychological distance between themselves and those they are called on to judge with informal norms that counsel judges to struggle against popular prejudices and preserve their impartiality.[77] And for over a century, judges have been impressed with the need to promote public confidence in the courts by watching what they say, where they go, and with whom they associate to preserve not just the reality but also the appearance of judicial independence, integrity, and impartiality.

This deeply entrenched normative structure is unlikely to topple simply because the Supreme Court wakes up one morning and declares that the government is forbidden from imposing formal discipline on isolated deviants who now have a First Amendment right to say what they please and associate with whom they wish—unless the bench and bar let it. After all, the norms at issue emerged long before formal disciplinary processes were even in existence.

Regardless, then, of who prevails in the ongoing battle between regulators and civil libertarians over the extent to which the state may control judicial speech to guard against the appearance of judicial impropriety, those who seek to restore public confidence in the courts in an age of skepticism would be well advised to return to the roots of a legal culture that has promoted judicial independence, integrity, and impartiality far longer than any system of enforceable rules. At those roots is a principle worth preserving and inculcating: that lawyers who don the robe are doing more than accepting a new job. They are accepting a new way of life, in which they should sometimes sublimate their rights for the greater good of the public they serve, by curtailing their actions, speech, and associations so as to earn and retain the public's trust.

Notes

1. For a detailed description of the cycles of anti-court sentiment in the federal system, *see* CHARLES GARDNER GEYH, WHEN COURTS AND CONGRESS COLLIDE: THE STRUGGLE FOR CONTROL OF AMERICA'S JUDICIAL SYSTEM (2006) (discussing six cycles of court-

directed hostility during the Jeffersonian era, the Jacksonian era, Reconstruction, the populist-progressive period, the Warrant Court era, and today).

2. AMERICAN BAR ASSOCIATION, JUSTICE IN JEOPARDY: REPORT OF THE COMMISSION ON THE 21ST CENTURY JUDICIARY 10 (2003) (JUSTICE IN JEOPARDY).

3. DANIEL BOORSTIN, THE IMAGE: A GUIDE TO PSEUDO-EVENTS IN AMERICA (1961).

4. LEE M. MITCHELL, WITH THE NATION WATCHING: REPORT OF THE TWENTIETH CENTURY FUND TASK FORCE ON TELEVISED PRESIDENTIAL DEBATES 44–45 (1979).

5. Edward R. Murrow. RTNDA Convention, Oct. 15, 1958 ("There are, it is true, occasional informative programs presented in that intellectual ghetto on Sunday afternoons. But during the daily peak viewing periods, television in the main insulates us from the realities of the world in which we live.").

6. Neil Hicky, *Money Lust: How Pressure for Profit is Perverting Journalism*, in THE POWER OF THE PRESS 36 (Beth Levy & Denise Bonilla, eds., 1999).

7. DORIS GRABER, MASS MEDIA AND AMERICAN POLITICS 93 (1989)

8. Gerry Yandel, *TV Watch*, ATL. J.CONST., June 23, 1992; CMPA Election Watch, Oct. 30, 2000 *available at* http://cmpa.com/election2004/JournalistsMonopolize.htm.

9. Edward Schoenbaum, *A Historical Look at Judicial Discipline*, 54 CHI.-KENT L. REV. 1, 13–15 (1977) (describing three procedures: the scire facias process for repealing a judge's letter of patent; removal on criminal conviction; and the Lord Chancellor's authority to remove county judges for misbehavior).

10. MARY VOLCANSEK, JUDICIAL MISCONDUCT: A CROSS-NATIONAL COMPARISON 68–74 (1996).

11. JEFFREY SHAMAN, STEVEN LUBET & JAMES ALFINI, JUDICIAL CONDUCT AND ETHICS §1.12 (3rd Ed. 2000).

12. Schoenbaum, *supra* note 9 at 4–5; *see also* Akhil Reed Amar, *A Neo-Federalist View of Article III: Separating the Two Tiers of Federal Jurisdiction*, 65 B. U. L. REV. 205, 227 n. 81 (1985).

13. SHAMAN, LUBET & ALFINI *supra* note 11 at §14.12.

14. Schoenbaum, *supra* note 9 at 8–9; William Ross, *The Resilience of Marbury v. Madison: Why Judicial Review Has Survived so Many Attacks*, 38 WAKE FOREST L. REV. 733, 741–42 (2003).

15. AMERICAN BAR ASSOCIATION, REPORT OF THE COMMISSION ON PUBLIC FINANCING OF JUDICIAL CAMPAIGNS 1–2 (2002).

16. Quoted in J. CAMPBELL, LIVES OF THE CHIEF JUSTICES OF ENGLAND 208 (1873).

17. "IV. That in the execution of justice I carefully lay aside my own passions"; "VI. That I suffer not myself to be prepossessed with any judgment at all, till the whole business, and both parties be heard"; "VII. That I never engage myself in the beginning of any cause, but reserve myself unprejudiced till the whole be heard"; "X. That I not be biased with compassion to the poor, or favor to the rich"; "XI. That popular or court applause, or distaste, have no influence into anything I do in point of distribution of justice"; "XII. Not to be solicitous of what men will say or think, so long as I keep myself exactly according to the rules of justice"; "XVI. To abhor all private solicitations . . . in matters depending."

18. "VIII. That in business capital, though my nature prompt me to pity, yet to consider that there is also a pity due to the country;" "IX. That I be not too rigid in matters conscientious, when all the harm is in diversity of judgment"; "XIII. If in criminals it be a measuring cast, to incline to mercy and acquittal;" "XIV. In criminals that consist merely in words when no harm ensues, moderation is no injustice"; "XV. In criminals of blood, if the fact be evident, severity is justice."

19. "II. That [the administration of justice] be done 1st, uprightly; 2ndly, deliberately; and 3dly, resolutely"; "V. That I be wholly intent upon the business I am about"; "XVIII. To be short and sparing at meals, that I may be fitted for business."

20. "I. That in the administration of justice, I am entrusted for God, the king, and country"; and "III. That I rest not upon my own understanding or strength, but implore and rest upon the direction and strength of God."

21. "XVII. To charge my servants: 1st, not to interpose in any business whatsoever; 2nd, not to take any more than their own fees; 3d, not to give any undue precedence to causes; 4th, not to recommend counsel."

22. VOLCANSEK, *supra* note 10 at 70–71.

23. The Bacon impeachment, however, warrants an asterisk on a list of judicial removals in England and the United States that is otherwise confined largely to cases of actual—not apparent—misconduct, which may help to explain why, after Bacon was removed, the king quickly intervened, released Bacon from the Tower of London, remitted his fine, and granted him a full pardon. *Id.*

24. Dimes v. Grand Junction Canal, 10 Eng. Rep. 301, 315 (H.L. 1852) (Campbell, concurring).

25. Reprinted in ADDRESSES AND ORATIONS OF RUFUS CHOATE 360--63 (6th Ed. 1891).

26. WILLIAM ROSS, A MUTED FURY 1 (1994).

27. 198 U.S. 45 (1905).

28. Roscoe Pound, *The Causes of Popular Dissatisfaction with the Courts*, reprinted in 20, JUDICATURE 178 (1936).

29. *Address of the President*, 33 REPORT OF THE 31ST ANNUAL MEETING OF THE AMERICAN BAR ASSOCIATION 341 (1908).

30. STEPHEN GILLERS & ROY D. SIMON, REGULATION OF LAWYERS: STATUTES AND STANDARDS 4 (2005).

31. Quoted in JOHN P. MACKENZIE, THE APPEARANCE OF JUSTICE 182 (1974).

32. 6 Cannon's Precedents §536 (1935).

33. Impeachment Charges Against Judge Kenesaw Mountain Landis, House Rep. No. 1407, 66th Cong. 3d Sess., March 2, 1921.

34. *Id.*

35. Quoted in MACKENZIE, *supra* note 31 at 181.

36. *Id.*

37. Canon 19 opined that to "avoid[] the suspicion of arbitrary conclusion [and] promote[] confidence in his judicial integrity," judges should explain the basis for their rulings. Canon 24 encouraged a judge not to incur obligations that would "appear to interfere with his devotion to the expeditious and proper administration

of his official functions." Canon 25 urged a judge to avoid creating "any reasonable suspicion that he is using the power or prestige of his office" to advance his private interests. Canon 26 counseled the judge against maintaining relationships that would "arouse the suspicion that such relations warp or bias his judgment." Canon 27 declared that a judge should refrain from holding fiduciary positions that would "seem to interfere with the proper performance of his judicial duties." Canon 28 warned judges against engaging in political activities that could give rise to the "suspicion of being warped by political bias." Canon 30 advised a candidate for judicial office to do nothing "to create the impression that if chosen, he will administer his office with bias, partiality or improper discrimination." Canon 31 provided that in jurisdictions where judges were authorized to practice law part-time, the judge should not "seem[] to utilize his judicial position to further his professional success." In Canon 33, the judge was encouraged to avoid conduct that could "awaken the suspicion that his social or business relations or friendships constitute an element in influencing his judicial conduct." Canon 34 provided that "in every particular [a judge's] conduct should be above reproach." And Canon 35 observed that allowing cameras in the courtroom "create[s] misconceptions . . . in the mind of the public and should not be permitted." AMERICAN BAR ASSOCIATION, CANONS OF JUDICIAL ETHICS (1924).

38. Robert Martineau, *Enforcement of the Code of Judicial Conduct*, 1972 UTAH L. REV. 410, 411.

39. *Id.*

40. MACKENZIE, *supra* note 31 (quoting Charles Boston, the chief drafter of the Canons of Judicial Ethics, as saying that by 1922 "the agitation for the recall appears to have diminished, and, perhaps, to have spent its force."). *See* Ross, *supra* note 26 at 311 (discussing the relationship between the Supreme Court majority's reversal of position on the constitutionality of New Deal legislation and the end of the cycle of court-directed hostility that had begun in 1890).

41. In re Filipiak, 113 N.E.2d 282, 284 (Ind. 1953) (Emmert, concurring); In re Heggerty, 241 So. 2d 469 (La. 1969); In re Somers, 182 N.W. 341 (Mich. 1971); Estate of Lynde, 250 N.Y.S. 2d 358 (N.Y. App. Div. 1964); La Rue v. Township of East Brunswick, 172 A. 2d 691 (N.J. App. Div. 1961); State v. Lawrence, 123 N.E. 2d. 271 (Oh. 1954); In re Stanley Greenburg, 280 A.2d. 370 (Pa. 1971); In re Gorsuch, 75 N.W. 2d 644 (S.D. 1956); Tharp v. Massengill, 28 P.2d 502 (Wa. 1933).

42. Whitney North Seymour, *The Code of Judicial Conduct from the Point of View of a Member of the Bar*, 1972 UTAH L. REV. 352, 352.

43. Canon 2B provided that a judge "should not convey or permit others to convey the impression that they are in a special position to influence him"; Canon 3C stated that "a judge should disqualify himself in a proceeding in which his impartiality might reasonably be questioned"; Canon 4 authorized a judge to engage in certain "quasi-judicial" activities "if in so doing he does not cast doubt on his capacity" to decide matters impartially; Canon 5A limited a judge's permissible extrajudicial activities to those that "do not detract from the dignity of his office," and Canon 5B

restricted a judge's civic and charitable activities to those that do not "reflect adversely on his impartiality," and Canon 5C imposed a similar limitation on a judge's financial dealings. Canon 6 authorized judges to receive compensation or reimbursement for extracurricular activities, if "the source of such paragraphs does not give the appearance of influencing the judge in his judicial duties or otherwise give the appearance of impropriety." Finally, Canon 7B declared that candidates for judicial office "should maintain the dignity appropriate to judicial office."

44. Peter Morgan, *The Appearance of Propriety: Ethics Reform and the Blifil Paradoxes*, 44 Stan. L. Rev. 593 (1992).

45. SHAMAN, LUBET & ALFINI, *supra* note 11 at §1.03.

46. LISA MILORD, THE DEVELOPMENT OF THE ABA JUDICIAL CODE 8 (1992).

47. JUSTICE IN JEOPARDY, *supra* note 2 at 57.

48. *Id*. At 58.

49. Alex Kozinski, *The Appearance of Propriety*, LEGAL AFFAIRS, February 2005 at 19; Morgan, *supra* note 44.

50. The vagueness problems discussed here can exceed the practical and become constitutional, insofar as subjecting judges to sanction for violating unduly vague rules deprives them of their right to due process of law as guaranteed by the Fourteenth Amendment to the U.S. Constitution. As discussed below, however, the courts have rejected constitutional objections to the appearance of impropriety rule; for that reason, vagueness is discussed here as a practical problem, rather than a constitutional one.

51. AMERICAN BAR ASSOCIATION, MODEL CODE OF PROFESSIONAL RESPONSIBILITY, Canon 9 (1969).

52. Woods v. Covington County Bank, 537 F.2d 804, 813 (5th Cir. 1976).

53. Restatement (Third) of the Law Governing Lawyers §5(c) (2000).

54. ABA Formal Op. 342, n. 17 (1975).

55. ABA Comm. On Evaluation of Model Rules of Prof'l Conduct 53 (Prop. Final Draft 1981).

56. Cynthia Jacob, *A Polemic Against R.P.C. 1.7(C)(2): The Appearance of Impropriety Rule*, THE NEW JERSEY LAWYER 23 (June 1996); Brian Buescher, *Out with the Code and in With the Rules: The Disastrous Nebraska "Bright Line" Rule for Conflict of Interest: A Direct Consequence of the Shortcomings in the Model Code*, 12 GEO. J. LEGAL ETHICS 717 (1999).

57. Nonjudicial activities of Supreme Court justices: Hearing on S. 1097 Before the Subcomm. On Separation of Powers of the Senate Comm. On the Judiciary, 91st Cong. 1st Sess. (1969).

58. Leslie Abramson, *Canon 2 of the Code of Judicial Conduct*, 79 MARQ. L. REV. 949, 955 (1996).

59. Letter from Ronald Minkoff, on behalf of the Association of Professional Responsibility Lawyers, to the ABA Joint Commission to Evaluate the Model Code of Judicial Conduct, Jun 30, 2004, at 6, 9.

60. *Editorial, Weakening the Rules for Judges*, N.Y. TIMES, May 22, 2004, at A16.

61. See polling data cited in Charles Garner Geyh, *Why Judicial Elections Stink*, 64 OH. ST. L. J. 43, 54–55 (2003).

62. For a summary of the First Amendment impediments to regulating judicial campaign finance, *see* AMERICAN BAR ASSOCIATION, REPORT OF THE COMMISSION ON PUBLIC FINANCING OF JUDICIAL CAMPAIGNS 34–37 (2002).

63. Administrative Office of the U.S. Courts, *News Release: Judicial Conference Opposes Sweeping Restrictions on Educational Programs*, Sept. 19, 2000.

64. Judges shall not: "convey the impression" that others are in a special position to influence the judge; "hold membership in any organization that practices invidious discrimination" on specified bases; "by words or conduct manifest bias or prejudice"; "initiate . . . ex parte communications"; "make any comment that might substantially interfere with a fair trial or hearing"; "make pledges, promises or commitments that are inconsistent with the impartial performance of the adjudicative duties of the office"; "commend or criticize jurors for their verdict"; "disclose . . . nonpublic information acquired in a judicial capacity"; "appear at a public hearing before . . . an executive or legislative body" except on specified subjects; "personally participate in the solicitation of funds" for civic or charitable organizations; or engage in a range of political activities except in specified circumstances.

65. 536 U.S. 765 (2002).

66. 867 So. 2d 1006 (Miss. 2004).

67. AMERICAN BAR ASSOCIATION, MODEL CODE OF JUDICIAL CONDUCT, Canon 2.E.(1)(e); *see also* JAMES ALFINI, CHARLES GARDNER GEYH & STEVEN LUBET, JUDICIAL CONDUCT AND ETHICS §4.02 (3d Ed. 2004 Supp).

68. *See, e.g.,* Matthew Medina, Note, *The Constitutionality of the 2003 Revisions to Canon 3(E) of the Model Code of Judicial Conduct*, 104 COLUM. L. REV. 1072 (2004).

69. Cheney v. United States District Court, 541 U.S. 913 (2004).

70. Tony Mauro, *Breyer Consulted Ethics Expert Over Sentencing Case Recusal*, LEGAL TIMES, Jan. 17, 2005.

71. *Id.*

72. 46 Am. Jur 2d Judges 91.

73. United States v. Will, 449 U.S. 200 (1980)(authorizing federal judges to decide case challenging congressional action depriving federal judges of statutory salary increase); Olson v. Cory, 26 Cal. 3d 672 (Cal. 1980) (rule of necessity authorizes state judges to hear case concerning cost of living adjustments for judges); Duplantier v. United States, 606 F.2d 654 (5th Cir. 1979), cert. denied, 449 U.S. 1076 (1981) (judge did not err in refusing to disqualify himself from case challenging the constitutionality of financial disclosure requirements imposed on federal judges).

74. Jonna Goldschmidt & Jeffrey Shaman, *Judicial Disqualification: What Do Judges Think?*, 80 JUDICATURE 68, 71 (1996).

75. Marla Greenstein, *Ethical Relativity*, 41 JUDGES J. 38, 38 (2002).

76. *Id.* (referring to issue as one of "ethical relativity"); In re Antonio, 612 A. 2d 650, 654 (R.I. 1992)("To hold that mere acquaintanceship between bench and bar requires recusal of the trial justice, particularly in a state the size of Rhode Island,

would result in a collapse of the state's judicial system"); In re McCutcheon, No. 3 JD 03 (Pa. Ct. of Jud. Discipline, April 15 2004) (it was proper for judge to hear the traffic case of his grandson's friend, "given the realities of the administration of justice in small towns").

77. *See, e.g.,* the rules of judicial conduct developed by Sir Matthew Hale, *supra* notes 16–21.

2 Politicizing the Process

The New Politics of State Judicial Elections

G. Alan Tarr

DURING THE TWENTIETH CENTURY, judicial reformers sought to de-politicize the selection of state court judges by persuading states to replace their existing systems, under which in most states judges were elected on either partisan or nonpartisan ballots with "merit selection." During the 1960s and 1970s, these reformers enjoyed considerable success. Whereas in 1960 only three states—Alaska, Kansas, and Missouri—employed merit selection in choosing state supreme court justices, by 1980 eighteen did so.[1] Moreover, even in states without merit selection, there seemed to be a movement away from partisan contests—for example, Georgia switched from partisan to nonpartisan election of judges in 1983. Thus, according to one observer during the 1970s, "of the total number of judicial elections held in the 50 states, closely contested, partisan 'unjudicial' judicial elections probably constitute no more than 5 to 7 percent of the total."[2] A more recent commentator concurred, noting that from 1980 to 1995 incumbent justices on state supreme courts were challenged only 61 percent of the time in partisan elections and only 44 percent of the time in nonpartisan elections.[3]

Distinguished Professor of Political Science and Director, Center for State Constitutional Studies, Rutgers University—Camden. I wish to thank Luke Bierman, Charles Geyh, and Aman McLeod for their helpful comments on an earlier draft of this chapter. Research for this article was supported in part by a fellowship from the National Endowment for the Humanities, and I gratefully acknowledge this support. The views expressed in this chapter are my own and do not necessarily reflect the views of the National Endowment for the Humanities.

Of course, states that switched to merit selection did not thereby eliminate judicial elections, as judges appointed under merit selection are obliged to run periodically in retention elections.[4] Yet this did not unduly concern judicial reformers, because they expected that retention elections would differ fundamentally from partisan and nonpartisan elections. They assumed that because retention elections were uncontested and because no individual was directly challenging an incumbent, this would reduce the likelihood of personal attacks. In addition, they believed that by removing the cue of party affiliation, retention elections would encourage voters to decide on the basis of qualifications and experience, rather than seeking to seat judges who shared their partisan affiliation or policy preferences. They further expected that voters would unseat judges only rarely, in those cases in which their performance in office was clearly unsatisfactory. Finally, they emphasized that defeat of incumbent judges would not elevate unqualified persons to the bench, because the nomination of their replacements would remain in the hands of impartial expert selection commissions. Taken altogether, the reformers expected that the movement toward merit selection heralded a de-politicization of judicial selection.[5]

What is most striking about judicial selection in the states in recent years, however, is not de-politicization but hyper-politicization. The reform movement's momentum has ceased. Since 1990, legislatures in North Carolina, Texas, and elsewhere have considered merit selection, only to reject it. In 2000, voters in every county in Florida rejected a constitutional amendment that would have allowed for a local option as to merit selection of trial judges, and in 2005 South Dakota voters rejected an amendment that would have changed the system of selection from nonpartisan election to merit selection.[6] Even more important, judicial elections in the states generally have become "noisier, nastier, and costlier," characterized by "pernicious rhetoric directed at courts and individual judges," by "relentless negativity," and by "dirty politics, even gutter politics."[7] This transformation raises important questions. Given the efforts of reformers to de-politicize state judicial selection, why have state judicial races become so politically charged? Why do states now "confront judicial election and retention election campaigns drowning in dollars and misleading advertisements"?[8] Is this politicization merely a temporary phenomenon, or does it reflect factors that are likely to have long-term impact? This chapter addresses those questions.

Politicization and Its Consequences

Currently, thirty-nine states use elections in either selecting or reselecting state supreme court justices, and in many states the races for seats on those courts have grown increasingly costly and contentious, closely resembling campaigns for other political offices. One factor contributing to this change is the increased use of television advertising in judicial races. Such ads, once rare, have become commonplace. Whereas in 2000, television ads aired in only one-fourth of contested state supreme court elections, in 2004 they aired in four-fifths of the states with contested elections. The television ads themselves have also become nastier and more negative. In West Virginia in 2004, for example, Jim Rowe defeated Justice Warren McGraw after groups supporting Rowe poured more than $2 million into a series of ads that accused the incumbent justice of being soft on child molesters. And in Michigan in 2004, ads targeting Justice Stephen Markman of the Michigan Supreme Court accused him of ruling that "it was legal for employers to harass women" and charged that he was "appointed in secret on orders of the insurance industry and large corporations." Four years earlier in Ohio, groups seeking to defeat Justice Alice Resnick broadcast the infamous "lady justice" ads, which depicted Justice Resnick as the statue of justice, peeking from under her blindfold as special interests placed bags of money on one side of her scales. The voice-over for the ad claimed that Justice Resnick had ruled nearly 70 percent of the time for lawyers who had contributed to her campaigns and concluded with "Alice Resnick. Is justice for sale?"[9]

Such ads are particularly likely to have a substantial effect in judicial elections, because voters typically lack independent information that they might use to assess or counter the claims found in the ads. Absent a major controversy, press coverage of the judiciary and of judicial campaigns is minimal or nonexistent. Most judges perform their work out of view of the press and public, so that when they run for reelection, voters usually do not even know their names, much less the quality of their service. In a Wyoming retention election, for example, more than half the voters admitted that they knew nothing at all about any of the candidates for retention.[10] Until the U.S. Supreme Court's ruling in *Republican Party of Minnesota v. White* (which will be discussed below) eased somewhat the restrictions on judicial candidates, candidates for judicial office could not easily address this information gap, because state codes of judicial conduct drastically restricted what they could say in a campaign. For example, unlike candidates for other offices, judges or prospective judges could not inform voters of how they would vote on forthcoming issues nor could they make promises of specific behavior to constituents. They could not even respond effectively to charges leveled against them by independent groups that are not subject to the same restrictions. They were largely limited to pledging to deal impartially with the cases coming before them. As a result, "political campaigns for judicial posts [were] generally about as exciting as a game of checkers played by mail."[11] And when both candidates made the same pledge of impartiality, they provided voters with little guidance for choosing between them.

Because of the limited information available from candidates even today, voters in judicial elections often lack a basis on which to evaluate the claims of television ads, and thus they are especially vulnerable to manipulative characterizations of a few decisions by interest groups. Ironically, given the agenda of judicial-selection reformers, this may be particularly true in retention elections and nonpartisan elections. Although party labels may offer an inexact indication of a judge's general orientation, they can serve as voting cues, enabling voters to base their decisions on the overall performance or expected performance of the judge. But when these cues are removed, voters are more "likely to cast ballots consistent with the balance of campaign messages they have received, giving a substantial advantage to the candidate best able to get his or her message out to voters."[12] Thus, the absence of party labels makes judges particularly susceptible to "electoral challenges based on narrow issues that arouse particular interest groups rather than the broad quality of their performance on the bench."[13] Moreover, the accusations against particular judges may have consequences beyond the particular race. As Frances Zemans has noted, "Though attacks may be focused on individual judges, their impact is general and magnified. It is generalized because the public makes little distinction among judges (or even among different jurisdictions)."[14]

Related to the increased use of television in judicial campaigns is the skyrocketing cost of such campaigns. In 1986, when groups and candidates in California spent more than $11.5 million in a retention election in which Chief Justice Rose Bird and two associate justices of the California Supreme Court were defeated, the figure seemed—and was—extraordinary.[15] It no longer is. In Illinois in 2004, for example, candidates, political parties, and interest groups together spent $9.3 million in a contest for a single seat on the Illinois Supreme Court. Although the amount spent in Illinois exceeded that in other states, virtually all states have experienced a sharp rise in expenditures in contested judicial races. For example, campaign expenditures for state supreme court races in Alabama rose 776 percent from 1986 to 1996.[16] In Ohio the highest spending for a supreme court race prior to 1980 was $72,000, but in 2000 candidates on average spent $640,000, and interest groups spent far more.[17] Even over shorter time frames, increases in expenditures have been dramatic. Whereas the aggregate spending in judicial races in the 1994, 1996, and 1998 election cycles totaled $73.5 million, the aggregate spending in the three most recent electoral cycles totaled $123 million, a rise of 67 percent. In 2004, nine of the twenty-two states that conducted contested judicial elections broke aggregate candidate fund-raising records.[18]

The increasing sums needed for successful campaigns require candidates for judicial office—or more accurately, their campaign committees—to be heavily involved in fund-raising. This need to raise large sums could tempt judges to tailor their decisions to attract the support of law firms or of interest groups for their reelection campaigns. Even when no corruption is involved, the spectacle of law firms and other groups contributing heavily to the campaigns of judges before whom they will appear can create the appearance of corruption. Thus, a 2002 poll by the American Bar Association found that 72 percent of respondents were concerned that judges having to raise funds might affect their impartiality, and a poll the same year by the Justice at Stake Campaign showed that 76 percent of respondents believed that judicial decisions were influenced at least in part by campaign contributions. Interestingly, respondents in the ABA poll were nonetheless more likely to trust elected than nonelected judges, and a 2005 Maxwell School Poll found that 75 percent of respondents rejected the idea of reducing the number of judges subject to election.[19]

Finally, it should be noted that the phenomenon of expensive and bitterly contested judicial races that rely heavily on negative advertising is spreading and that it is no longer confined to those states that select judges through partisan elections. At one time, it was assumed that one could avoid politicization of judicial elections by opting for merit selection or nonpartisan elections, and data seemed to support the assumption.[20] For example, a study of retention elections for judges from 1964 to 1998 found that only 52 of the 4,558 judges running in retention elections were not retained (1.1 percent), and those defeats generally resulted from judicial misbehavior, rather than from ideological opposition to the judges.[21] Indeed, the mean affirmative vote for candidates who stood for retention from 1964 to 1994 was 74.9 percent.[22] But in recent years there appears to be a convergence among electoral systems, such that state supreme court justices running in nonpartisan elections or retention elections may face the same expensive, vituperative challenges that were previously confined to partisan races. The 1986 race in California pioneered the practice of groups organizing to target sitting justices in retention elections, but it is no longer unique. In 1996, interest groups successfully targeted Justice David Lanphier in Nebraska and Justice Penny White in Tennessee, and in 2005, interest groups fueled the voter anger that led to defeat for Justice Russell Nigro in Pennsylvania. In other instances, groups have mounted major but unsuccessful challenges in retention elections, failing to unseat Chief Justice Leander Shaw in Florida in 1990 and Justice Sandra Newman in Pennsylvania in 2005.

Interest groups and political parties have intervened to influence the outcomes of nonpartisan elections as well. Thus, businesses affiliated with the Ohio Chamber of Commerce spent millions on ads for an Ohio Supreme Court race in 2000, and more than $3 million was spent in Michigan the same year to fill three supreme court positions.[23] In 2000, both the Republican and Democratic parties endorsed candidates in a nonpartisan election for the Idaho Supreme Court, and one candidate launched his campaign by speaking at a Republican Party fund-raising banquet.[24] Although appellate court elections in Georgia are nominally nonpartisan, in 2004 the Democratic Party undertook direct expenditures in support of Justice Leah Sears, who was seeking reelection, and Jesse Jackson was featured in automated phone calls on behalf of Court of Appeals candidate Howard Mead. This led Republican Governor Sonny Perdue to suggest he might support a constitutional amendment to turn Georgia judicial elections back into partisan contests, if partisanship could not be eliminated from the purportedly nonpartisan races.[25]

One must be careful not to overstate the case—thus far the politicization of retention elections and nonpartisan elections has been episodic rather than endemic. Nonetheless, the trend lines are clear. Moreover, even episodic instances of politicization have consequences that reach far beyond the particular race. Justices running for reelection in a state with retention or nonpartisan elections can never be sure whether they will be the focus of a concerted campaign to defeat them. For example, those who unseated Justices White and Lanphier launched their attack only two months prior to the election, when it was too late for the incumbents to raise adequate funds to mount a response.[26] In such circumstances, justices facing retention elections may well find it prudent to build up a campaign war chest, both to discourage efforts to unseat them and to ensure that if they are targeted, they will have resources available to respond to attacks. Thus, fearful of opposition by anti-abortion groups that ultimately did not materialize, California Chief Justice Ronald George raised $886,936 and Justice Ming Chin $710,139 for their retention elections in 1998.[27] Uncertainty about the likelihood of a challenge may also affect judicial behavior: judges may seek to avoid decisions that will bring the wrath of interest groups down on them. The prospect of an election in which a single decision can be taken out of context and used to attack a judge may have a chilling effect on judicial independence. In a series of interviews conducted with judges who ran in retention elections from 1986 to 1990, 15 percent indicated that as the election approached, they sought to avoid controversial cases and rulings, while another 5 percent indicated that they became more conservative in sentencing in criminal cases.[28] Even judges who seek to avoid being influenced by the prospect of a reelection campaign worry that they cannot be sure that it does not subconsciously influence their judgments.[29]

Finally, judges may retire rather than face a contentious reelection fight. Thus, after interest groups engineered the defeat of Justice Penny White in a 1996 retention election, Justice Lyle Reid, the likely next target of those who had defeated Justice White, decided not to seek retention. His withdrawal shows that challenges to incumbents may have effects that extend beyond the occasional defeat of a sitting justice. Indeed, this seems to be the aim of those groups that target sitting justices. They wish not only to unseat the "offending" judge but also to send a message to other members of the court and thereby to change its decisional orientation.

The Origins of Politicization

State judicial selection does not occur in a political vacuum. Rather, political developments within particular states inevitably influence judicial selection, whether it be by election or appointment. In addition, the same factors that have affected American politics and law nationally in recent decades have also left their mark. Thus, as the character of American politics and law has changed, these changes have inevitably and inescapably affected state judicial selection as well.

Partisan Shifts

One dramatic change during the latter half of the twentieth century was the spread of two-party competition throughout the nation. Many states that once were dominated by a single party, particularly in the South and in New England, now regularly conduct highly competitive elections.[30] This is important because, perhaps not surprisingly, a major factor affecting the level of partisan and group conflict in the selection of judges is the overall level of partisan and group competition within a state. In states in which a single party predominates, conflict and competition in judicial elections—as in other elections—tend to be limited. But in states in which party competition is intense and in which parties establish clear ideological identities, that intensity tends to spill over into judicial elections. In Pennsylvania, for example, Republicans and Democrats vigorously compete for the governorship and for control of the state legislature, and they compete just as vigorously for control of the state's courts. From 1979 to 1997, there were elections for nine vacant seats on the Pennsylvania Supreme Court, all hotly contested races, with Republicans winning five seats and Democrats four.[31]

Politicization of judicial races is particularly likely when a state shifts from dominance by a single party to more balanced party competition. In such circumstances, the emerging political party seeks to gain control of all the institutions of state government, including the state supreme court. Texas has long elected its judges in partisan elections, but prior to 1980, the Texas Democratic Party dominated politics in the state, and so judicial elections tended to be uncontested, low-key affairs.[32] As one participant noted: "Forty-four years ago, I participated in a judicial campaign in Dallas. We put up a few billboards, pasted fliers on telephone poles, and passed out small handbills. Our successful campaign cost a few thousand dollars."[33] Only with the rise of the Texas Republican Party did this situation change. The emergence of the Republicans as a viable political alternative encouraged vigorous party competition for all offices, including seats on the state bench. As a result, six incumbent justices of the Texas Supreme Court and numerous lower-court judges were defeated in their reelection bids from 1980 to 1998. In fact, the political transformation in Texas may ultimately lead to sustained Republican control of the judiciary. None of the eighteen judges elected statewide in Texas in 2000 was a Democrat, and in the 2000 elections, no Democrat ran for any of the three open seats on the Texas Supreme Court. In 2002 Republicans were elected in all five races for the supreme court, all with 57 percent or more of the vote, and in 2004 Republicans won all three vacant seats, in two instances running unopposed.[34]

A similar pattern appears to be developing in Alabama. Judicial candidates run in partisan elections, but historically only Democrats stood a chance of serving on the Alabama Supreme Court.[35] But with the inroads by the Republican Party in the South, the composition of state high courts in the region has begun to change, including in Alabama. In 2002 Justice Harold See fought off a major challenge by a Democratic opponent, and in 2004 the Republicans captured all three open seats on the court, winning more than 55 percent of the vote in all three races. Indeed, the most hotly contested race occurred in the Republican primary, where Tom Parker defeated an incumbent justice, Jean Williams Brown, who had voted for the removal of Chief Justice Roy Moore after he refused to remove a courtroom display of the Ten Commandments. Thus, as of 2005, Republicans occupied all seats on the Alabama Supreme Court.[36]

A shift in the partisan balance of power in a state can also increase the level of political conflict between a state legislature and the state supreme court beyond the normal friction inherent in a system of separation of powers. The partisan and ideological composition of a state legislature can change quickly, given the relatively short terms that legislators serve. In contrast, appellate judges tend to serve longer terms—the median term for state supreme court judges is eight years, and most justices serve more than a single term—so turnover on the state bench is more gradual. As a result, when a major political shift occurs in a state, the state's judges may be perceived—whatever their mode of selection—as out of step with the state's newly regnant political forces. Thus, after they gained control of the state legislature in 1996 and the governorship in 1998, Republicans in Florida tended to view the Florida Supreme Court, even though selected by merit selection, as a "remnant of the heyday of Democratic dominance" in Florida.[37] Attributing a partisan cast to merit selection is hardly a new phenomenon—after the institution of the first merit selection system in Missouri in 1940, critics charged that it was actually "a self-perpetuating Democratic political system."[38]

Accompanying the increased partisan competitiveness of recent years has been a shift in the ideological distance separating the Democratic and Republican parties. This is not altogether surprising. When the Democratic Party controlled the "solid South," the conservatives from that region tempered the liberalism of the party nationally. But with both parties competitive throughout much of the country, the effect is that liberals have gravitated toward the Democratic Party and conservatives toward the Republican Party, thus strengthening the ideological identity of each party and accentuating the lack of common ground between the parties. This is reflected in the increasingly party-based voting in Congress.[39] It is also reflected in the opinion gap between Democrats and Republicans on a wide range of issues. As Gary Jacobson has observed, "partisan polarization in Congress reflects electoral changes that have left the parties with more homogeneous and more dissimilar electoral coalitions."[40] This political polarization has sharpened interparty conflict, which is reflected in bitter and personal political rhetoric and in "gotcha" politics. Thus, the politicization of judicial elections replicates the increasingly bitter partisan and ideological conflict present in the nation as a whole.

State Supreme Court Involvement in Public Policy

A second major development affecting state judicial selection is the increasing involvement of state supreme courts, particularly in recent decades, in addressing legal issues with far-reaching policy consequences, such as school finance, tort law, abortion, capital punishment, the rights of defendants, and same-sex marriage. In part, this increased judicial involvement reflects a worldwide movement toward expanding judicial power or judicial activism, which has been encouraged by increasing reliance on the courts by groups seeking political advantage or policy goals.[41] In part, too, it reflects factors peculiar to the United States, such as the American penchant for judicializing political conflicts.[42] But in large measure the changes in the agendas of state supreme courts reflect institutional and legal developments occurring in the states.

One crucial factor has been the change in the size and character of the caseloads of state supreme courts.[43] During the late nineteenth century, state supreme courts struggled with overwhelming caseloads, dominated by minor disputes and private law (primarily commercial) cases. Typically the sole appellate court in the state, the state supreme court exercised no control over its docket and typically found itself facing a severe backlog of cases. Given these caseload pressures, justices had little opportunity to concern themselves with the development of the law of the state. During the twentieth century, however, most states instituted intermediate appellate courts to handle routine cases, thereby relieving the burden on state supreme courts. The establishment of intermediate appellate courts not only diverted less important cases from state supreme courts but also encouraged a reduction in the mandatory jurisdiction of those courts.[44] When states gave courts more control over their dockets, this provided the opportunity, although not necessarily the incentive, for greater activism. State supreme courts became "less concerned with the stabilization and protection of property rights, more concerned with the individual and the downtrodden, and more willing to consider rulings that promote social change."[45] The reduction in caseload pressures also freed justices to concentrate on shaping the law of the state—indeed, "the architecture of the system [told] the judges of the top court to be creative."[46]

This creativity expressed itself initially in the field of tort law. Since the end of World War II, state supreme courts have revolutionized the field of tort law, transforming standards for determining liability, abolishing longstanding immunities, eliminating common law limitations on causes of action, and generally making it easier for plaintiffs to pursue their claims. Writing in 1969, one scholar observed that the "most striking impression that results from reading the weekly outpouring of torts opinions . . . is one of candid, openly acknowledged, abrupt change."[47] Beginning in the 1980s, state legislatures attempted to rein in these court-initiated changes by enacting "tort reform" statutes that sought to restrict recovery and shift the law in ways favorable to defendants in tort cases. The plaintiffs' bar responded by challenging many of these statutes as unconstitutional. For example, they argued that statutory limits on punitive or noneconomic damages violated state constitutional guarantees of jury trial because they limited the discretion of jurors in awarding damages. And they contended that statutes of limitations and statutes of repose violated the "open courts" provisions of state constitutions, which guarantee that the courts be available for the redress of injuries.[48] These arguments enjoyed considerable success: during the 1980s and 1990s, supreme courts in twenty-six states struck down more than ninety tort reform statutes.[49] The success of these constitutional challenges and the ensuing conflict between state legislatures and supreme courts, as well as between pro-plaintiff and pro-defendant interest groups, provided a major impetus for the politicization of judicial races.

Even more important in providing opportunities for state supreme courts to shape state law was the emergence of the new judicial federalism—that is, the renewed reliance by state courts on state declarations of rights to provide protections unavailable under the U.S. Constitution.[50] This new judicial federalism emerged in the early 1970s, following the appointment of Chief Justice Warren Burger to succeed Earl Warren on the U.S. Supreme Court. Civil liberties and social reform groups, concerned about what they expected to be a major shift in orientation on the U.S. Supreme Court, began to look to state courts as a new arena in which to pursue their goals. Initially, the preponderance of claims involved the rights of defendants in criminal cases, and this has remained a major focus of the new judicial federalism.[51] But quite quickly the range of novel and controversial claims brought before state supreme courts expanded to include such hot-button issues as public school finance, abortion, the death penalty, same-sex marriage, and tort reform. When state supreme courts ruled on those issues, they often upset prevailing policies and practices within their states.[52] For example, since 1973, fifteen state supreme courts have invalidated the system of school finance in their states, requiring a major increase in state funding for education and redistribution of those funds among various districts.[53] And the courts' controversial rulings have also upset—and activated—important groups within state populations. Sometimes these groups responded by amending state constitutions to overturn judicial rulings, as occurred with rulings striking down the death penalty in California and Massachusetts.[54] But more frequently these groups have responded by seeking to ensure that jurists sympathetic to their views were placed on the bench or by seeking to defeat those justices who ruled contrary to their views by galvanizing public sentiment against the "offending" jurists.

Group Involvement in Judicial Selection

As this suggests, another key development affecting the politics of state judicial selection has been the increased involvement of interest groups in the process of judicial selection and the increased intensity of that involvement. This is not limited to the states. At the federal level, President Ronald Reagan's nomination of Robert Bork in 1987 generated a major lobbying and publicity campaign by liberal groups determined to deny him a seat on the Supreme Court, and this successful effort marked a turning point in interest-group activity relating to federal judicial appointments. Since the Bork nomination, groups have mobilized over not only Supreme Court nominees but also over lower court appointments, and they have pressured senators to take an active role in opposing or supporting presidential choices.[55]

Interest groups at the state level whose concerns are affected by court rulings have also recognized that they have a stake in who serves on the state bench, and they have tried to influence its composition no matter what the selection system. In some instances, groups have formed in response to particular judicial rulings, targeting particular justices. For example, a group calling itself "And for the Sake of the Kids" played a major role in the defeat of Justice McGraw in West Virginia. More frequently, however, it is preexisting groups that are activated by adverse rulings. Some of these groups are state specific. For example, after the Florida Supreme Court in 1990 struck down a state law requiring minor girls to obtain parental consent before obtaining abortions, the Florida Right to Life Committee sought to defeat Chief Justice Leander Shaw, the author of the majority opinion. Others are national groups that have focused their energies in states whose courts are ruling on issues affecting their members. For example, the Chamber of Commerce in 2000 spent lavishly in judicial campaigns in Michigan, Ohio, and Alabama to try to fill the bench with justices who would uphold defendant-friendly tort reforms. This does not mean, of course, that these groups are always successful in their opposition—Chief Justice Leander Shaw was reelected with 59 percent of the vote, and Justice Alice Resnick of the Ohio Supreme Court, who had been targeted by the Chamber of Commerce, won with 57 percent of the vote. However, interest group opposition to their candidacies did change the intensity and character of the reelection process, because those groups had the resources to increase the salience of the judicial races and because they were not bound by the ethical restrictions on campaign messages imposed on judges and judicial candidates.

The interplay of politicians and interest groups is important as well. Politicians may seek to court groups by seizing on a single controversial ruling as a weapon to attack judges, regardless of the legal merits of the ruling. As Justice Hans Linde put it, "Voters are invited to feel angry at a decision and to vent that anger against any judge who participated in it."[56] In addition to court bashing in order to score points with voters, politicians may seek popular support by placing themselves in the forefront of efforts to deny judges reelection. This has occurred most often with rulings that involve the death penalty or the rights of defendants. Thus, Governor Don Sundquist allied himself with the Tennessee Conservative Union and with victims' rights groups in opposing Justice Penny White because of an opinion that she joined, holding that rape was not in all cases an aggravating factor in murder cases. And Mississippi politicians joined with the state prosecutors' association in spotlighting an opinion by Justice James Robertson that noted that the death penalty could not be imposed on rapists whose victims survived the attack.

The increased involvement of interest groups in state judicial elections is likely to continue because, as Charles Sheldon and Linda Maule have noted, "[i]nterest groups have discovered that contributions to court contests have a pay-off similar to contributions to legislative races."[57] Indeed, the payoff may even be greater. A change in a single seat in the state legislature may have only a minimal effect, but replacement of a single justice can have dramatic effects. Were the Alabama, Ohio, and Texas supreme courts to cease dealing with torts and tort reform, one suspects that the plaintiffs' bar and business groups would no longer offer huge campaign contributions to candidates for seats on those courts. But as long as those courts—and others—continue to address legal issues that are simultaneously contentious policy issues, they will attract the attention and involvement of interested groups.

Republican Party of Minnesota v. White

Historically, state codes of judicial conduct imposed severe constraints on what those seeking or holding judicial office could say in judicial campaigns. They could not comment on pending cases, take positions that appeared to commit them on issues that might come before the court, appear at political functions, or make promises of conduct in office.[58] However, in *Republican Party of Minnesota v. White* (2003), the U.S. Supreme Court dealt a serious blow to these restrictions, upholding a challenge under the First Amendment to the "announce clause" of the Minnesota Code of Judicial Conduct, which prohibited judicial candidates from announcing their views on contested issues that might come before the courts.[59] Speaking for a five-member majority, Justice Antonin Scalia argued that "[w]e have never allowed the government to prohibit candidates from communicating relevant information to voters during an election."[60]

The long-term legal significance of *White* remains unclear. The Court majority expressly distinguished the announce clause from provisions that prohibited judges from making pledges or promises of conduct in office, and it did not rule on the constitutionality of the latter restrictions. Doubtless future cases will compel the Court to address the constitutionality of those restrictions, as well as other limitations on judicial candidates. Indeed, anti-abortion and conservative groups in five states have already filed suit challenging rules that prohibit candidates for judicial office from taking public positions on controversial political and legal issues likely to come before the court.[61] But whatever the legal ramifications of *White*, its political consequences are clear: it has further contributed to the politicization of state judicial elections. By striking down the announce clause, the Supreme Court gave judicial candidates greater freedom of speech. Yet this freedom has proved a mixed blessing for judges. Before *White*, the code of judicial conduct protected judicial candidates, who were able to plead that they were legally prohibited from discussing their views. In the wake of *White*, they can no longer make that claim. In this changed environment, interest groups have aggressively sought to elicit the views of judicial candidates through questionnaires and in public forums, and they have publicized those views to the voting public. Once one candidate responds to questions about her views, the pressure on other candidates to be similarly forthcoming is intense. These views, then, rather than the more outcome-neutral standard of judicial qualifications, may increasingly become the basis on which campaigns for judicial office are waged.

Public Perceptions of Courts

Finally, the politicization of judicial elections has both influenced and been influenced by changing public perceptions of law and of judges. Those who oppose the election of judges have traditionally argued that appropriate accountability is nonetheless ensured for lower court judges, because their decisions are subject to appellate review. Even for appellate judges, accountability is ensured because they remain accountable to the law. Thus, opponents of judicial elections insist that safeguarding judges' responsiveness to the law, rather than to public opinion or to personal values, is crucial to ensuring the impartial administration of justice. Implicit in this rule-of-law argument are two key assumptions, namely, that the law provides a standard that can guide judicial decisions and that it is possible to assess judicial fidelity to the law. Yet both these assumptions have become less widely accepted. In part, this skepticism may reflect a more general decline of confidence in the major institutions of American society. But in part, it reflects developments within the legal community that have filtered down to the general public.

Within the legal community, assessment of judicial fidelity to law has been complicated by a breakdown of consensus about how one interprets the law or, indeed, what constitutes interpretation as opposed to lawmaking. This is true not only with regard to constitutional interpretation—consider the debates over constitutional theory since the 1980s—but with regard to statutory interpretation and the development of the common law as well.[62] This breakdown dates from the early twentieth century, when the Legal Realists launched their assault on legal formalism, marking the "jurisprudential divide between the old order and modernity."[63] Legal Realism demonstrated that law was not a closed system of legal rules and persuasively argued for the indeterminacy of law and for the role of subjectivity in the decisional process. But its constructive work did not equal its critical contribution. It succeeded in destroying the edifice of legal orthodoxy but not in replacing it.

One may well question whether the American public ever fully accepted the picture of totally apolitical judicial decision making traditionally espoused by the legal profession. Charles Geyh has documented several periods of intense public criticism of federal judges and their rulings, and similar discontent has been voiced in the states as well.[64] But what is clear is that the contemporary American public has certainly learned the lessons of Legal Realism. Although most Americans have never witnessed state judges in operation nor read judicial opinions they have written, poll data reveal a deep skepticism about the impartiality of state courts and their ability to administer justice evenhandedly. Thus, in a 2005 Maxwell School poll, a majority of respondents agreed with the view that "in many cases judges are really basing their decisions on their own personal beliefs," and 82 percent of respondents believed that the partisan background of judges influenced their rulings a lot or at least some.[65] A poll for Justice at Stake reported similar findings: 64 percent of respondents agreed that "there are too many activist judges who make rulings that follow their own views rather than the law," and 60 percent thought "too many judges are legislating from the bench and making laws instead of interpreting the laws."[66]

Whatever the accuracy of these perceptions, they have important implications. The perception that judicial decisions generally reflect judicial predilections or idiosyncrasy rather than simply the legal merits of the case weakens considerably the rule-of-law argument for judicial independence. For this perception encourages the conclusion that judicial decisions are not fundamentally different from those of other political actors.[67] Yet once this is accepted, it follows easily that judges should be assessed on the basis of their political orientations and judicial decisions on the basis of whether one agrees with the outcomes.

The Future?

As Justice Harold See's contribution to this volume makes clear, not everyone views the politicization of judicial elections in the states as cause for alarm.[68] Some may well applaud politicization as promoting greater popular control over the judiciary. For proponents of judicial accountability, the escalation in the costs of judicial campaigns is a positive development, because it signals that races for judicial office have become more competitive, and greater competitiveness translates into more meaningful choices for voters. If the fear of electoral defeat induces candidates to spend more money on campaigns, this should make judicial elections more salient and should ensure that more information is transmitted to voters. If rules governing campaign speech are relaxed, this too should ameliorate the flow of information and encourage more informed voter choice. So should greater involvement by interest groups in judicial races.

Opponents of politicized judicial selection have been vocal in registering their dismay, but the remedies available to them are limited. Groups such as the American Bar Association and the American Judicature Society continue to recommend that states adopt merit selection. However, given the unlikelihood of that occurring in the near future, they have sought ways to reduce the politicization of state judicial contests or to curtail the effects of such politicization. For example, the ABA has recommended that judicial terms be lengthened and that judges not stand for reelection, fearing that the reselection process is far more vulnerable to politicization than the process of initial selection.[69] The ban on successive terms makes considerable sense—it is the norm for constitutional courts in Europe—but no states have shown an interest recently in increasing the insulation of judges through longer terms, and judges themselves may be less than enthusiastic about giving up the possibility of more than one term in office.[70] The ABA has further recommended that states unwilling to embrace merit selection should replace partisan elections with nonpartisan ones and that public financing be instituted for appellate races to safeguard judicial candidates against illicit influences. Yet only North Carolina has taken these steps in recent years. Moreover, even if public financing is instituted, it does not protect against independent spending by private groups seeking to influence the membership of state supreme courts. Indeed, it is precisely the possibility of interest group involvement in judicial campaigns, safeguarded by the First Amendment from the strictures that can be imposed on judicial candidates, that frustrates most efforts to combat the politicization of judicial elections.

Finally, opponents of judicial elections have sought to limit the effects of politicization by encouraging a strengthening of recusal rules and supporting the disqualification of judges from cases involving issues on which they expressed views during their election campaigns. Despite the immediate appeal of this new "disqualification regime," it is hardly a complete solution. Indeed, as Charles Geyh has noted, the potential impact of mass disqualifications on the administration of justice may well trigger a rethinking of the requirements of judicial impartiality.[71]

In sum, the genie cannot be put back in the bottle. The same factors that have encouraged the politicization of judicial selection in the states are likely to continue to influence judicial selection for the foreseeable future. The only question is whether this politicization will undermine the quality of those selected as state judges and impair their impartiality, as critics of judicial elections fear, or whether, as Justice See and others have suggested, it will promote meaningful accountability without impeding the impartial administration of justice.

Notes

1. Information on judicial selection systems in the various states is available at the website of the American Judicature Society, *available at* http://www.ajs.org.

2. Henry R. Glick, *The Promise and Performance of the Missouri Plan: Judicial Selection in the Fifty States*, 32 U. MIAMI L. REV. 509, 519 (1978).

3. Melinda Gann Hall, *State Supreme Courts in American Democracy: Probing the Myths of Judicial Reform*, 95 AM. POL. SCI. REV. 324 (2001); *see also* Chris Bonneau and Melinda Gann Hall, *Predicting Challengers in State Supreme Court Elections: Context and the Politics of Institutional Design*, 56 POL. RES. Q. 337–49 (2003), *and* Chris W. Bonneau, *Patterns of Campaign Spending and Electoral Competition in State Supreme Court Elections*, 25 JUST. SYS. J. 21 (2004).

4. According to one expert, 87 percent of state judges currently run for election or reelection. *See* Roy A. Schotland, *Comment*, 61 LAW & CONTEMP. PROBS. 149, 154–55 (Summer 1998).

5. *See Merit Selection: The Best Way to Choose the Best Judges*, American Judicature Society, *available at* http://www.ajs.org/js/ms_descrip.pdf. As Michael Dimino notes: "The push for merit selection . . . rests . . . on the determination that public input is bad for the judicial system and must be tolerated only as a political compromise. This is clear once one sees the degree to which success under the merit selection system is equated with the retention of incumbents." *See* Michael R. Dimino, *The Futile Quest for a System of Judicial 'Merit' Selection*, 67 ALB. L. REV. 803, 813 (2004). For a more general analysis of the claims of proponents of merit selection, *see* Aman McLeod, *If at First You Don't Succeed: A Critical Analysis of Judicial Selection Reform Efforts*, 107 W. VA. L. REV. 499 (2005). For a classic account of merit selection, which concludes that it changes the politics of judicial selection, rather than eliminating politics from judicial

selection, *see* RICHARD A. WATSON & RONDAL G. DOWNING, THE POLITICS OF THE BENCH AND BAR: JUDICIAL SELECTION UNDER THE MISSOURI NONPARTISAN COURT PLAN (1969).

6. *See* Seth Andersen, *Examining the Decline in Support for Merit Selection in the States*, 67 ALB. L. REV. 793 (2004), *and* Luke Bierman, *Beyond Merit Selection*, 29 FORDHAM URB. L. J. 851 (2002). The Florida proposal lost in every county and averaged only a 32 percent approval rate. *See* http://www.ajs.org/js/FL_history.htm.

7. DEBORAH GOLDBERG ET AL., THE NEW POLITICS OF JUDICIAL ELECTIONS 2000 8 (2000) *available at* http://faircourts.org/files/JASMoneyReport.PDF; Paul J. De Muniz, *Eroding the Public's Confidence in Judicial Impartiality: First Amendment Jurisprudence and Special Interest Financing of Judicial Campaigns*, 67 ALB. L. REV. 763, 764 (2004); Paul D. Carrington, *Judicial Independence and Democratic Accountability in Highest State Courts*, 61 LAW & CONTEMP. PROBS. 79, 111 (1998); *and* Clive S. Thomas et al., *Interest Groups and State Court Elections: A New Era and Its Challenges*, 87 JUDICATURE 135, 138 (2003).

8. Stephen B. Burbank & Barry Friedman, *Reconsidering Judicial Independence*, *in* JUDICIAL INDEPENDENCE AT THE CROSSROADS: AN INTERDISCIPLINARY APPROACH 37 (Stephen B. Burbank & Barry Friedman eds., 2002).

9. Information and data in this paragraph are drawn from DEBORAH GOLDBERG ET AL., THE NEW POLITICS OF JUDICIAL ELECTIONS 2004 1–12 (2004) *available at* http://www.justiceatstake.org/files/NewPoliticsReport2004.pdf, *and from* Roy A. Schotland, *Financing Judicial Elections*, *in* FINANCING THE 2000 ELECTION 220–22 (David B. Magleby, ed., 2002).

10. Kenyon N. Griffin & Michael J. Horan, *Patterns of Voter Behavior in Judicial Retention Elections for Supreme Court Justices in Wyoming*, 67 JUDICATURE 68, 72 (1983). For a less pessimistic view, *see* Nicholas P. Lovich, *Citizen Knowledge and Voting in Judicial Elections*, 73 JUDICATURE 28, 32–33 (1989).

11. William C. Bayne, *Lynchard's Candidacy, Ads Putting Spice into Judicial Race*, COMMERCIAL APPEAL, Oct. 29, 2000, at DS1, quoted in Schotland, *supra* note 9 at 213.

12. Charles H. Franklin, *Behavioral Factors Affecting Judicial Independence*, in Burbank & Friedman, *supra* note 8, at 152.

13. *Id.* at 154. See more generally, PHILIP L. DUBOIS, FROM BALLOT TO BENCH: JUDICIAL ELECTIONS AND THE QUEST FOR ACCOUNTABILITY (1980).

14. Frances Kahn Zemans, *The Accountable Judge: Guardian of Judicial Independence*, 72 S. CAL. L. REV. 625, 640 (1999).

15. On the California campaign, *see* John H. Culver & John T. Wold, *Rose Bird and the Politics of Judicial Accountability in California*, 70 JUDICATURE 81 (1986), *and* John T. Wold & John H. Culver, *The Defeat of the California Justices: The Campaign, the Electorate, and the Issue of Judicial Accountability*, 70 JUDICATURE 348 (1986).

16. *Merit Selection in the States: Alabama*, American Judicature Society, *available at* http://www.ajs.org/js/AL.htm.

17. Roy A. Schotland, *To the Endangered Species List, Add: Nonpartisan Judicial Elections*, 39 WILLAMETTE L. REV. 1397, 1405, n. 34 (2003); *and* GOLDBERG *supra* note 7, at 10.

18. GOLDBERG, *supra* note 9, at 13–19.

19. The ABA poll results are available at http://www.abanet.org/media/aug02/apnewsconfrevised8-8.html. Last visited on August 14, 2006. Justice at Stake, National Survey Results (2001), *available at* http://faircourts.org/files/JASNationalSurveyResults.pdf. These data are reported and discussed in McLeod, *supra* note 5, at 509. Campbell Public Affairs Institute, the Maxwell Poll on Civic Engagement and Inequality (Oct. 2005) (margin of error ± 5 percent), *available at* http://www.maxwell.syr.edu/campbell/Poll/2005Poll/MaxwellPoll.pdf. Last visited on August 14, 2006.

20. Many of the states with partisan election of judges were located in the South, and for most of the twentieth century those states were Democratic strongholds, so opposition to Democratic nominees for judgeships was often token at best.

21. Larry T. Aspin, *Trends in Judicial Retention Elections, 1964–1998*, 83 JUDICATURE 79 (1999).

22. Larry T. Aspin et al., *Thirty Years of Judicial Retention Elections: An Update*, 37 SOC. SCI. J. 1 (2000).

23. G. Alan Tarr, *Rethinking the Selection of State Supreme Court Justices*, 39 WILLAMETTE L. REV. 1445,1446–47 (2003); TRACIEL V. REID, THE POLITICIZATION OF JUDICIAL RETENTION ELECTIONS: THE DEFEAT OF JUSTICES LANPHIER AND WHITE, RESEARCH ON JUDICIAL SELECTION 1999 (2000); *and* GOLDBERG *supra*, note 7.

24. Anthony Champagne, *National Summit on Improving Judicial Selection: Interest Groups and Judicial Elections*, 34 LOY. L. A. L. REV. 1391, 1402 (2001).

25. Jim Wooten, *Voters in Dark on Judge Races*, ATL. J. CONST., Nov. 28, 2004, *available at* http://www.ajc.com/opinion/content/opinion/wooten/2004/112804.html (last visited on August 14, 2006), *and* Brian Basinger, *Perdue Looks at Partisan Judicial Races*, AUGUSTA CHRON., May 23, 2005, *available at* http://chronicle.augusta.com/stories/052405/met_4227612.shtml.

26. Harold See, "An Essay on Judicial Selection" in this volume.

27. Schotland, *supra* note 17, at 1407, n. 40.

28. Larry T. Aspin & William K. Hall, *Retention Elections and Judicial Behavior*, 77 JUDICATURE 306, table 4 (1994). Other studies have produced similarly troubling findings. *See, e.g.*, Paul Brace & Melinda Gann Hall, *Studying Courts Comparatively: The View from the American States*, 48 POL. RES. Q. 13–24 (1995); Carol Ann Traut & Craig F. Emmert, *Expanding the Integrated Model of Judicial Decision Making: The California Justices and Capital Punishment*, 60 J. POL. 1177 (1998); *and* Gregory A. Huber & Sanford C. Gordon, *Accountability and Coercion: Is Justice Blind When It Runs for Office?* 48 AM. J. POL. SCI. 247–63 (2004). Surveying the effects of elections on judicial behavior, one scholar concluded: "Retention elections have the same potential for intimidation and a chilling effect on judicial decisionmaking as direct elections." *See* Stephen B. Bright, *Can Judicial Independence Be Attained in the South: Overcoming History, Elections, and Misperceptions about the Role of the Judiciary*, 14 GA. ST. U. L. REV. 817, 859 (1998). For consideration of the implications of these findings, see Peter M. Shane, *Interbranch Accountability in State Government and the Constitutional Requirement of Judicial Independence*, 61 LAW & CONTEMP. PROBS. 21 (Summer 1998).

29. Gerald F. Uelman, *Otto Kaus and the Crocodile*, 30 LOY. L. A. L. REV. 971 (1997).

30. *See* EARL BLACK & MERLE BLACK, THE RISE OF THE SOUTHERN REPUBLICANS (2002), *and* DAVID LUBLIN, THE REPUBLICAN SOUTH: DEMOCRATIZATION AND PARTISAN CHANGE (2004).

31. James Eisenstein, *Financing Pennsylvania's Supreme Court Candidates,* 84 JUDICATURE 10, 12 (2000).

32. Kyle Cheek & Anthony Champagne, *Money in Texas Supreme Court Elections, 1980–1998,* 84 JUDICATURE 20, 22 (2000).

33. Thomas et al., *supra* note 7 at 137.

34. On the shift in Texas, *see* Anthony Champagne & Kyle Cheek, *The Cycle of Judicial Elections: Texas as a Case Study,* 29 FORDHAM URB. L. J. 907, 929 (2002). For more recent election results, *see* Texas State Supreme Court Elections Data 2004, *available at* http://www.justiceatstake.org/contentViewer.asp>breadcrumb=4,126,111,462. Last visited on August 14, 2006.

35. *See* G. ALAN TARR & MARY CORNELIA ALDIS PORTER, CHAPTER 3, STATE SUPREME COURTS IN STATE AND NATION (1988).

36. *See* Alabama State Supreme Court Elections Data 2004, *available at* http://www.justiceatstake.org/contentViewer.asp>breadcrumb=4,124,47,489. Last visited on August 14, 2006.

37. Rebecca Mae Salokar & Kimberly A. Shaw, *The Impact of National Politics on State Courts: Florida After Election 2000,* 23 JUST. SYS. J. 57, 59–60 (2002).

38. Quoted in RICHARD A. WATSON & RONDAL G. DOWNING, THE POLITICS OF THE BENCH AND THE BAR: JUDICIAL SELECTION UNDER THE MISSOURI NONPARTISAN COURT PLAN 55 (1969).

39. *See* Nolan McCarty et al., *The Hunt for Party Discipline in Congress,* 95 AM. POL. SCI. REV. 673–87 (2001), *and* James M. Snyder, Jr. & Tim Groseclose, *Estimating Party Influence in Congressional Roll Call Voting,* 44 AM. J. POL. SCI. 193–211 (2000). For a more general perspective, *see* KEITH T. POOLE & HOWARD ROSENTHAL, CONGRESS: A POLITICAL-ECONOMIC HISTORY OF ROLL-CALL VOTING (1997).

40. Gary Jacobson, *Party Polarization in National Politics: The Electoral Connection, in* POLARIZED POLITICS: CONGRESS AND THE PRESIDENT IN A PARTISAN ERA 25 (Jon R. Bond & Richard Fleisher, eds., 2000).

41. *See* RAN HIRSCHL, TOWARD JURISTOCRACY: THE ORIGINS AND CONSEQUENCES OF THE NEW CONSTITUTIONALISM (2004), *and* THE GLOBAL EXPANSION OF JUDICIAL POWER (C. Neal Tate & Torbjorn Vallinder, eds., 1995). On the greater reliance by groups on courts in seeking political goals, a phenomenon characteristic of the United States but increasingly common in other systems as well, *see* CHARLES R. EPP, THE RIGHTS REVOLUTION: LAWYERS, ACTIVISTS, AND SUPREME COURTS IN COMPARATIVE PERSPECTIVE (1998).

42. As Alexis de Tocqueville noted 170 years ago: "there is hardly a political question in the United States which does not sooner or later turn into a judicial one." *See his* DEMOCRACY IN AMERICA 270 (1969).

43. The analysis in this paragraph follows that of two articles written by Robert A. Kagan, Bliss Cartwright, Lawrence M. Friedman, & Stanton Wheeler, *The Business*

of State Supreme Courts, 1870–1970, 30 STAN. L. REV. 121 (1977), and *The Evolution of State Supreme Courts*, 76 MICH. L. REV. 961 (1978).

44. *See* Roger D. Groot, *The Effects of an Intermediate Appellate Court on the Supreme Court Work Product: The North Carolina Experience*, 7 WAKE FOREST L. REV. 548–72 (1971); Victor Eugene Flango & Nora F. Blair, *Creating an Intermediate Appellate Court: Does It Reduce the Caseload of a State's Highest Court?* 64 JUDICATURE 74–84 (1980); *and* John M. Scheb & John M. Scheb II, *Making Intermediate Appellate Courts Final: Assessing Jurisdictional Changes in Florida's Appellate Courts*, 67 JUDICATURE 474 (1984).

45. Kagan et al., *supra* note 43, at 155.

46. PAUL D. CARRINGTON, DANIEL J. MEADOR, & MAURICE ROSENBERG, JUSTICE ON APPEAL 150 (1976).

47. ROBERT E. KEETON, VENTURING TO DO JUSTICE: REFORMING PRIVATE LAW 3 (1969).

48. Robert S. Peck, *In Defense of Fundamental Principles: The Unconstitutionality of Tort Reform*, 31 SETON HALL L. REV. 672 (2002).

49. For a listing of these cases, *see* Victor E. Schwartz & Leah Lorber, *Judicial Nullification of Civil Justice Reform Violates the Fundamental Federal Constitutional Principle of Separation of Powers: How to Restore the Right Balance*, 32 RUTGERS L. J. appendix (2002).

50. For an overview and citation to much of the pertinent literature, *see* G. ALAN TARR, UNDERSTANDING STATE CONSTITUTIONS 161–70 (1998).

51. *See* BARRY LATZER, STATE CONSTITUTIONS AND CRIMINAL JUSTICE (1993).

52. This statement leaves unaddressed the reasons why state supreme courts were willing to respond to the novel claims being advanced under state declarations of rights. What was crucial was the availability of a model as to how state judges could go about developing a civil-liberties jurisprudence. Only when circumstances brought a combination of state constitutional arguments, plus the Warren Court's example of how courts might develop such constitutional guarantees, could a state's civil-liberties jurisprudence develop. *See* TARR, *supra* note 50, at 164–65.

53. The literature on this litigation is vast. Useful overviews that emphasize the political dynamics of these cases include MATTHEW H. BOSWORTH, COURTS AS CATALYSTS: STATE SUPREME COURTS AND PUBLIC SCHOOL FINANCE EQUITY (2001), and DOUGLAS REED, ON EQUAL TERMS: THE CONSTITUTIONAL POLITICS OF EDUCATIONAL OPPORTUNITY (2001).

54. *See* CAL. CONST., art. 1, §. 27, *overruling* People v. Anderson, 493 P.2d 880 (Cal. 1973), and MASS. CONST., Declaration of Rights, art. 26, amendment 1116, *overruling* District Attorney v. Watson, 411 N.E.2d 1274 (Mass. 1980).

55. NANCY SCHERER, SCORING POINTS: POLITICIANS, ACTIVISTS, AND THE LOWER FEDERAL COURT NOMINATION PROCESS (2005).

56. Hans A. Linde, *The Judge as Political Candidate*, 40 CLEV. ST. L. REV. 1, 7 (1992).

57. CHARLES H. SHELDON & LINDA S. MAULE, CHOOSING JUSTICE: THE RECRUITMENT OF STATE AND FEDERAL JUDGES 76 (1998).

58. AMERICAN BAR ASSOCIATION, JUSTICE IN JEOPARDY: REPORT OF THE COMMISSION ON THE 21ST CENTURY JUDICIARY 29 (2002) (JUSTICE IN JEOPARDY).

59. Republican Party of Minnesota v. White, 536 U.S. 765 (2002).

60. *Id.*, at 781.

61. Nicole Tsong, *Anti-Abortion Group Wants Judges' Views*, ANCHORAGE DAILY NEWS, Nov. 20, 2004, at A1, *and* Emily Heller, *Judicial Races Get Meaner*, NAT'L L. J., Oct. 5, 2004, *available at* http://www.law.com/jsp/article.jsp?id=1098217051328.

62. For an overview of the constitutional theory debates, *see* MICHAEL J. GERHARDT, CONSTITUTIONAL THEORY: ARGUMENTS AND PERSPECTIVES (1993). For different perspectives on statutory interpretation, see WILLIAM N. ESKRIDGE, DYNAMICS OF STATUTORY INTERPRETATION (1994) *and* ANTONIN SCALIA, A MATTER OF INTERPRETATION: FEDERAL COURTS AND THE LAW: AN ESSAY (1997).

63. LAURA KALMAN, THE STRANGE CAREER OF LEGAL LIBERALISM 13 (1996). Other key studies of Legal Realism include MORTON HORWITZ, THE TRANSFORMATION OF AMERICAN LAW, 1870–1960: THE CRISIS OF LEGAL ORTHODOXY (1992), AND JOHN SCHLEGEL, AMERICAN LEGAL REALISM AND EMPIRICAL SOCIAL SCIENCE (1995).

64. *See* CHARLES GARDNER GEYH, WHEN COURTS AND CONGRESS COLLIDE: THE STRUGGLE FOR CONTROL OF AMERICA'S JUDICIAL SYSTEM (2006), *and* Geyh, "Preserving Public Confidence in an Age of Individual Rights and Public Skepticism," in this volume. For studies documenting popular skepticism of the impartiality of state judges over time, *see, e.g.,* RICHARD E. ELLIS, THE JEFFERSONIAN CRISIS: COURTS AND POLITICS IN THE YOUNG REPUBLIC (1971); Theodore W. Ruger, *"A Question Which Convulses the Nation": The Early Republic's Greatest Debate about the Judicial Review Power*, 117 HARV. L. REV. 826 (2004); and WILLIAM G. ROSS, A MUTED FURY: POPULISTS, PROGRESSIVES, AND LABOR UNIONS CONFRONT THE COURTS, 1890–1937 (1994).

65. The Maxwell Poll, *supra* note 19.

66. Justice at Stake National Survey, *supra* note 19.

67. This is not the only possible conclusion. Even admitting the inevitability of judicial choice, one might still seek to reduce external influences, such as campaign contributions and interest-group pressures, on those choices.

68. Harold See, "An Essay on Judicial Selection," in this volume.

69. American Bar Association, *supra* note 58, at 67–82.

70. For a discussion of the advantages of a single, nonrenewable term for state supreme court judges, drawing on the European experience in staffing constitutional courts, see Tarr, *supra* note 23, at 1465–69.

71. See Geyh, "Preserving Public Confidence in the Courts."

II VIEWS FROM THE BENCH

3 An Essay on Judicial Selection

A Brief History

Harold See

IN THE YEARS IMMEDIATELY FOLLOWING the adoption of the Constitution of the United States, the states virtually uniformly used the pattern of appointed judges that the federal government had adopted. At that time, only Vermont selected any of its judges by election.[1] Every state that entered the Union before 1845 did so with an appointed judiciary.[2]

In 1812 Georgia became the first state to amend its constitution to provide for the election of some judges.[3] In 1832, Mississippi became the first state to choose all of its judges through contested elections.[4] During the period of Jacksonian democracy, which called for popular control over all aspects of government, most states went to an elected judiciary.[5] By the time of the Civil War, the great majority of states elected their judges.[6] Every state that entered the Union between 1846 and 1912 provided for judicial elections.[7]

In 1906 Roscoe Pound delivered an address in which he called for reforms to state court systems to limit political influences on state judges.[8] In 1913, he helped found the American Judicature Society. His cofounder, Albert M. Kales, was made responsible for drafting a new procedure for selecting state judges. Kales devised a system, called "merit selection," of appointing judges

Harold See is a justice on the Supreme Court of Alabama. Justice See would like to thank the anonymous reviewer and Professor Roy Schotland for their valuable comments, and to thank Bud Barnes, Matt Bauer, Joi Montiel, and Mitria Wilson for their research assistance. Any views expressed in this essay are not official views or those of the court on which Justice See serves, but are offered for consideration for their value in improving the judicial system.

for a term that is followed by a retention election.[9] Missouri was the first state to adopt the plan and, thus, Kales's plan came to be called the "Missouri plan."[10] For eighteen years no state followed Missouri's lead; however, from 1958 to 1976, nineteen additional states adopted some variation of the Missouri Plan.[11] In the last thirty years, only one additional state has done so.[12]

Selection Methods

In looking at the selection of judges,[13] there are two critical issues: by whom the selecting is done and what restrictions there are on the appointment.[14] A judge may be selected by representatives of one of the three branches of government. Thus, the selection may be made by the governor, as is the practice in twenty-six states.[15] Or, it may be made by the legislature—the practice in two states.[16] Finally, the selection may be made by the judiciary itself; however, this method is practiced rarely in the United States and then only for courts of limited jurisdiction.[17] The selection of a judge also may be made by some body other than one of the branches of government. Again, while such a practice is conceptually possible, it is not the practice in any state.[18] There may be restrictions on who may be selected for a judicial position. Typically judges must be selected from among lawyers,[19] but it may be further limited. It is common in those states in which the governor selects judicial appointees to restrict the governor's selection to the names on a list composed by a judicial selection committee.[20] The committee is commonly representative of a number of constituencies. Thus, the state bar association may select a certain number of members, the governor selects others, and, perhaps, a judges' association or other groups or officeholders select still others. It is common to have non-lawyers as well as lawyers as members of the judicial selection committee.[21] In practice, however, lawyers selected by the state bar association typically dominate such committees.[22] Thus, one would expect the list presented to the governor to be composed largely of lawyers with whom the state bar association is comfortable.[23]

Not only may there be prior restrictions on whom the governor may select, but there may be subsequent restrictions as to who may serve. Thus, for example, the governor may select someone to serve as a judge, but that selection may be in some way conditioned on the approval of the legislative branch. Senatorial approval of the presidential appointment of an Article III federal judge is the most widely recognized example of such a procedure.

Judges, instead of being selected by one of the three branches of government or by a commission, may be selected (or retained) directly by the public by election. There are three principal forms of election. Election may be partisan, nonpartisan, or without an opponent—that is, "on one's record."[24] It is helpful to define terms. Clearly, we do not want partisan judges who will decide cases based on whether the parties or the lawyers are Republicans or Democrats. However, it is equally true that we do not want a partisan school board member who will give educational opportunity based on political affiliation, or a partisan attorney general who will prosecute or not depending on the political affiliation of the wrongdoer. The public generally does not look fondly on overtly political actors,[25] regardless of the manner of their selection. The reference to the partisan election of judges improperly carries with it the connotation of partisan judges; however, "partisan" denotes only the method of selection, not the nature of service. Partisan election of judges means no more than that the judges run for election under party labels. Nonpartisan election means that judges run without party labels. Running "on one's record" means that the voters vote yes or no—conceptually "running on one's record" may be partisan with one political party supporting and the other opposing retention of an incumbent judge, or it may be nonpartisan. In practice, it has been nonpartisan.[26]

Methods by which judges are selected and those by which they are either retained or replaced, at least conceptually, may be combined in various ways; however, although a large number of combinations is possible, only a limited number is of practical concern. Thus, the initial selection of a judge is typically (1) by popular election, which may be partisan or nonpartisan; (2) by gubernatorial appointment, with or without confirmation by the legislative branch, and either from a list prepared by an independent commission or in the sole discretion of the governor; or (3) by the legislature. The judge, once appointed, serves either for life or for a period of years.[27] Where she serves for a period of years, at the expiration of her initial term she either stands for reappointment or for election or "retention," either against an opponent, or "on her record" without an opponent.[28] Thus, for example, the Missouri Plan ("merit selection") combines a number of these features. First, a commission prepares a list of names. The governor selects one of the names for appointment. That selection may require legislative approval.[29] The appointee serves an initial term.[30] At the expiration of the initial term, the appointee must stand for a popular retention election—an up or down vote on whether the judge is to be retained in office for an additional term—in which he, typically, runs unopposed "on his record."[31]

Requirements for a Strong Judiciary

> In a government framed for durable liberty, not less regard must be paid to giving the magistrate a proper degree of authority, to make and execute the laws with rigour, than to guarding against encroachments upon the rights of the community. As too much power leads to despotism, too little leads to anarchy, and both eventually to the ruin of the people. (Papers of Alexander Hamilton, II, 650–51; newspaper article, July 12, 1781)

Our constitutional structure recognizes both the importance of a strong central government and the need to protect the citizenry from it. It is by the principles of the separation and balance of powers among the three branches of government that we attempt to achieve this proper balance:

> Separation of powers was designed to implement a fundamental insight: Concentration of power in the hands of a single branch is a threat to liberty. The Federalist states the axiom in these explicit terms: "The accumulation of all powers, legislative, executive, and judiciary, in the same hands . . . may justly be pronounced the very definition of tyranny." . . . [The Framers] used the principles of separation of powers and federalism to secure liberty in the fundamental political sense of the term, quite in addition to the idea of freedom from intrusive governmental acts. The idea and the promise were that when the people delegate some degree of control to a remote central authority, one branch of government ought not possess the power to shape their destiny without a sufficient check from the other two. In this vision, liberty demands limits on the ability of any one branch to influence basic political decisions.[32]

It is the insight of Hamilton in Federalist Number 78 "that the judiciary is beyond comparison the weakest of the three departments of power; that it can never attack with success either of the other two; and that all possible care is requisite to enable it to defend itself against their attacks."[33]

How do we achieve a strong and vital judiciary? I would look for what I will call independence, legitimacy, and quality. The American Bar Association undertook a multi-year project of advocacy for an independent judiciary.[34] Indeed, our common-law predecessors struggled for centuries to produce a judiciary that was not merely an arm of the king.[35] Our own scheme of the separation and balance of powers requires a judiciary that is sufficiently independent to perform its constitutional role. I will, therefore, list independence as the first criterion by which to evaluate a system of judicial selection.

All power ultimately derives from the people. That is particularly true in a government founded in democratic principles. As Madison noted, the judiciary is peculiarly without sources of power; therefore, it is peculiarly dependent on popular legitimacy.[36] Thus, independence and legitimacy are criteria that I believe we should consider when deciding how we should select and retain judges.

Finally, strength alone is not sufficient. It is strength applied to perform a particular role in divided government that we desire. There has been a great deal of complaint—since the days of the Warren Court by political conservatives, and in the 1930s, and again recently by political liberals—about activist judges who substitute their will for that of the legislature or of the established law. This is not a complaint that can be addressed by weakening the judiciary; instead, we should seek a judiciary that is strong enough in knowledge and judgment to understand its role in our constitutional republic and that is strong enough in character not to yield to the temptation to abuse the power it has.[37] I will call this standard "quality." Thus, I identify three criteria for the evaluation of the factors of judicial selection: independence, legitimacy, and quality. Each of us has his or her own notion of what the terms independence, legitimacy, and quality mean. My understanding of them in the context of judicial selection and retention will become clearer as we proceed.

Independence

The concept of "independence" is central to Americans' self-concept; however, to apply it we must ask, how much independence, and independence from what?[38] We want an independent judiciary, but not one that is too independent.

1. Structural Independence
Madison said of Montesquieu's maxim that "there can be no liberty . . . if the power of judging be not separated from the legislative and executive powers" that Montesquieu "did not mean that these departments ought to have no *partial agency* in, or no *controul* over the acts of each other."[39] Madison explained that "unless these departments be so far connected and blended, as to give to each a constitutional controul over the others, the degree of separation which

[Montesquieu's] maxim requires as essential to a free government, can never in practice, be duly maintained."[40] In order to protect our freedom, we want each branch of government to have a certain degree of independence from the others; also, in order to protect our individual freedom, we want each branch of the government to be to a certain degree answerable for its actions.[41]

The Constitution of the United States assures federal judges life tenure and no diminution in their compensation during their tenure in office.[42] Hamilton believed this an "excellent barrier to the encroachments and oppressions of the representative body" and the "best expedient which can be devised in any government, to secure a steady, upright and impartial administration of the laws."[43]

On the other hand, checks and balances intended to limit the independence of the various branches of the government affect the judiciary. It is the president who, with the advice and consent of the Senate, appoints judges to the bench,[44] and it is the Congress, with the approval of the president, that sets their salaries and appropriates their budget.[45] And, it is the Congress that has the power to impeach and remove judges.[46] It is also the executive and legislative branches that establish the laws that judges are to enforce and the rules by which they are to proceed in that enforcement. And, it is the executive that also has the discretion to prosecute[47] and the power to pardon.[48]

We want judicial independence to a degree, but just as we do not want the judiciary to be too independent, we do not want the individual judges who make up the judiciary to be too independent. Therefore, we have appellate courts to correct departures and collegial appellate courts so that no individual appellate judge can wander off too far. And, although we do want judges to have a degree of independence from the legislative and executive branches of the government, we do not want them to be independent of the law; we want them to be its servants. In fact, it is precisely because we want judges to be free to follow the law that we want them to be in a significant measure independent of those other branches of the government that would make judges servants of their interests.

2. Popular Independence

During the period of Jacksonian democracy, states began to adopt elective judiciaries with the belief that elected judges would be more accountable to voters.[49] Some are of the view that states intended "the elective system to insulate the judiciary not from the people, but rather from the branches that it was supposed to restrain."[50] The reformers distrusted both judges and legislators, and elections were touted as a way of making judges more accountable to the people and more independent of the other branches.[51] Many felt it was impossible to create a judiciary completely free of influence; they merely believed it better that the influence come from the people than from the legislature.[52]

Whether one holds with the notion that judges should be accountable directly to the people or only indirectly through an appointment-for-life and impeachment process, depends, I submit, on one's view of the wisdom of the citizenry. The drafters of the Constitution of the United States held a cautious view.[53] They were familiar with how history had dealt with popular republics—their seemingly inevitable slide into tyranny.[54] And, they had had recent experience with Shay's Rebellion.[55] Thus, the Constitution provided for an electoral college to select a president[56] and for the state legislatures to elect senators.[57] Moreover, although representatives were to be elected every two years so that they would represent the popular will,[58] senators were to serve six-year terms[59] to provide them a certain insulation from the vicissitudes of popular will.[60] The life tenure of judges and the congressional—not popular—power of impeachment are consistent with this cautious view of popular wisdom. Jacksonian democracy, on the other hand, had a more positive view of popular wisdom, and state judicial selection was changed from appointment to popular election for a term.

The argument is often made—at least in private, if seldom in print—that the public lacks the understanding of the judicial function that is needed to make wise selections of judges. The argument is that the public will choose judges who promise them the results they want instead of judges who promise only to apply the law and who display the qualities that will enable them to do so.[61] If the distinction the critics of judicial elections raise is one between the public that wants results rather than good judges, and, for example, the president and Senate that want only good judges and are not concerned with the results that a judge may produce, then there is some contemporary evidence that the drafters of the Constitution may have had it backward.[62]

More generally, this is the issue that separates the drafters of the Constitution from the Jacksonians. I will not attempt to resolve the issue here; however, because we are comfortable with arguments supporting the positions taken by the drafters of the Constitution, I will note that the Jacksonian position is not without its own justification. We now trust citizens to understand the legislative function, and, at least at the state level, the executive function, and therefore to vote directly for their legislators and many executive officers (governor, lieutenant governor, attorney general, treasurer).[63] We have trusted the voters in most states for over a 150 years to elect at least some of their judges,[64] and we have not witnessed a general collapse of government, or even of the judiciary.[65] Moreover, the justification for appointment and life tenure of the federal bench is not necessarily applicable to a state judiciary. There is a difference between a state judiciary that swears obedience not only to the federal constitution but also to the state constitution, and a federal judiciary—selected from and residing within the state—that depends on independence from any state constituency in order to assure the implementation of the Article VI Supremacy Clause of the federal constitution.

3. Application

a. Appointment.   How well does the system of appointing judges serve the independence function? Alabama Governor George Wallace once observed, I suspect only partly in jest, that the appointment of a judge creates a dozen enemies (those who wanted and expected to be appointed but were not) and one ingrate. The fact that a judge who is appointed is considered an ingrate suggests that judges once appointed exercise some degree of independence, but Governor Wallace's statement fairly shouts that the appointing authority intended something else.

One would have to be totally blind to the press coverage of the federal judicial appointment process to believe that those engaged in it do not look for judges they believe will perform the judicial function with an eye toward the same results that the appointing authority would like to see.[66] Thus, I would suggest that appointment by a chief executive mitigates against judicial independence, at least in the short run. This is not to suggest that the new judge will not be acting independently, but that the result will tend to be what it would have been had the judge not been acting independently, because the judge will have been selected with that result in mind.

Legislative appointment is less problematic from the perspective of appointments being result oriented. It is more difficult to find a consensus in a large group than it is in a single individual; therefore, there would almost certainly be less on which the legislature would agree as it selects its appointee. On the other hand, the legislature has much greater means of enforcing its will on the judiciary than does the executive. The legislature has the continuing power of the purse and the power to promulgate legislation and rules,[67] not to mention the power of impeachment. Therefore, adding appointment—with an eye toward selecting judges who will defer to the legislature—to that continuing legislative power may tend to produce a judiciary that is less independent of another branch than does gubernatorial appointment.[68]

Gubernatorial appointment with legislative advice and consent should serve as something of a check on the governor's ability to appoint judges who will be in some measure subservient to the governor,[69] but is unlikely to make the judges less grateful for the appointment, if that is a concern. On the other hand, to the extent that the executive and the legislative branches are successful in weeding out the candidates that each branch considers objectionable, we would expect to find the judiciary composed of those most likely to defer to, rather than to check, either of the other branches.[70] Gubernatorial appointment from a short list prepared by a judicial selection committee dramatically limits the ability of the governor to select someone that she trusts to do her will. It vests that power instead to a large measure in the committee. Therefore, the composition of that committee is of critical importance. Some governors appoint such a committee.[71] In those cases, the selection of potential appointees depends critically on the governor.[72] A committee that will provide the governor with the name he has chosen in advance is no more than a smoke screen. One that is composed of a cross section of "leading lights" is apt to select "leading light" candidates who share their views, and to eschew candidates with more common views, while a committee composed of representatives of certain interest groups is likely to name candidates that the interest groups believe will rule in ways that are important to those groups.

Most such committees, however, are dominated by the organized bar.[73] Some have non-lawyer representatives, but the non-lawyers are usually in the distinct minority, while the majority, or key plurality, is representative of the leadership of the state bar organization.[74] Therefore, we would expect the candidates on the committee's list to be lawyers with whom the leadership of the state bar organization is comfortable,[75] that is, that the committee would have a tendency to select candidates who are most like them and who share their values. Whatever other effects state bar judicial selection may have on the balance of powers among the branches of government, one would expect that practicing lawyers, who are used to dealing directly or indirectly with courts, would have more confidence in the judicial than in the other two branches of government, and would have a magnified view of the proper role of that branch of the government.

b. Popular election.   Consistent with the presumption that those who do the selecting will select judges that they believe will do what they want them to do, the advantage of popularly elected judges is that, like the legislature, a diversity of interests is represented. In fact, the electorate is so much more numerous than the legislature that even more interests will be represented.[76]

Moreover, as I noted above, there is no reason to believe that the electorate will be any less interested in a judiciary that plays its proper role in the separation and balance of powers designed into the state constitution than is the governor or the legislature; however, the electorate has no vested interest in a judiciary that is subservient to either of the other two branches. In fact, its interest is to the contrary.

The pubic has an interest in preserving its own freedom by preserving a judiciary that can and will play its proper role in the constitutional structure of checks and balances.[77] Each of the other branches has a competing interest in furthering its own ability to accomplish its own objectives, and a nominating committee has a competing interest in furthering the objective of its own profession or class.

There is an additional independence-related advantage to the popular election of judges: if judges are elected, they have a popular constituency to which they can appeal if they are in a conflict with one of the popular branches of government.[78] Elected judges are not strangers to the public, but are people with whom the public is familiar from their last election, in the same way that legislators and others are known—if not by everyone, at least by key individuals in the politically aware and active population. Moreover, not only do the citizens know their judges, but the judges also know the voters and their concerns, and, thus, one would expect, know how to communicate with them. It is true, of course, that this advantage can rather easily be overvalued, since the nature of the judicial function does not permit judges to engage in the politics that is the staple of the political branches. Nonetheless, it is a factor to be considered in evaluating the independence of the judicial branch.

One charge often brought against the election of judges is that large sums of money are contributed to the candidates, and that this makes the judges beholden to contributors instead of to the law. The social science research is to the contrary. Melinda Gann Hall reports:

> Empirical research on the effects of judicial selection processes has been quite consistent in finding that methods of judicial recruitment do not affect either the quality of the bench or judicial outcomes. . . . Likewise, studies demonstrate

selection methods do not affect the tendency for state supreme courts to rule in favor of particular categories of litigants. Based on the evidence to date, the conclusion reasonably could be drawn that selection mechanisms simply do not have much of an impact on the operation of state judiciaries.[79]

I have personally seen no evidence that campaign contributions affect how a judge votes; though, of course, campaign contributions are no doubt made to candidates whom the contributor believes share the contributor's judicial philosophy. Money put into a judge's campaign—as contrasted with money put into a judge's pocket—that benefits a judge only in that it helps the individual to become a judge, can influence the judge only to the extent that she is willing to "sell out" in order to get the job. That is, the individual must want the title or the salary so badly that she is willing to subvert the job in order to get it. The title of "judge" will almost certainly lose its luster if it is tainted by rulings contrary to law that favor one's contributors. Similarly, the salary can be an incentive to grant favors in return for campaign contributions only if the judge is unable to earn that much in private practice.[80] It is, therefore, unsurprising that actual judicial scandals appear not to involve campaign funding but instead to be cases of bribery and corruption that promise substantially greater personal financial rewards.[81]

G. Alan Tarr in this volume argues a somewhat different point, that the process of standing for election and the prospect of being the target of a challenge pushed by a special interest group "may have a chilling effect on judicial independence."[82] Tarr cites a series of interviews that show that 15 percent of judges running in retention elections from 1986 to 1990 sought to avoid controversial cases and rulings "as the election approached."[83] These decisions, then, may well have been rendered in the days following the election—a regrettable practice, but not the demise of an independent judiciary. I did once hear a more troubling story—I hasten to emphasize that it is an undocumented anecdote—of a trial court judge who was alleged to have said that he decided a case contrary to the law and was going to let the appellate court straighten it out because he knew there would be a public outcry. This judge was alleged to be a judge in elective judicial office. Such conduct is inexcusable; however, I submit that a judge who was willing to rule contrary to what he believed the law is so that he could keep his office—if that was the motivation, then that same judge, if he were assured his office by lifetime tenure, would also be willing to sell his professional soul to avoid public criticism, to be thought well of by his country club friends, to be popular at the family reunion, or for myriad other reasons. The problem here is not that the judge must run for election,[84] but that he lacks character[85] and that he should be removed from office. I also hasten to point out that the data recited by Tarr demonstrate that the overwhelming majority of respondents apparently did not consider the prospect of a retention election to have a "chilling" effect on their judicial independence.

c. Retention.   Judges may be selected by appointment or election, and may be retained for another term by appointment or election. The benefits and evils of each method should be substantially the same whether used for initial selection or for retention.[86] However, initial selection and retention are for a term (of years, or for a life term). Alexander Hamilton, in advocating for the life tenure provision of the Constitution rather than for temporary commissions for federal judges, said that:

> Periodical appointments, however regulated, or by whomsoever made, would in some way or other be fatal to their necessary independence. If the power of making them was committed either to the executive or legislature, there would be danger of an improper complaisance to the branch which possessed it; if to both, there would be an unwillingness to hazard the displeasure of either; if to the people, or to persons chosen by them for the special purpose, there would be too great a disposition to consult popularity, to justify a reliance that nothing would be consulted but the constitution and the laws.[87]

The longer the term, the greater the independence and the less the accountability of the judge; the shorter the term, the greater the accountability to the retention authority and the less the independence from that authority. Limiting a judge to a single term, whatever its length, similarly increases independence and decreases accountability, because the judge has little incentive to please a retention authority.[88]

Legitimacy

Alexander Hamilton states in Federalist Number 78 that,

> Whoever attentively considers the different departments of power must perceive, that, in a government in which they are separated from each other, the judiciary, from the nature of its functions, will always be the least dangerous to the political rights of the Constitution; because it will be least in a capacity to annoy or

injure them. The Executive not only dispenses the honors, but holds the sword of the community. The legislature not only commands the purse, but prescribes the rules by which the duties and rights of every citizen are to be regulated. The judiciary, on the contrary, has no influence over either the sword or the purse; no direction either of the strength or of the wealth of the society; and can take no active resolution whatever. It may truly be said to have neither FORCE nor WILL, but merely judgment; and must ultimately depend upon the aid of the executive arm even for the efficacy of its judgments.[89]

As Hamilton points out, the judiciary can do nothing by its own power, except to speak. How then can the judiciary offer a counterpoise to the other branches of the government? While it is true that the executive holds the sword and that the legislative commands the purse and prescribes the rules, ultimately all power is popular power. The judiciary can command and the legislative and executive be expected to comply only so long as the public demands such compliance, and that will happen only if the people hold the voice of the judiciary to be legitimate. The question, then, is whether it matters to the legitimacy of the judiciary whether judges are appointed by the executive, by the legislature, or by the people by popular election.

1. Appointment

Appointment of judges by either of the other two branches lends some of that branch's legitimacy to the judicial branch. The legislative is the branch closest to the people, but it is the executive that generally is considered the appointing department of government. Gubernatorial appointment with the advice and consent of the legislative branch would appear to lend the most legitimacy to the judiciary, since it gives to the judiciary the blessing of both of the other two branches. Governors with the power of appointment sometimes seek the advice of an appointment committee to send to the governor a short list from which the governor makes a selection. This step is taken presumably to add legitimacy to the choice. That is, the appointment is represented to be one that is based on the merit of the candidate. That such a representation could add legitimacy to the choice is compelling evidence that the governors of those states—astute politicians of their constituencies to have made it to the governor's office—believe that the public expects judges to be something other than politicians.

Why not then formalize this process into a selection committee as the Missouri Plan does? The problem is that when the committee is selected by the governor, the governor must be attentive to whether those selected to serve on the committee will add to or detract from the legitimacy of his choice. A commission that is dominated by lawyers, and, in particular, the organized bar, may enhance or it may detract from legitimacy, depending on the public's sense of lawyers as servants devoted to the interests of the public at large, or as opportunists devoted to their own well-being even at the expense of the public.[90]

2. Popular Election

A popularly elected judiciary draws legitimacy, as do the other two branches of government, from the electorate. Thus, the legitimacy is direct, not derivative.

Elections, however, involve campaigns. Two criticisms are often made of popular election of judges that I believe involve concerns about legitimacy: (1) the amount of money spent on elections and (2) the tone of those elections. The first criticism is that partisan elections attract large campaign contributions that undermine public confidence in the impartiality of the judiciary.[91] The criticism is not so much with the money itself, but that it creates the impression that judges are being bought, and, therefore, detracts from the legitimacy of the judicial branch.

This criticism of partisan elections presumes that money is attributable to the presence of political parties. Political parties, and factions within those parties, however, are merely evidence of competing interests. There is no reason to believe that the nonpartisan election or the appointment of judges will somehow attract less money than will their election with a party label. If it is worth a million dollars to some interest to elect or to defeat a particular candidate for a judicial position, it is worth a million dollars whether the candidate has a party label or not. And, for that matter, if it is worth a million dollars to have the candidate elected or defeated, then it is worth a million dollars to have that candidate appointed or defeated for appointment. However, it is true that the money spent on an election is more likely to be reported and may otherwise be more obvious.

The implicit proposition is that because the strength of the judiciary depends on the public perception of its integrity, it is preferable to have a selection system that hides the money and the clash of interests groups from public view. This argument I call the whited sepulcher theory of judicial legitimacy:[92] it is better to have a system that superficially appears to be free of politics and money than to have one in which the money spent and the struggle waged is in public view. The whited sepulcher approach probably does offer some advantage in popular confidence in the short term; the question is whether a system dependent on public ignorance can be a stronger one in the long term.

A similar analysis must be applied to the tone of elections. The real complaint is not that ugly things are said about a person. Such information is needed. If a new school principal is appointed and it turns out that he is a convicted sex offender, the appointing person or body will be roundly condemned for the failure of investigation, particularly if there were rumors to that effect going around. The incentive in making appointments is, "if there are any red flags, don't hire him." The criticism, thus, is not that the decision maker should be denied information, but that, with that information made public, the tone of judicial campaigns could cause the voters to lose confidence in the judiciary.[93] The public could learn that judges have feet of clay—that he beats his wife, that she has a drug dependency problem, that he always rules for this interest, or that she is three years behind on her docket. Because the judiciary depends on public confidence for its legitimacy, we must conceal the negative: Again, the whited sepulcher theory.

I will be accused of being unfair to the argument that the opponent of elections is not opposed to "that information" being made public, but, rather, that it is the (amorphous) "tone" of the election that causes the problem. Perhaps the objection is to judges "looking like politicians." This, however, is again the debate over the ability of the voter to evaluate a judicial candidate. Will the voter reject a judicial candidate who does not act like a judge: a candidate who promises anything more than to apply the law, one who displays an injudicious temperament, or one who makes untrue and unfair allegations against an opponent?

I am not aware of social science research on the outcomes of judicial elections where one side does not merely point out relevant facts about the other, but descends into ad hominem attacks and outright falsehoods, but it is my observation that such campaigns lose—not every time, perhaps, but in the overwhelming number of cases. It may be simply that it is the candidate who already is losing who launches such an attack, or it may be that the public either simply does not like such an attack by someone who seeks to be a judge, because it appears unjudicial, or it may be that the public is wise enough to see through the tactic.

The criticism that it is partisan elections that lower the tone of judicial selection presumes that tone is attributable to the presence of political parties. Political parties, and factions within those parties, however, are merely evidence of competing interests. If parties were the reason for ugly election campaigns, then we would not expect to see negative campaigns until the general election when the two parties meet. Yet, instances of ugly primary campaigns are too numerous to require recitation. In fact, instances of ugliness now are commonplace in the federal appointment process in the total absence of judicial elections.[94] The simple fact is that the tone of a judicial selection depends not on party but on interests. If a particular judicial candidate for election or appointment is viewed as important to a significant financial or social interest (tort liability, abortion, immigration), then we can expect the tone of the selection process to decline.

Thus, the tone of the selection process does not appear to be tied to the type of selection process that is employed.[95] However, just as public election makes more obvious the money that goes into the selection process, so the open process of judicial elections makes more obvious the tone of the campaign. In an appointive system, the attacks on a candidate are focused on the decision maker, and the public may be largely unaware of them. But, just as with money, the attacks have not gone away. The question, then, is whether in the long term attempting to conceal the workings of the system improves legitimacy. Does the public believe that the federal judiciary is more legitimate than the state judiciaries because the tone of federal appointments is better than the tone of state elections? Is one system more likely than the other to lead to improvements in tone? It is at least arguable that as the public rejects judicial candidates who wage ugly campaigns, the candidates will learn and the tone will improve. In the appointive process, because of its secrecy, it is hard for us to know whether the appointing authorities reject those on whose behalf an ugly campaign is launched, and it would be difficult for future candidates to learn of that fact.

Quality

The quality of the judiciary depends on the quality of the judges who compose it. As we noted above, the legitimacy of the judicial branch depends in large measure on the power of the logic and language of its voice. Moreover, it is the character of those who occupy the bench that prevents the abuse of their position and thereby the ultimate weakening of the judicial branch.

1. Appointment

A governor or a legislature acting independently or in concert to select judges is free to do the research and to select the person whom it believes is the best candidate, and it presumably will do so in accordance with its notion of what is best. Unfortunately, as is discussed above, its interests are not in total concert with those of the judicial branch or with those of the people. This problem is not rectified by interposing an independent committee between the potential candidates and the governor.

A judicial selection committee could be composed of non-lawyers, or it could be composed predominantly of lawyers.[96] The advantage of such a committee, however, is usually said to be that lawyers are those most familiar with other lawyers and that they know what a good judge is;[97] therefore, it is lawyers who should choose the names from which the governor must pick. The evidence does not bear out this hypothesis. Melinda Gann Hall has said,

> To the extent that quality can be measured objectively, however, the evidence to date suggests that the Missouri Plan does not fulfill its promise. In a comprehensive study of state supreme courts, Glick and Emmert (1987) conclude that the professional credentials (e.g., prestige of legal education, legal and judicial experience) of judges are quite similar, regardless of the method of selection.[98]

Glick and Emmert recognize that they cannot measure objectively characteristics such as judicial temperament or fair-mindedness, but point out that research indicates that merit panels also encounter difficulty measuring such intangible judicial characteristics and instead rely on explicit "resumé-type" credentials such as those measured in their research (education or amount and type of legal and judicial experience).[99]

It is important to remember that, even if the state bar association leaders do have special knowledge, they are not only lawyers all in the same profession, but they are also in positions of leadership within that profession. What lawyers value may not be what is valued by the rest of society, and lawyers' professional interests may not coincide with the interests of the rest of society.[100] Thus, the "quality" for which judges are being selected may not be the quality that is most important to the constitutional purpose.

2. Popular Election

Judicial selection may be by election: partisan, nonpartisan, or, in the case of retention, on the judge's record without an opponent. A common argument against the popular election of judges is that the voter cannot name even one of her state supreme court justices; therefore, it is suggested, she lacks the ability to vote for that office.[101] The problem with this argument is that it proves too much. I am confident that a random poll would demonstrate that the average citizen cannot name his school board members; yet, we elect school board members. The implication of the argument that school board members therefore should be appointed might not sound too shocking. But, how many of that same sample could name their state representative to the legislature? Would anyone seriously argue that, because the average citizen cannot name his representative to the state legislature, state legislators should be appointed by the governor, perhaps selecting from among three to five names submitted by a committee appointed by various state officers and groups that appear regularly before the legislature?[102]

If electoral government works, then there must be something to it besides the ability to recite the names of all the elected officials. I have suggested elsewhere that the electoral process for judges may well be essentially a popular veto process.[103] That is, as long as the public has not heard anything about a sitting judge that causes it concern, the judge is voted back into office, but the public wishes to preserve its right to vote out of office a judge (or an entire court, seriatim) with whom it has concern. Such a function does not require that the voter be able to recite the names of any judges except the one he intends to vote against, or the one with whom he intends to replace that judge.

I noted above that a common complaint against the election of judges is that too much money flows into judicial races and that that undermines confidence in the judiciary.[104] It is interesting that it seems to be the same people that make that argument who also argue that people do not know who their judges are. When more money is spent on advertising, more people know the candidate. If that is not true, then how does the critic advocate informing the several million people of the average state, or the 647,000 people of the average congressional district, about candidates for public office?[105]

It is reported that more money was raised for campaigns for the supreme court in Alabama than for the supreme court races in any other state in the 2000, 2002, and 2004 cycles.[106] In Alabama, a combined total of $19,635,899 was reported spent on such races in those three election years that represent the election, or reelection, of all nine justices.[107] The Supreme Court of Alabama is the head of one of the three coequal branches of the state government. The governor and the legislature are the heads of the other two. In 2002, $29,885,139 was spent on the Alabama governor's race, and $22,035,756 was spent on Alabama's legislative races.[108] Thus, in the 2000, 2002, and 2004 races, the candidates for the supreme court spent less than did either the gubernatorial or the legislative candidates. An argument could be made that not enough is being spent on judicial races, if we really want the public to be as informed about judicial candidates as it is about nonjudicial candidates, so that when the public makes its choices the best qualified judges will be selected.

We have noted that the other major complaint against the election of judges is that campaigns have, or can have, an ugly tone. Of course, we noted that this phenomenon is not limited to election. However, from the standpoint of having available the information needed for an informed choice, negative information on a candidate (he is a convicted sex offender being considered for the juvenile court) may be as significant as positive information (he graduated from law school with honors). Where there is interest in a candidate's selection, however, both relevant and irrelevant information, both truth and falsehood will circulate. The principal difference between appointment and election is that in an appointment process some of the ugliest attacks will take place behind closed doors and even the candidate may never be aware of them; the attacks need only reach the key decision makers. In an elective process, the voters are the key decision makers; therefore, attacks must be public if they are to have their desired effect.

Thus, the advantage of an elective process is that the candidate knows of the attack and has the opportunity to address it and to correct false information. In an appointive process, to the extent that the attack is focused on the decision makers, the candidate may never have the chance to respond. In addition to the fairness issue, there is a weakness in the appointive process to the degree that decisions are more likely to be based on incomplete information.[109]

There are some practical differences in method of selection. If a candidate is up for appointment, the money spent to obtain or defeat that appointment is far more likely to be hidden from public view—appearing, for example, undifferentiated among the contributions to the governor, if the donor wishes to influence future gubernatorial appointments, or to key legislators, if the donor wishes to influence future legislative appointments. Or, it will appear as "third-party" expenditures on ads.[110] Or, it will be spent to promote "whisper" campaigns and to influence key supporters of the decision maker. In the case of an appointing commission, the expenditures and efforts may be made long in advance, as an interest group attempts to "capture" the commission by influencing the appointing authority or authorities.

Another practical difference is that in a retention election the judge is relatively helpless against a well-timed attack. Where there is no opposition, it is difficult to raise money. In a contested election, the opponent must declare himself; in a Missouri Plan retention election, the opposition can remain silent until just before the election. Thus, a well-funded opposition is able to launch an attack when it is too late for the candidate to raise the money necessary to fund a response.[111]

A nonpartisan election favors incumbents, because the incumbent has had the time in office to develop a network of friends and supporters. A challenger must develop such a network in order to launch a meaningful challenge. In a partisan election, the challenger is helped in launching a campaign by the party network that is already in place for all elections. By going to the party to which the incumbent judge does not belong, the challenger can find knowledgeable people who are interested in judicial elections and are willing to work on or contribute to the campaign. Therefore, it is not surprising that incumbent judges favor nonpartisan over partisan elections.[112]

This systemic bias in favor of incumbent judges may be an argument in favor of nonpartisan elections, but, of course, we have not created the judiciary for the benefit of judges. The real question is not what is better for incumbent judges, but what is better for the public—partisan, nonpartisan, or "on one's record" election or retention of judges.

If, as I suggested above, the public in a certain state wants little more than the opportunity to vote out a judge that it has learned it does not want, then at first blush it appears that the aptly named retention election—running on one's record—is the perfect fit. This conclusion, however, overlooks an important part of the process—the generation of information. An opponent has an incentive to supply the public with information and the candidate an incentive to respond with more information. In an election without an opponent, the incentive is to say nothing—the overwhelming percentage of retention election candidates are retained,[113] as we would expect if no information at all is generated about them, but there is an incentive for an organized and funded opposition to supply one-sided information too late for a response from the candidate.[114] Therefore, the retention election fails in its purpose if it is intended to give the public a meaningful opportunity to evaluate the performance of a judge: the incentives are to provide no information or one-sided information.

In a contested election each candidate has an incentive to present her case for herself and against her opponent, thereby fulfilling the information function. If party labels are allowed, this is an additional source of information not available in nonpartisan elections where party endorsements are not permitted.[115] The fact that a candidate is the candidate of one party rather than another says something about that candidate's judicial philosophy. If it did not, we would not see party-line votes on judicial nominees to the federal bench. We may debate what the party labels mean, but it is practical nonsense to say that they provide no information.

I have heard it argued that a party label can be misleading.[116] I agree; I have seen it. But, any single piece of information can be misleading. If we believe in the First Amendment's guarantee of freedom of speech, then we must believe that "the usual cure for false speech is more speech," not suppression.[117]

The quality of judges on the bench depends not only on the quality of the choice made among those in the pool, but also on the quality of the pool from which the choice is made. It is argued that potential candidates are discouraged from making themselves available because of the tone of elections. This is no doubt true, but, like so much else, it is true not only of elections but also of appointments. We do not know how many potential candidates have been lost to us because of some particular judicial election they have observed; neither do we know how many potential candidates for appointment have been lost to us because of the recent U.S. Senate hearings.

It is not the method of selection that is to blame. Where a person's reputation has been destroyed among those on whom her career depends so that she will not be selected by a judicial selection committee or appointed by the governor, the word spreads. Public service, unfortunately, carries with it a price—and for all of us, a cost. But the cost is not attributable to method of selection.

My former colleague on the bench, Hugh Maddox, who served for over thirty years in a partisan election state, once told me that he had been through campaigns with a primary opponent but no general election opponent, with a general election opponent but no primary opponent, with a primary opponent and a general election opponent, and, with no primary opponent and no general election opponent. He observed that, everything considered, he liked the last one best. Who would decline to run if guaranteed no opposition? It is not the method of selection that deters potential candidates, it is the presence and the strength of the opposition.

My review of the methods of selection and retention suggests that the quality of judges should not be expected to decline simply because they are selected by popular election. The social science research fully supports this conclusion:

> Empirical research on the effects of judicial selection processes has been quite consistent in finding that methods of judicial recruitment do not affect either the quality of the bench or judicial outcomes. Earlier studies, as well as more recent work, all determine that background characteristics of judges are similar regardless of method of judicial selection. Likewise, studies demonstrate selection methods do not affect the tendency for state supreme courts to rule in favor of particular categories of litigants. Based on the evidence to date, the conclusion reasonably could be drawn that selection mechanisms simply do not have much of an impact on the operation of state judiciaries.[118]

Conclusion

I have considered the elements of judicial selection in light of the check-and-balance function of the judiciary in our tripartite system of government. I reach no global answer to the question of which system is "best." The citizens of different states may have different values and assemble the elements of a judicial selection system differently. One thing is clear, however: uncritical condemnation of the election of judges that addresses that system's apparent faults while ignoring its strengths, and a similar uncritical advocacy of the Missouri Plan based on attention to its supposed advantages while ignoring its faults, is naive.

There are trade-offs between appointment and election. Popular election would appear to enhance independence from the other two branches of government and enhance the judiciary's ability to check and balance the other branches. Whether legitimacy is enhanced by one method over the other depends on whether the other branches are able to bestow on the judiciary a legitimacy that is greater than that bestowed directly by popular election. Finally, insofar as it is measurable, the quality of judges appears to be unaffected by the method of selection; however, as Glick and Emmert, conclude:

> We believe the data employed here is substantial and realistically raises concerns about the openness of merit selection in comparison with other recruitment methods. Since the credentials of merit selection judges are not superior to nor

substantially different from those of other judges, the claims for merit selection and the need for bar leaders to have special influence in order to guarantee the selection of superior judges are questionable.[119]

Thus, it is difficult to defend the Missouri Plan for selecting and retaining judges. On the other hand, despite their shortcomings, strong arguments can be made for either the appointment of judges or for their popular election. It has not been my purpose in this essay, however, to advocate for or against any selection and retention system. Rather, it has been my purpose to raise considerations that I believe are important and that I do not hear in the popular debate on judicial selection and retention.

Notes

1. Republican Party of Minnesota v. White, 536 U.S. 765 (2002); Steven P. Croley, *The Majoritarian Difficulty: Elective Judiciaries and the Rule of Law*, 62 U. CHI. L. REV. 689 (1995) both citing E. HAYNES, SELECTION AND TENURE OF JUDGES 99–135 (1944).

2. Caleb Nelson, *A Re-Evaluation of Scholarly Explanations for the Rise of the Elective Judiciary in Antebellum America*, 37 AM. J. LEGAL HIST. 190, 190 (April 1993).

3. Republican Party of Minnesota v. White, 536 U.S. at 2540 citing HAYNES, *supra* note 1.

4. *See* Nelson, *supra* note 2. There is some debate about which states had partially elective judiciaries at what time, and about which states were first to have a fully or partially elected bench. *See* Croley, *supra* note 1, at n. 73.

5. *See* Croley, *supra* note 1, at 716; Kermit L. Hall, *Progressive Reform and the Decline of Democratic Accountability: The Popular Election of State Supreme Court Justices, 1850–1920*, 1984 AM. B. FOUND. RES. J. 345, 346–47. Hall's thesis is that lawyers led the reform of state judicial election systems in order to strengthen the judiciary, professionalize the bench, and erode the influence of partisan politics in elections. However, by the turn of the century, he suggests, the lawyer reformers came to believe that professional accountability and popular accountability were increasingly at odds, and thus the zeal for an elected judiciary faded with a new, developing, and mostly urban culture of legal professionalism. *Id.* at 348–49.

6. Republican Party of Minnesota v. White, 536 U.S. at 2540 citing Haynes, *supra* note 1, and Larry Berkson, *Judicial Selection in the United States: A Special Report*, 64 JUDICATURE 176 (1980). *See also* Nelson, *supra* note 2, at 190 ("As the nation approached the Civil War, two of every three states elected their lower courts and three of every five states elected their supreme courts.")

7. *See* Nelson, *supra* note 2.

8. Roscoe Pound, *The Causes of Popular Dissatisfaction with the Administration of Justice*, 8 BAYLOR L. REV. 1, 23 (1956) (reprinting a speech given by Pound to the American Bar Association).

9. *See* Croley, *supra* note 1.

10. *See* Berkson, *supra* note 6.

11. *See* Daniel W. Shuman & Anthony Champagne, *Removing the People from the Legal Process: The Rhetoric and Research on Judicial Selection and Juries*, 3 PSYCHOL. PUB. POL'Y & L. 242, 243 (1997).

12. Rhode Island established a merit selection plan in 1994. AMERICAN JUDICATURE SOCIETY, JUDICIAL SELECTION IN THE STATES: APPELLATE AND GENERAL JURISDICTION COURTS (January 2004).

13. It is possible to create a continuum of methods of judicial selection ranging from direct partisan election to gubernatorial appointment for life, with the Missouri Plan in the middle of that continuum drawing elements from each of the polar systems; however, such a continuum is a bit misleading because it mixes method of selection with method of retention. *See* Harold See, *Comment: Judicial Selection and Decisional Independence*, 61 LAW & CONTEMP. PROBS. 141, 143 (1998).

With fifty states, appellate courts, general jurisdiction courts, and specialty courts, a thorough treatment of the issues raised by the myriad schemes for selection and retention quickly becomes Gordian. The U.S. Department of Justice and the American Judicature Society both have prepared charts that categorize the various methods of judicial selection used throughout the country; however, the reader should be cautioned that these charts sometimes fit irregular pegs into square holes. *See* BUREAU OF JUSTICE STATISTICS, U.S. DEPARTMENT OF JUSTICE, STATE COURT ORGANIZATION 2004 (August 2006), *available at* http://www.ojp.usdoj.gov/bjs/pub/pdf/sco04.pdf, and AMERICAN JUDICATURE SOCIETY, JUDICIAL SELECTION IN THE STATES: APPELLATE AND GENERAL JURISDIC-TION COURTS (2004), *available at* http://www.ajs.org/js/JudicialSelectionCharts.pdf.

14. In order to address what I believe are the most salient concerns, I leave much untreated: for example, I do not separately address the method of filling unexpired terms even though incumbency can play an often decisive role in a later election or appointment.

15. BUREAU OF JUSTICE STATISTICS, UNITED STATES DEPARTMENT OF JUSTICE, STATE COURT ORGANIZATION 2004, Table 4, Selection of Appellate Court Judges. The number increases to twenty-eight if Puerto Rico and the District of Columbia are included. Appellate judges in the District of Columbia are appointed by the president with approval of the Senate.

Because of the large number of ways in which the various components of judicial selection may be combined, and because a state may employ different practices with respect to the selection of trial and appellate judges, different sources quote different numbers of states as selecting judges by gubernatorial appointment. The number of states indicated in the above text, twenty-three, choose appellate judges by gubernatorial appointment. The disparity among sources can also be attributed to the fact that the process of gubernatorial appointment is not uniform throughout the states that use it. *See infra* note 20. Also adding to the disparity in numbers among sources is the fact that, while a state may employ one method of selection initially, it might employ an alternative method in filling midterm vacancies.

16. Virginia initially selects trial and appellate judges through legislative appointment, which is also how South Carolina selects its circuit and family court judges. BUREAU OF JUSTICE STATISTICS, UNITED STATES DEPARTMENT OF JUSTICE, STATE COURT ORGANIZATION 2004, Table 4, Selection of Appellate Court Judges and Table 6, Selection of Trial Court Judges.

17. For example, in Hawaii, the chief justice appoints district and family court judges. AMERICAN JUDICATURE SOCIETY, JUDICIAL SELECTION IN THE STATES: APPELLATE AND GENERAL JURISDICTION COURTS, and, in Montana, the chief justice appoints the water court judge. BUREAU OF JUSTICE STATISTICS, UNITED STATES DEPARTMENT OF JUSTICE, STATE COURT ORGANIZATION 2004, Table 4.

Many foreign jurisdictions allow their judiciary to appoint at least some of their judges. *See* G. Alan Tarr, *Rethinking the Selection of State Supreme Court Justices*, 39 WILLAMETTE L. REV . 1445, 1465–66 (2003) ("Still other countries, such as Spain and Italy, employ a mixed system of selection, with some judges named by the executive, some named by the judiciary, and some elected by super-majorities in parliament."); *see also* APPOINTING JUDGES: A JUDICIAL APPOINTMENT COMMISSION FOR NEW ZEALAND? MINISTRY OF JUSTICE OF NEW ZEALAND (April 2004), *available at* http://www.justice.govt. nz/pubs/reports/2004/judicial-appointment (comparing different forms of judicial selection). The Judiciary of the Republic of Bulgaria, for instance, is headed by the Supreme Judicial Council, which has the power to appoint, promote, and terminate all judges, prosecutors, and magistrates. Membership on the Supreme Judicial Counsel is limited to experienced and reputable attorneys, and the counsel consists of eleven members appointed by the legislature and eleven appointed by judicial bodies, in addition to the minister of justice, who has no vote. CONSTITUTION OF THE REPUBLIC OF BULGARIA, art. 129, 130 (2005).

18. *See generally* AMERICAN JUDICATURE SOCIETY, JUDICIAL SELECTION IN THE STATES: APPELLATE AND GENERAL JURISDICTION COURTS. However, as we will note later, an independent commission may submit a very short list of names, for example, three names, to the governor for the governor to appoint one of them to the office. This effectively places meaningful choice in an independent commission, but reserves the final selection to the executive branch.

19. BUREAU OF JUSTICE STATISTICS, UNITED STATES DEPARTMENT OF JUSTICE, STATE COURT ORGANIZATION 2004, Table 5, Qualifications to Serve as an Appellate Court Judge, and Table 7, Qualifications to Serve as a Trial Court Judge.

20. In twenty-two of the twenty-six states that initially appoint appellate judges by gubernatorial appointment, the gubernatorial appointment is preceded by a nomination by a judicial selection committee. Seven of those twenty-two states require senate approval of the governor's selectee. The District of Columbia also requires Senate approval of the nominee that the president chooses from those nominated by a judicial selection committee. BUREAU OF JUSTICE STATISTICS, UNITED STATES DEPARTMENT OF JUSTICE, STATE COURT ORGANIZATION 2004, Table 4, Selection of Appellate Court Judges.

21. *See generally,* AMERICAN JUDICATURE SOCIETY, JUDICIAL MERIT SELECTION: CURRENT STATUS (2003), Table 2, Composition of nominating commission.

22. Federalist Society, White Paper Task Force, *The Case for Partisan Judicial Elections*, 33 U. TOL. L. REV. 393, 401 (2002) (stating that the best explanation for the fact that the nominating commission route has likely failed to live up to businesses' expectations is that the nominating commissions are dominated by lawyers). Although the process for selecting commission members typically assures or virtually assures a majority of lawyers on the commission. Even if it does not, we would expect that lawyers, whose profession is advocacy, would dominate the commission's selection of nominees.

23. *The Case for Partisan Judicial Elections, supra* note 22, at 363 ("'Merit Plans' have a built-in bias toward whatever group of lawyers control local bar associations.").

24. *See generally,* Owen G. Abbe & Paul S. Hernson, *How Judicial Election Campaigns Have Changed*, 85 JUDICATURE 286 (2002).

25. *See, e.g.,* Paul Marcus and Vicki Waye, *Australia and the United States: Two Common Criminal Justice Systems Uncommonly at Odds*, 12 TUL. J. INT'L & COMP. L . 27, 109 (2004) ("Australian population might describe politicians and bureaucrats with a disdain similar to that expressed by Americans.").

26. However, it may not stay that way. *See* Republican Party of Minnesota v. White, 416 F.3d 738, 754 (8th Cir. 2005) ("Inasmuch, then, as the partisan-activities clause seeks, at least in part, to keep judges from aligning with particular views on issues by keeping them from aligning with a particular political party, the clause is likewise 'barely tailored' to affect any interest in impartiality toward parties [and] it is not narrowly tailored to any such interest and fails under strict scrutiny.").

27. Many states, such as Massachusetts and New Hampshire, have set a maximum age beyond which the judge may not serve. BUREAU OF JUSTICE STATISTICS, UNITED STATES DEPARTMENT OF JUSTICE, STATE COURT ORGANIZATION 2004, Table 5, Terms of Appellate Court Judges.

28. It may also be worth noting that removal during the term may be by impeachment or by a judicial discipline commission.

29. This is the procedure in ten states, Puerto Rico, and the District of Columbia. BUREAU OF JUSTICE STATISTICS, UNITED STATES DEPARTMENT OF JUSTICE, STATE COURT ORGANIZATION 2004, Table 5, Terms of Appellate Court Judges.

30. In the states where a retention election follows the initial appointment, the first term for a Supreme Court justice is as follows: two years (Indiana), three years (Nebraska and Utah), six years (Arizona, Florida, Kansas), eight years (Iowa, South Dakota, Wyoming), ten years (Alaska, Colorado, Maryland), and twelve years (Missouri). The first term for trial court judges varies greatly; but it is most commonly four or six years. BUREAU OF JUSTICE STATISTICS, UNITED STATES DEPARTMENT OF JUSTICE 1998, STATE COURT ORGANIZATION, Table 5, Terms of Appellate Court Judges. The Justice Department report includes Illinois and Pennsylvania as states in which the initial term is ten years; however, these are not states in which supreme court justices are initially appointed.

31. Jay A. Daugherty, *The Missouri Non-Partisan Court Plan: A Dinosaur on the Edge of Extinction or a Survivor in a Changing Socio-Legal Environment*, 62 MO. L. REV. 315, 319 (1997).

32. Clinton v. New York, 524 U.S. 417, 450–51 (1998) (Kennedy, J., concurring).

33. THE FEDERALIST NO. 78, at 523 (Alexander Hamilton) (Jacob E. Cooke, ed., 1961).

34. The American Bar Association Commission on the 21st Century Judiciary was convened to "study, report and make recommendations to ensure fairness, impartiality and accountability in state judiciaries" and culminated in thirty-one recommendations to the states. AMERICAN BAR ASSOCIATION, JUSTICE IN JEOPARDY: REPORT OF THE AMERICAN BAR ASSOCIATION COMMISSION ON THE 21ST CENTURY JUDICIARY (2003). *See also* AN INDEPENDENT JUDICIARY: REPORT OF THE ABA COMMISSION ON SEPARATION OF POWERS AND JUDICIAL INDEPENDENCE (1997).

35. HANNIS TAYLOR, THE ORIGIN AND GROWTH OF THE ENGLISH CONSTITUTION: AN HISTORICAL TREATISE (1898). One of the grievances in the Declaration of Independence was that King George III "has obstructed the administration of justice, by refusing his assent to laws for establishing judiciary powers. He has made [j]udges dependent on his [w]ill alone, for the tenure of their offices, and the amount and payment of their salaries." THE DECLARATION OF INDEPENDENCE (U.S. 1776).

36. THE FEDERALIST NO. 49, at 341 (Madison) ("We have seen that the tendency of republican governments is to an aggrandizement of the legislative, at the expense of the other departments. The appeals to the people therefore would usually be made by the executive and judiciary departments."); *see also* THE FEDERALIST NO. 78, at 529 (Hamilton) ("[T]he judiciary, from the nature of its functions, will always be the least dangerous to the political rights of the Constitution. . . . It may truly be said to have neither FORCE nor WILL, but merely judgment; and must ultimately depend upon the aid of the executive arm even for the efficacy of its judgments.").

37. There is nothing peculiar in the role of a judge that makes the judge singularly needy of character, understanding, and wisdom; we depend on the character, understanding, and wisdom of the officials in all three branches of the government, and, ultimately, on the character, understanding, and wisdom of the citizens who directly or indirectly select these officials.

38. *See* See, *Comment: Judicial Selection and Decisional Independence, supra* note 13, at 145 (1998):

There are two perspectives from which we may address the structural aspects of the proper balance between control of judicial power—or, to use the language of this symposium, "judicial accountability"—and its exercise. The first perspective is that of the separation of powers. That is, we may consider the appropriate level of institutional independence of the judiciary from the other branches of government.

The second perspective is that of the democratic principle. That is, we may address the degree to which it is appropriate to remove each branch of government from the direct and immediate control of the people.

39. THE FEDERALIST NO. 47, at 325 (Madison).

40. THE FEDERALIST NO. 48, at 332 (Madison).

41. *See supra* note 38.

42. U.S. CONST. art. III, § 1.

43. THE FEDERALIST NO. 8, at 522 (Hamilton).

44. U.S. CONST. art. II, § 2.

45. U.S. CONST. art. II, § 9, cl. 7.

46. U.S. CONST. art. I, § 2, cl. 5.

47. U.S. CONST. art. II, § 2 ("[H]e shall take Care that the Laws be faithfully executed.").

48. U.S. CONST. art. II, § 2.

49. Lee Epstein et al., *Selecting Selection Systems, in* JUDICIAL INDEPENDENCE AT THE CROSSROADS: AN INTERDISCIPLINARY APPROACH 198 (Stephen B. Burbank & Barry Friedman, eds., 2002).

50. *Cf.* Hall, *supra* note 5, at 348 ("These pragmatic judicial reformers believed that the democratic goal of popular accountability and the professional goal of an able, powerful judiciary were reciprocal and reinforcing.").

51. Nelson, *supra* note 2, at 205.

52. *See* Nelson, *supra* note 2, at 205–219 ("To be sure, since 'one object of the judiciary was to protect the people from the other branches of the government,' it was essential that the judiciary be 'above the control of the legislative and executive departments.'") (quoting two Illinois reformers) (footnotes omitted).

53. For example, in advocating for the election of the president through the electoral college, rather than by popular election, Hamilton wrote that

> the immediate election should be made by men most capable of analizing [sic] the qualities adapted to the station, and acting under circumstances favourable to deliberation and to a judicious combination of all the reasons and inducements, which were proper to govern their choice. A small number of persons, selected by their fellow citizens from the general mass, will be most likely to possess the information and discernment requisite to so complicated an investigation.

THE FEDERALIST NO. 68, at 458 (Hamilton).

54. *See* THE FEDERALIST NO. 63, at 422–31 (Madison) discussing the difference between a republic and a direct democracy. Also, Benjamin Franklin said, when asked by a citizen what kind of a government the representatives at Philadelphia had provided, "A republic, if you can keep it." 3 THE RECORDS OF THE FEDERAL CONVENTION OF 1787 app. A, at 85 (Max Farrand, ed., 1911).

55. Stewart Jay, *Origins of Federal Common Law*, 133 U. PA. L. REV. 1003, 1116 (1985) ("The fresh memory of Shay's Rebellion was not the least of the weights that the Framers carried with them to Philadelphia.") citing Corwin, *The Progress of Constitutional Theory Between the Declaration of Independence and the Meeting of the Philadelphia Convention*, 30 AM. HIST. REV. 511, 533–34 (1925).

56. U.S. CONST. art. II, § 1.

57. U.S. CONST. art. I, § 3. This provision of the Constitution was superseded by the Seventeenth Amendment, which provides for election by the people. U.S. CONST. amend. XVII.

58. U.S. CONST. art. I, § 2.

59. U.S. CONST. art. I, § 3.

60. THE FEDERALIST NO. 63, at 422–31 (Madison).

61. Michael R. Dimino, Sr., puts the argument in print. *The Worst Way of Selecting Judges—Except All the Others That Have Been Tried*, 32 N. KY. L. REV. 267 (2005) ("We all know the defects of judicial elections. The public is too ignorant of the legal system, the candidates, and the law to make wise choices; consequently, judges are elected often because of their famous names, ethnicities, position on the ballot, party affiliation, and the like, rather than through an assessment of merit.").

62. Dimino, *supra* note 60, at 284. ("[I]t is undeniable that . . . the attitudes of the judges forecast their decisions on the bench. And if the average voter does not understand this confluence of legal realism and political science, one can be sure that Presidents and Senators do.") citing Barry Friedman, *Mediated Popular Constitutionalism*, 101 MICH. L. REV. 2596, 2609 (2003) (finding that studies show the "popular influence" on the Supreme Court is because the President, who appoints [Justices], "appoint[s] people whose views are congenial.").

63. Dimino, *supra* note 60, at 299. ("Voter ignorance, however, has not stopped us from extending universal suffrage in legislative and executive races, where the public votes with the same visceral, half-informed opinions as determine their votes in judicial races.").

64. See previous discussion noting that, at the time of the Civil War, a majority of the states provided for the popular election of some judges.

65. There is commentary to the contrary. *See, e.g.*, AMERICAN BAR ASSOCIATION, JUSTICE IN JEOPARDY: REPORT OF THE AMERICAN BAR ASSOCIATION COMMISSION ON THE 21ST CENTURY JUDICIARY (2003).

66. *See, e.g.*, Bruce Fein, *Squandering a Supreme Opportunity*, WASH. TIMES, Sept. 30, 2005 (suggesting that Justice Sandra Day O'Connor's retirement from the Supreme Court provides the Bush Administration with an opportunity to "move the Court towards original meaning."); Michael McGough, *Roberts to Face Tough Questions*, PITT. POST-GAZETTE, Sept. 12, 2005, at A1 (reporting that a number of senators intended to question the nominee for the position of Chief Justice of the United States, John Roberts, to ensure that his views on the right to privacy, the separation of church and state, and laws against sex discrimination were consistent with their own).

67. THE FEDERALIST NO. 78, at 522–23 (Alexander Hamilton) ("The legislature not only commands the purse, but prescribes the rules by which the duties and rights of every citizen are to be regulated.").

68. *See* DANIEL R. PINELLO, IMPACT OF JUDICIAL-SELECTION METHOD ON STATE SUPREME COURT POLICY: INNOVATION, REACTION, AND ATROPHY 130 (1995) (finding that legislatively appointed judges are the most deferential to the legislative and executive departments).

69. Indeed, this was, in part, the framers' rationale in adopting the bifurcated executive and legislative appointment process used in the federal system. *See* THE FEDERALIST NO. 76, at 513 (Hamilton) (suggesting that the Senate's role in the confirmation process "would be an excellent check upon a spirit of favoritism in the President" and would further prevent the possibility that the "disposition of offices would be governed by . . . his private inclinations and interests").

70. King Henry VIII and St. Thomas More, however, may be remembered for the proposition that there are no guarantees. *See generally*, DEREK WILSON, IN THE LION'S COURT: POWER, AMBITION, AND SUDDEN DEATH IN THE REIGN OF HENRY VIII (2003).

71. For example, the governor of Wisconsin created the state's judicial selection committee by executive order and selects each of the committee members. *See* Nathan S. Heffernan, *Judicial Responsibility, Judicial Independence and the Election of Judges*, 80 MARQ. L. REV. 1031, 1048 (1997).

72. *See* Madison B. McClellan, *Merit Appointment Versus Popular Election: A Reformer's Guide to Judicial Selection Method in Florida*, 43 FLA. L. REV. 529, 548 (1991) ("[T]he Governor's dominant influence over the [nominating] commission often allows the Governor to control the list of nominees.").

73. *The Case for Partisan Judicial Elections, supra* note 22, at 401.

74. *See generally*, AMERICAN JUDICATURE SOCIETY, *supra* note 21, at Table 2. I also would note that lawyers are trained and experienced advocates; therefore, it should not take a majority of lawyers to carry the argument.

75. Federalist Society, White Paper Task Force, *The Case for Judicial Appointments*, 33 U. TOL. L. REV. 353, 363 ("'Merit Plans' have a built-in bias toward whatever group of lawyers control local bar associations.").

76. As Madison explained, "[e]xtend the sphere, and you take in a greater variety of parties and interests." THE FEDERALIST NO. 10, at 64 (Madison).

77. *See* Elizabeth A. Larkin, *Judicial Selection Methods: Judicial Independence and Popular Democracy*, 79 DENV. U. L. REV. 65, 85 (2001) (Noting that "[e]lections provide an aspect of judicial accountability and popular democracy that is absent in lifetime appointment systems.").

78. *See* Otto B. Mullinax, *Judicial Revision—An Argument Against the Merit Plan for Judicial Selection and Tenure*, 5 TEX. TECH L. REV. 21, 25 (1973). *Cf.* G. Alan Tarr, *Politicizing the Process: The New Politics of State Judicial Elections*, in this volume at 59 (arguing that the politicization of judicial elections can arise when an "emerging political party seeks to gain control of all the institutions of state government, including the state supreme court.").

79. Melinda Gann Hall, *Electoral Politics and Strategic Voting in State Supreme Courts*, 54 J. POL. 427, 428 (1992).

80. Chief Justice John Roberts wrote in the 2005 Year-End Report on the Federal Judiciary that judges' salaries are too low: "If Congress gave judges a raise of 30 percent tomorrow, judges would—after adjusting for inflation—be making about what judges made in 1969." The report is available on the Supreme Court's website *at* http://www.supremecourtus.gov/publicinfo/year-end/2005year-endreport.pdf. "At the time of the 1990 enactment to increase federal judicial salaries, it was widely observed that the young law clerks working at the elbows of Supreme Court justices would in their first year in the private sector earn more than an associate judge of the United States Supreme Court." Paul D. Carrington, *Butterfly Effects: the Possibilities of Law Teaching in a Democracy*, 41 DUKE L. J. 741, 780 n. 206 (1992) citing Joseph Deitch, *New Jersey*

Q & A: Harold A. Ackerman; Seeking a Raise for Federal Judges, N.Y. TIMES, Aug. 20, 1989, at 12NJ3.

81. For example, in 1969, two Illinois Supreme Court justices were accused of rendering a favorable verdict in exchange for receiving gifts. Now-Justice John Paul Stevens was asked to head the investigation into the alleged improprieties. The commission's findings led to the resignation of the two justices. KENNETH A. MANASTER, ILLINOIS JUSTICE: THE SCANDAL OF 1969 AND THE RISE OF JOHN PAUL STEVENS (2001).

"In the past decade or so we have had evidence of criminal bribery in Chicago's Operation Greylord, in Miami, San Diego, and Youngstown, Ohio, to name a few places." David Barnhizer, *"On the Make": Campaign Funding and the Corrupting of the American Judiciary*, 50 CATH. U. L. REV. 361, 365 n. 10 (2001).

Barnhizer opines without offering any evidence—in fact, he states that there is no empirical evidence—that campaign funding is corrupting the judiciary. Not only does Barnhizer offer no empirical evidence beyond speculating as to what could happen, but he does not even offer any anecdotal examples of campaign funding induced corruption. He does, however, offer the following evidence of bribery and corruption: Alex Roth, *Judges Gain Little on Appeal: 2 Ex-jurists, Disbarred Attorney Are Resentenced*, SAN DIEGO UNION-TRIB., June 13, 2000, at A1 (reporting criminal bribery in San Diego); *Corruption Inquiry Ends After 10 Years*, FLA. TODAY, June 4, 2000, at 8 (reporting the sentence of Judge Alfonso Sepe after his admission of taking a $125,000 bribe in a criminal drug trial); Mark Gillispie, *3 More Officials Face Charges: Corruption of Judiciary Probe Continues*, THE PLAIN DEALER (Cleveland), Oct. 26, 1999, at 3B ("Two more judges and a former assistant county prosecutor were implicated in a growing federal investigation into judicial corruption in Mahoning County yesterday."); Robert Becker, *Convicted Judge Seeks $113,222: Shields Contends State Owes Pension Payout*, CHI. TRIB., Apr. 26, 2000, at 1. Barnhizer, *supra* note 80, at 365 n. 10.

82. Tarr, *supra* note 78, at 58.

83. This concern differs from that associated with the influence of campaign contributions; contrary to the case with campaign contributions, the judge would be following what she believes to be the will of the electorate. As Bonneau suggests, "Incumbents chosen in competitive races are more likely to defer to their constituencies when casting votes on controversial issues rather than choosing policy preferences that better reflect their personal preferences. . . . [However,] while state court races are becoming more expensive, they are not also necessarily becoming more competitive." Chris W. Bonneau, *Patterns of Campaign Spending and Electoral Competition in State Supreme Court Elections*, 25 JUST. SYS. J. 21, 28–29 (2004).

84. See Melinda Gann Hall, *Electoral Politics and Strategic Voting in State Supreme Courts*, 54 J. POL. 427, 428 (1992)("studies demonstrate selection methods do not affect the tendency for state supreme courts to rule in favor of particular categories of litigants. Based on the evidence to date, the conclusion reasonably could be drawn that selection mechanisms simply do not have much of an impact on the operation of state judiciaries.").

85. See the discussion of quality below.

86. A system, like the Missouri Plan, should have the benefits of one method for initial appointment and the benefits of the other method for retention, but it also will incorporate the evils of both methods.

87. THE FEDERALIST NO. 78, at 529 (Hamilton).

88. *See* AMERICAN BAR ASSOCIATION, JUSTICE IN JEOPARDY: REPORT OF THE AMERICAN BAR ASSOCIATION COMMISSION ON THE 21ST CENTURY JUDICIARY, at 26–27 (2003) (recommending that judges be appointed without the possibility of reselection because it is "then that judges are subject to a loss of tenure as the consequence of their decisions.").

89. THE FEDERALIST NO. 78, at 529 (Hamilton).

90. In a survey of the public perception of lawyers, only 19 percent of respondents indicated they were "extremely" or "very confident" in the legal profession, while 33 percent indicated such confidence in the judiciary in general and 31 percent held such confidence in state and local courts. Lawyers fared better only than the media. Sixty-nine percent of respondents agreed with the proposition that lawyers are more interested in making money than in serving their clients; and 57 percent agreed that most lawyers are more concerned with their own self-promotion than with their clients' best interests. AMERICAN BAR ASSOCIATION, SECTION OF LITIGATION, PUBLIC PERCEPTIONS OF LAWYERS: CONSUMER RESEARCH FINDINGS 6, 29 (2002).

91. *See* Dimino, *supra* note 60, at 301 ("Unquestionably, campaign contributions create a serious risk of undermining public confidence in the impartiality of judicial decisions"); *see also The Case for Judicial Appointments, supra* note 74, at 377–80 (2002). *But see* Tarr, *supra* note 78, at 56 (citing data in an American Bar Association poll that while almost three-fourths of respondents expressed concern that the need to raise funds would affect a judge's impartiality, a majority still trusted elected judges more than non-elected judges).

92. Roundtable, *Judicial Elections and Free Speech: Ethics and a Judge's Campaign Rhetoric*, 33 U. TOL. L. REV. 315, 318 (2002). As a panelist, I explained that the "whited sepulcher" argument is that

> we cannot let the electorate know the truth about our judicial system—that is, see the "bones" in the tomb. We do not want the public to know how far behind we are on cases or see the money and the "politics" behind the elections for fear that the public may lose confidence in our judiciary. Yet, the same "bones" are present in a system of judicial appointment as in one of judicial election; it is just that the tomb has a coat of whitewash on it when judges are appointed, so we are happy. I believe that the more important issue is how we are actually performing in our jobs, regardless of whether we are appointed or elected. Ultimately, the bones in the sepulcher are going to come into public view. So why do we try to hide them? Why shouldn't we instead be forthcoming with the public, recognize the judiciary's shortcomings, and then stand up and strive to make improvements? I believe this can, and should, be accomplished, in part, through the use of campaign speech in judicial elections.

See Matthew 23:27 ("ye are like unto whited sepulchers, which indeed appear beautiful outward, but are within full of dead men's bones, and of all uncleanness").

93. AMERICAN BAR ASSOCIATION, JUSTICE IN JEOPARDY: REPORT OF THE AMERICAN BAR ASSOCIATION COMMISSION ON THE 21ST CENTURY JUDICIARY, at 26–27 (2003).

94. *See* Lyle Denniston & Arch Parsons, *Rights Groups Await NAACP's Call on Thomas Nomination*, BALT. SUN, July 31, 1991, at 3A.

95. Tarr expresses a similar view with respect to partisan versus nonpartisan elections, suggesting that "supreme court justices running in nonpartisan elections may face the same expensive, vituperative challenges that were previously confined to partisan races." Tarr, *supra* note 78, at 57.

96. If such a committee is composed of non-lawyers, then its interests will diverge from those of the people in accordance with its composition; and, if it is dominated by lawyers then its interests can be expected to reflect those of the lawyers appointed to it. If it is dominated by the leadership of the state bar association, it is likely to reflect that interest, experience, and knowledge. I have spoken with judges who are very highly regarded by their fellow judges, but who have said that they would never have been selected by the committee because they were never active in the state bar association, preferring instead to devote themselves to other community activities.

97. "[T]he use of a judicial nominating commission composed primarily of lawyers is seen as bringing a degree of expertise to the process of picking judges." *The Case for Partisan Judicial Elections, supra* note 22, at 396.

98. Melinda Gann Hall, *State Supreme Courts in American Democracy*, 95 J. POL. 315 (2001).

99. Glick & Emmert, *Selection Systems and Judicial Characteristics: The Recruitment of State Supreme Court Judges*, 70 JUDICATURE 229–35 (1986).

100. *See The Case for Partisan Judicial Elections, supra* note 22, at 401–02 (taking the position that businesses cannot assume that the defense bar will adequately represent the interests of business and of consumers on a nominating commission because the "practicing bar, as a whole, is well to the left of the American public as a whole.")

101. Daniel W. Shuman & Anthony Champagne, *Removing the People from the Legal Process: The Rhetoric and Research on Judicial Selection and Juries*, 3 PSYCHOL. PUB. POL'Y & L. 242, 244 (1997) ("One criticism of popular selection of judges is that voters do not know for whom they are voting.") citing Alan T. Klots, *The Selection of Judges and the Short Ballot*, 38 J. AM. JUD. SOC'Y. 134 (1955); Glenn R. Winters, *How Much Do Voters Know or Care About Judicial Candidates?*, 38 J. AM. JUD. SOC'Y. 141 (1955). It has been said that, in Alabama during the 2000 election cycle, candidates for five supreme court positions spent more money than was spent by all judicial candidates in any other state, yet 90 percent of Alabama's voters "could not name a single candidate except for the chief justice's position." Roy A. Schotland, *Financing Judicial Elections, 2000: Change and Challenge*, 2001 L. REV. MICH. ST. U. DET. C. L. 849, 855 n. 26 (2001) citing Editorial, *This Is No Way to Choose Who's on Appeals Courts*, MOBILE REG., Nov. 8, 2000, at 12A.

102. In addressing arguments against campaign speech, I have said:

Tell me who your state treasurer is. Name your public service commissioners. Do you know who is on your school board? Few citizens know these officials, yet for some reason we think it is acceptable to elect them. Why is it then, that because we aren't intimately familiar with all of the candidates in a judicial election, we should prohibit those candidates from talking about themselves or talking about their opponents? Isn't the answer to this absence of information, more speech, not less?

Harold See, *When Free Speech and Ethical Standards Collide*, 3 ENGAGE: J. FEDERAL-IST SOC'Y PRACTICE GROUPS, 224 (Aug. 2002).

103. I believe citizens are capable of determining who is not performing the judicial function in the way they believe the judicial function should be performed. And, in fact, I think we frequently see that. Judges are usually simply re-elected; but, if there is a problem, then the public has the power, through either contested election or retention election, to say, "No, we don't think you're doing the job right, and so we're going to remove you." If we believe that a rational public could believe that it is capable of making such an evaluation, then it seems to me we have to concede that a rational public could choose to have an elective system.

See, *When Free Speech and Ethical Standards Collide supra* note 101, at 224 (Aug. 2002).

104. *See The Case for Partisan Judicial Elections, supra* note 22, at 374–80.

105. One measure that has been adopted in several states is the distribution of voter guides by the state. Whether this is an effective substitute for media exposure is doubtful or we would not likely see government agencies undertaking public education media campaigns. It also raises the specter of government censorship; though, thus far in the states in which it is being tried that has not been a complaint of which I am aware.

106. DEBORAH GOLDBERG ET AL., THE NEW POLITICS OF JUDICIAL ELECTIONS 2004: HOW SPECIAL INTEREST PRESSURE ON OUR COURTS HAS REACHED A "TIPPING POINT"—AND HOW TO KEEP OUR COURTS FAIR AND IMPARTIAL, at 14, figure 9 (2004); DEBORAH GOLDBERG ET AL., THE NEW POLITICS OF JUDICIAL ELECTIONS 2002: HOW THE THREAT TO FAIR AND IMPAR-TIAL COURTS SPREAD TO MORE STATES IN 2002, at 18, figure 9 (2002); and DEBORAH GOLD-BERG ET AL., THE NEW POLITICS OF JUDICIAL ELECTIONS: HOW 2000 WAS A WATERSHED YEAR FOR BIG MONEY, SPECIAL INTEREST PRESSURE, AND TV ADVERTISING IN STATE SUPREME COURT CAMPAIGNS, at 11, figure 5 (2000).

107. *Id.* In Illinois $19,079,552 was raised in supreme court races, and in Ohio $15,819,111 was raised in supreme court races during these years.

108. Office of the Secretary of State, State of Alabama. There was no race for governor and were no legislative races in 2000 or 2004. The 2006 governor's race was significantly less expensive than the 2002 race. The candidates for governor received $16,318,812 in contributions and spent $19,875,209 on their campaigns. The 2006 su-preme court races for five seats on the court, including the chief justice's seat, were, to the contrary, expensive in historical perspective. The supreme court candidates re-ported receiving $11,929,707 and spending $12,386,547.05. Thus, if we were to compare the total spending in the 2002, 2004, and 2006 supreme court races, $22,290,896.68, with the total amount spent on the 2006 governor's race, we would find rough parity. The 2006 figures for the legislative races are currently unavailable; however, it appears

that the 2006 legislative races were, like the judicial races and unlike the governor's race, unusually expensive campaigns.

109. Although a single decision maker can go through more information than the electorate is likely to consider, in practice the actual decision maker is likely to do the same thing that the electorate will, that is, to rely on recommendations from those she trusts. The voter similarly will rely on recommendations from the newspaper, AARP, a union or employer, a friend or relative, or a coworker or business associate who has gathered the more detailed information.

110. For example, a study undertaken by the Brennan Center for Justice and Justice at Stake found that $1,303,928 was spent by third-party interest groups on television advertisements alone during the confirmation of Chief Justice John Roberts. The same study found that third-party interest groups spent $2,407,392 on television advertisements during the confirmation of Justice Samuel Alito. Press Release, Brennan Center for Justice & Justice at Stake, Three Nominations Reveal Contrasting Influence of Interest Groups in High Court Nomination Process (Jan. 31, 2006), available at *http://www.justiceatstake.org/contentViewer.asp*?breadcrumb=7,55,750.

111. Paul D. Carrington, *Judicial Independence and Democratic Accountability in Highest State Courts*, 61 LAW & CONTEMP. PROBS. 79, 108 (Summer 1998). In Missouri, the incumbent judge is further disadvantaged by an ethical prohibition against the raising of money before there is "active opposition" to the judge's retention. Mo. Code of Judicial Conduct Canon 5B(3) (2006) ("An incumbent judge who is a candidate for retention in or reelection to office without a competing candidate, and whose candidacy has drawn active opposition, may campaign in response thereto and may obtain publicly stated support and campaign funds in the manner provided in Canon 5B(2).").

112. *See* See, *Comment: Judicial Selection and Decisional Independence, supra* note 13, at 145 (1998) ("Each step from life tenure toward contested election with the support of a party mechanism enhances the ability of a challenger."); *see also* Chris W. Bonneau, *Patterns of Campaign Spending and Electoral Competition in State Supreme Court Elections*, 25 JUST. SYS. J. 21, 29–30 (2004) (discussing data that suggest that the "incumbency advantage" is stronger in nonpartisan races than partisan ones). The only actual data with which I am familiar as to which system incumbent judges prefer are in a questionnaire distributed some years ago to Alabama trial court judges.

113. "Less than one percent of all judges standing for retention elections have been removed through that process." *The Case for Partisan Judicial Elections, supra* note 22, at 401. *See also The Case for Judicial Appointments, supra* note 74, at 377–80 ("almost 99 percent of judges are returned to office in retention elections").

114. For example, Penny White of the Tennessee Supreme Court and Rose Bird of the California Supreme Court lost retention elections due to the late attacks.

> In most cases, such attack campaigns do not surface until relatively late in the electoral season so that the judge seeking electoral retention may awaken one morning to a campaign for his removal without having had a clue it was coming. When such campaigns are begun late in the season, the judge is virtually powerless due to lack of time and resources to mount an effective campaign. Former Chief Justice Rose Bird and two

of her colleagues were removed from office in California by this means, and Justice Penny White of Tennessee was likewise removed by this method. There are others.

Chief Justice Joseph E. Lambert of the Supreme Court of Kentucky, *Contestable Judicial Elections: Maintaining Respectability in the Post-White Era*, 94 KY. L. J. 1 (April 14, 2005) (footnotes omitted) citing John H. Culver & John T. Wold, *Judicial Reform in California, in* JUDICIAL REFORM IN THE STATES 139, 154–55 (Anthony Champagne & Judith Haydel, eds., 1993); *see also* Peter D. Webster, *Selection and Retention of Judges: Is There One "Best" Method?*, 23 FLA. ST. U. L. REV. 1, 36 (1995) ("Because of ethical restraints and other factors, the justices were ill-prepared to do battle."); John D. Fabian, *The Paradox of Elected Judges: Tension in the American Judicial System*, 15 GEO. J. LEGAL ETHICS 155, 156–57 (2001).

The same phenomenon contributed to the 1996 defeat of Justice David Lanphier of the Nebraska Supreme Court:

> Although Nebraska election law required Justice Lanphier to file an official notification of his intent to seek retention in the November 1996 election, that same law placed no legal obligation on Citizens [for Responsible Judges] to file its intent to challenge Lanphier's retention. Therefore, Lanphier was unaware that Citizens was mounting a campaign to unseat him. Citizens publicly announced its challenge to Lanphier's retention only two months before the November election, allowing the group to accumulate money and develop a strategy long before Lanphier even learned of the campaign. Lanphier's supporters, taking the month following Citizens' announcement to organize Nebraskans, were left with only a month to respond to Citizens' charges, to present Lanphier as an effective judge, and to educate the electorate about the benefits of an independent judiciary.

Traciel V. Reid, *The Politicization of Retention Elections: Lessons from the Defeat of Justices Lanphier and White*, 83 JUDICATURE 68 (1999).

115. *But see supra* note 26.

116. *See e.g.*, Leslie Southwick, *The Least of Evils for Judicial Selection*, 21 MISS. C. L. REV. 209, 220 (2002); Roy A. Schotland, *Financing Judicial Elections, 2000: Change and Challenge*, 2001 L. REV. MICH. ST. U. DET. C. L. 849, 890.

117. *See e.g.*, Briggs v. Ohio Elections Com'n, 61 F.3d 487, 492 (6th Cir. 1995).

118. *See* Melinda Gann Hall, *supra* note 78, at 428. *See also*, Glick & Emmert, *supra* note 98 ("Our research confirms previous studies which find little evidence that selection systems produce judges with markedly different or superior judicial credentials or that they vary on most other background characteristics.").

One of the most widely cited contributors to the literature on this topic, Harry Stumpf, has written:

> [O]ne can determine whether different selection mechanisms tend to produce different types of individuals as measured by . . . variables [such as] educational attainments, prior judicial experience, the absence of parochialism, and so on. . . . And if the Missouri Plan is supposed to produce decidedly superior judges, these results might be expected to show up in such data. However, the research reported thus far does not lend much support to this claim.

Not only is there little evidence of the superiority of judges selected by the merit system (although there is some evidence to the contrary), there is in fact little to show that judicial selection mechanisms make any difference at all!

. . . if merit selection produces better judges, social science research has thus far failed to substantiate the claim.

The Case for Partisan Judicial Elections, supra note 22, at 399 quoting HARRY P. STUMPF, AMERICAN JUDICIAL POLITICS 171 (1988) (citing Henry R. Glick, *The Promise and the Performance of the Missouri Plan: Judicial Selection in the Fifty States,* 32 U. MIAMI L. REV. 509 [1978]).

The conclusions of social science research have been described more recently as follows: "the quality of judges in a merit-selection system are no better than those selected by voters, and . . . the retention-election system is a sham." Daniel W. Shuman & Anthony Champagne, *Removing the People from the Legal Process: The Rhetoric and Research on Judicial Selection and Juries,* 3 PSYCHOL. PUB. POL'Y & L. 242, 248 (1997).

119. Glick & Emmert, Selection Systems and Judicial Characteristics: The Recruitment of State Supreme Court Judges, 70 JUDICATURE 229–35 (1986).

4 Judicial Independence

The Courts and the Media

James E. Graves, Jr.

J<small>UDICIAL INDEPENDENCE</small> has been defined as the freedom of the judiciary to render justice fairly, impartially, in accordance with the law and the U.S. Constitution, without threat, fear of reprisal, intimidation, or other influence or consideration.

Challenges to judicial independence at the federal and state level include the unwarranted criticism of the judges, single-issue campaigns against sitting judges, inadequate funding of the judiciary, judicial recall elections, proposed term limit constitutional amendments, partisan delay in confirmation of federal judicial nominees, threats of impeachment and calls for resignation, and reductions in state and federal sentencing power and discretion. The implications of these challenges to our justice system are far-reaching and undermine court legitimacy and democratic ideals.

In the context of a discussion of judicial independence, a look back at the decision in *Brown v. Board of Education*[1] is very illuminating. As a member of the Mississippi Supreme Court, an African American man, and an American citizen, I have a profound respect for the beliefs and principles set forth in the U.S. Constitution. I also have a profound respect for the institutions that support, maintain, and facilitate our democracy, the U.S. Supreme Court among them. On May 17, 1954, this institution made a decision that affected boys and

---

Justice of Mississippi Supreme Court.

girls, men and women, students and teachers—indeed, all who make up this great country that we call America.

The decision in *Brown v. Board of Education* was tremendously important to the civil rights movement. While most experts attribute the birth of the movement to Rosa Parks's refusal to give up her seat on a city bus in Montgomery, Alabama, in December 1955, others might argue that the Court's announcement of the *Brown* verdict marked the true beginning of the civil rights effort. *Brown* preceded the Montgomery bus boycott by approximately eighteen months. And although the civil rights movement may have been born on December 1, 1955, in Montgomery, Alabama, the decision in *Brown* certainly accelerated the gestation period preceding the birth.

We celebrate the *Brown* decision because we recognize the importance of education in a democracy. There are three most important institutions in our society: churches, families, and schools. Of the three, schools were the most appropriate for government intervention to facilitate the end of the Jim Crow system in this country. Indeed, the nine justices on the U.S. Supreme Court recognized the importance of the decision to overrule racial segregation in public education. We cannot dismiss the fact that Justice Hugo Black was a former Ku Klux Klansman from Alabama. Yet he voted in favor of the decision in *Brown* along with the other eight justices on the Court. We should also remember that Justice Robert H. Jackson was hospitalized with a heart attack in May 1954. However, he checked himself out of the hospital on the day of the *Brown* announcement. He clearly recognized the importance of the show of unity, solidarity, and unanimity that was so essential to the citizens of our democracy. The justices were nine white men from different parts of the country who joined together and did the right thing for the good of America.

It was some sixteen years after the *Brown* verdict that I, as a schoolboy in Mississippi, actually experienced the effect of the Supreme Court's decision. When I started my Christmas vacation in December 1969, I left an all-black rural high school with an all-black faculty and staff. In January 1970, when Mississippi finally integrated its schools after much litigation, I returned to an all-black student body with an integrated faculty and an all-black staff. Despite the implementation of the Court's order in *Brown*, all of the white students who were zoned to attend my rural high school had instead enrolled in private schools. Many of these private schools sprang up almost overnight to absorb the white student population that otherwise would have been required to attend a majority-black school.

Still, the decision in *Brown* was the beginning of the end of Jim Crow in the South. If historian Lerone Bennett Jr. is correct that the warrant against Rosa Parks was the seal on the death certificate of the Jim Crow South, then the signature of those nine justices on the *Brown* decision was at least the signature on the birth certificate for integration in public institutions in our society. The *Brown* ruling teaches so many other lessons aside from its obvious impact and the unequivocal statement that separate is not equal. One of the most salient is that nine people of diverse backgrounds—and of a different race than those who sought relief in the *Brown* lawsuit—determined to do what was good for those plaintiffs, what was good for those schools, and ultimately, what was good for our democracy.

Brown also teaches a second and very important lesson on the role and function of the judicial branch of government. Many people often overlook the fact that the judiciary is one of three coequal branches of government. (Despite this status, in most states, the allocation for judicial expenditures is less than 1 percent of general fund budgets.) When most people think of government, they think of either the legislative branch or the executive branch. But the judiciary affects or influences the lives of most of our citizens on a daily basis. Just a casual reading of the newspaper will reveal that a number of matters are either in court, headed to court, or were in court. This is not necessarily a function of what some may label a litigious society, but rather the function of our constitutional, democratic form of government. Our system is designed so that the courts resolve disputes. Our system is designed so that the courts resolve issues of constitutional interpretation. And our system is designed so that the courts mete out justice. Justice is the cornerstone of our democracy. Indeed, it was a desire for justice, fairness, and equality that led to the birth of this nation.

A third and no less important lesson of *Brown* is that schools are a very important part of our democracy. There is a tendency nowadays on the part of some to neglect public education. Yet democracy does not function properly where its citizenry is uninformed and uneducated. People need to know, understand, and believe in their government in order for it to function properly. An uninformed citizenry leads to a dysfunctional democracy. In many ways, we have become a nation in which a system designed to be run by a majority of its citizens is in fact run by a minority of the citizens. There is increased voter apathy, increased disillusionment with government, and increased withdrawal from participation. Those things are unacceptable in a functional and functioning democracy. *Brown* should serve to remind us of the importance of education in our country, our democracy, and in our communities.

Surely we all agree that civic virtue, defined as knowledge of the public good and a sustained desire to achieve it, is beneficial. Those nine justices on the Supreme Court in May 1954 exemplified civic virtue. And their decision promoted it. It was unreasonable for the South to maintain a separate and unequal system of education. It is reasonable that a democratic government should seek to equally inform, educate, and enlighten all of its citizens. For, as James Madison is widely reputed to have said, the "diffusion of knowledge is the only true guardian of liberty."

There is a danger in both individual amnesia and collective amnesia. It is important to remember history. It often serves to educate us, to inspire us, and to motivate us. Those nine justices who decided the *Brown* case were thoughtful and deliberative in looking forward. We should be mindful and studious in looking back.[2]

Unquestionably, some personal views were set aside in the interest of justice. In light of the Court's earlier precedent in *Plessy v. Ferguson*,[3] those justices were certainly labeled judicial activists. What was then viewed by so many as "activism" is now highly praised as "justice."

A judicial activist is any judge who makes a decision with which a very vocal group, large or small, disagrees. However, there is today almost universal praise for the decision and almost universal disdain for the Jim Crow system that compelled it. "Judicial activism" is usually associated with liberals, but lately conservatives have been far more likely to strike down laws passed by Congress.

According to Yale Law Professor Paul Gewirtz, Justice Clarence Thomas has voted to invalidate 65 percent of the laws that have come before him in cases while those justices least likely to do so were Ruth Bader Ginsburg and Stephen Breyer.[4]

There have been several major attempts throughout our history to interfere with judicial independence. This is not a new issue. Judges are often accused of being activists, unaccountable, and out of the mainstream.

The framers of our Constitution struck a balance between accountability and judicial independence. Hence, federal judges have the security of a lifetime appointment, which is made by the executive branch with the advice and consent of the legislative branch. In other words, elected officials who are accountable to the people make the decisions regarding service in the judicial branch. It is indeed a system that facilitates judicial independence.

The judicial independence of state courts is an entirely different matter—but not really. It's different because most states have elections for state court judges. It's not different because citizens want justice in whatever court they find themselves, whether by chance or by choice.

Regarding the federal courts in the civil rights era, Stephen Bright wrote in a *Georgia State University Law Review* article that:

> Federal courts had to enforce the Constitution in these and other areas because the state courts simply were not independent and did not enforce the law. A Georgia Supreme Court justice acknowledged that the elected justices of that court may have overlooked errors, leaving federal courts to remedy them via habeas corpus, because [federal judges] have lifetime appointments. Let them make the hard decisions.[5]

However, in state court elections, the landscape has changed dramatically in the last ten to fifteen years. Many states still have judicial elections. And now more than ever before, special interest groups seek to secure the election, not of fair and impartial judges but of judges who will decide in their favor. From oil, tobacco, and pharmaceutical companies, to the insurance defense bar, to prosecutors, to the religious right, to labor unions, to the plaintiffs' personal injury bar, to medical doctors and other health care providers, all seek to control the courts and the judges. So a judge can (1) try to please everybody, (2) try to please whoever has the most money, (3) try to please whoever controls the most votes, or (4) try to serve the interest of justice. The correct choice is obvious. In order to minimize attacks on judicial independence, the courts must do a better job of educating the public about the work that judges do. The media is essential in this educational process.

The courts and the media generally have an uneasy relationship. A large percentage of what the media deems newsworthy emanates from the courts. The courts (judges) are very apprehensive about talking to the press either because of judicial canons that discourage or prohibit it or because of concerns that the coverage will show the judge in a negative light. The fact is both the media and the courts need each other. The media needs to be able to competently report on an institution that is the source of so much news, and the courts need to educate the public about the courts. A recent American Bar Association survey examined the public's confidence (or the lack thereof) in the judicial system.[6] The survey revealed that people would most like to learn about the courts from judges. However, for the reasons stated above, judges are the people who are least likely to talk about the courts. They should. While I agree that it is inappropriate for judges to discuss active cases with the press, I see nothing wrong with a judge talking to the media about court process, procedure, and basic legal principles. There is an obvious benefit when those who report on the courts have some general knowledge of the courts and legal procedures.

Judges should use the media to disseminate information about the courts and what they do. The more knowledge people have about the court system, then the more likely they are to support it. That is why after the conclusion of every jury trial, I would take the time to talk to jurors about whatever they wanted to talk about, as long as the subject matter was appropriate within the bounds of law and ethics. That is to say, I would never offer a comment about the correctness of the verdict although that was one of the most often asked questions, but I would discuss the process.

The goal was to educate lay people about the judicial system. Almost without exception, serving on a jury enhanced and deepened a citizen's appreciation for the worth and value of our judicial system. However, inasmuch as everyone does not get an opportunity for jury service, then the most effective way to share information about the courts is through the media. The judicial branch of government is the least understood of all three branches. Knowledge of the system only serves to increase the public's confidence in the system. Judges should learn to respect that reporters have deadlines. So a call back to a reporter two days later may be worthless. Judges should develop relationships with their local media. Not for the good of the judge but for the good of the institution.

Judicial Elections versus Judicial Appointments

The debate continues. I have been appointed by two different governors, in two different decades, to two judicial positions. I was first appointed to serve as a circuit judge in 1991. After serving as a circuit judge for ten years, I was then appointed to the Mississippi Supreme Court. In both instances, I was appointed to fill a vacancy and in both instances, I eventually had to stand for election. In Mississippi, judicial elections are nonpartisan. While there are no party primaries, judicial elections are, for the most part, the same as all other elections in Mississippi. However, nothing is more politicized than a judicial appointment.

The 1991 Appointment

By executive order, Governor Ray Mabus created a judicial selection committee that screened applicants for all judicial appointments to be made by the governor. That committee was a large and diverse group of lawyers and lay people. There was a lengthy application form. The committee screened the applications and determined which applicants would be invited to an interview before the committee. The committee, after interviewing those applicants, would score, rank, and submit the top three applicants to the governor for his review. The governor, although his executive order did not require, would then make a selection from among the three names submitted for his review. Obviously, this process was designed to maximize input, to objectively review applicants, and to facilitate a process that resulted in merit selection. To varying degrees of success, all of those goals were accomplished. But I still made numerous telephone calls to friends and supporters of the governor, seeking their support and assistance in obtaining the gubernatorial appointment. I was told that calls and letters of support from friends and supporters of the governor were important, despite the judicial selection committee. Raw politics.

I was appointed in February 1991. In September 1991, I was elected in a special election. It was a contested election where I had a single opponent. I ran again in 1994 and 1998. I was unopposed.

The 2001 Appointment

Governor Ronnie Musgrove had no judicial selection committee. I was interviewed by Governor Musgrove during the selection process. I was not privy to any of the other phases of either his decision-making process or his selection process. However, on November 1, 2001, I was appointed to the Mississippi Supreme Court. Clearly, the process worked. Surely, friends and supporters of the governor sought to influence his decision regarding the gubernatorial appointment.

I then stood for election in November 2004. I had three opponents in the general election. In order to avoid a runoff election, it was necessary for a single candidate to receive at least 50 percent of the popular vote. I received 48 percent. The runoff election was two weeks after the general election.

Frankly, I much prefer standing before the people.

Based on my experience, the electoral process is a purer form of attaining a public office. In a participatory democracy, where citizen involvement is essential, an election obviously involves more active citizen participation than does an appointment. I am of the opinion that a democracy becomes dysfunctional when a small minority of its citizens set policy and choose leaders. The electoral process provides an opportunity for more citizen participation, and those kinds of opportunities are almost always positive.

Conclusion

Justice Rehnquist said in his remarks on judicial independence in March 2003:

> I suspect the Court will continue to encounter challenges to its independence and authority by the other branches of government because of the design of our Constitutional system. The degree to which that independence will be preserved will depend again in some measure on the public's respect for the judiciary. Maintaining that respect and a reserve of public goodwill, without becoming subservient to public opinion, remains a challenge to the federal judiciary.[7]

And I would add, to the state judiciary as well.

Chief Justice Francis Nyalali of the United Republic of Tanzania put it this way:

> The people have to value an independent judiciary and be willing to defend it. And to win public affection, we, the judges, must do our jobs well. The courts must work. People must feel that they can resolve disputes satisfactorily and in a reasonable amount of time. If they do, then the people will support us. You see, it is really the quality of justice that determines whether we remain independent.[8]

> Judges and justices must conduct themselves, both in their on court activities and judicial decisions and in their everyday lives, in a manner that fosters public confidence in the judiciary. Unfortunately, a few pander to special interests and thereby lessen the public's confidence in what is a venerable institution in our democracy. While the institutions are much larger and much more important than any of the individuals among us who serve, it is important to remember that individuals can dilute the quality of justice that is handed down by these institutions. It is important that those of us who serve seek to rise to the level of quality that the citizens deserve and expect.

Notes

1. 347 U.S. 483 (1954).

2. James E. Graves, Jr., *A Look Back at Brown v. Board of Education*, 43 JUDGES' J. 25 (Spring 2004).

3. 163 U.S. 537 (1896).

4. Nicholas D. Kristof, *Drop the Judicial Activism*, INT'L HERALD TRIB., Oct. 5, 2005, at 7.

5. Stephan B. Bright, *Can Judicial Independence Be Attained in the South? Overcoming History, Elections, and Misperceptions about the Role of the Judiciary*, 14 GA. ST. UNIV. L. REV., 817, 840.

6. AMERICAN BAR ASSOCIATION, PERCEPTIONS OF THE U.S. JUSTICE SYSTEM 1 (1999), *available at* http://www.abanet.org/media/perception/perceptions.pdf. Last visited August 14, 2006.

7. Chief Justice William Rehnquist, Remarks at the Symposium on Judicial Independence, University of Richmond T. C. Williams School of Law (Mar. 21, 2003) *available at http://www.supremecourtus.gov/public*info/speeches/sp_03-21-03.html.

8. NATIONAL CENTER FOR STATE COURTS, MEMORANDUM ON FOSTERING JUDICIAL INDEPENDENCE IN STATE AND FEDERAL COURTS 4 (Feb. 27, 1998), *available at* http://ncsconline. org/WC/Publications/KIS_JudInd_S98-0281_Pub.pdf.

5   Politics and the Confirmation Process

Thoughts on the Roberts and Alito Hearings

John M. Walker, Jr.

RESPECT FOR THE AUTHORITY of the law depends on judicial modesty—judges performing their proper role within the judiciary's institutional limitations. Yet judicial modesty does not engender respect for the rule of law unless the public is aware of that constraint and realizes its significance in shaping judicial behavior. A recent poll by the Syracuse University Maxwell School of Citizenship and Public Affairs suggests that there is much ground to cover toward this goal. According to the survey, of people who read a newspaper at least several times a month, more than 57 percent agree that judges base their decisions on their personal beliefs rather than "the law and the Constitution."[1] For those who watch the local or national news each night, the percentage is 62 percent.[2] It is now common to hear judges characterized in political terms—"for" or "against" abortion, sweeping presidential power, large corporations, or the little guy—with no regard to the adjudication process. In this chapter, I use the confirmation hearings of Chief Justice John Roberts and Justice Samuel Alito as an opportunity for reflection on how the confirmation process for Supreme Court justices shapes the public's view of judicial legitimacy.

Circuit Judge, United States Court of Appeals for the Second Circuit and former Chief Judge (2000–2006). The assistance of J. Cam Barker in the preparation of this essay is gratefully acknowledged.

Recap: Politics in the Confirmation of Lower-Court Judges

I have written on this topic before. Three years ago, I reflected on the cabined nature of the judicial role and how the Senate confirmation process for lower-court nominees distorts the public's perception of that role.[3] The premise for my concern was and remains that centuries-old observation that the authority of the law and its courts rests on principles, not politics.[4]

Many constraints set the judiciary apart from the political branches. First, in resolving legal issues, judges look for guidance to a limited set of sources, with primacy always given to the language used by the people's representatives.[5] Of course, judges are not legal automatons, reflexively and mindlessly applying legal texts to decide the controversy presented by the parties. Within the common-law tradition, in addition to textual interpretation, we reason from precedents, background materials, and legal theories when confronted with uncertainty. Lower-court judges are further constrained by rulings of higher courts. Although debate continues over the permissible sources for legal reasoning and the weight to be given them, most judges agree that our goal is to objectively discern the meaning of legal dictates, influenced by a discrete universe of material. Indeed, the democratic nature of our Constitution, to which the power of judicial review is an exception, limits our role to interpreting only sources of law enacted by the people's representatives,[6] with resort to deductive reasoning to fill in any holes. Second, the judicial role is constrained by the requirement that we publicly explain our decisions, in writing, accounting for binding and persuasive legal sources and how they influence our judgment. Unlike actors in the political branches, judges may not simply pronounce a decision without explaining its justification. Third, judges are cabined by the reactive nature of our decision-making role. The judicial power is invoked not by judges but by parties who present us with cases or controversies. We rely as well on the parties to provide us with the functional requisites of informed adjudication—a concrete set of facts and the adversarial presentation of legal arguments.[7] Federal judges may not issue advisory opinions but are limited to deciding questions that affect the outcome of a live controversy between adverse litigants.[8] In short, we may not deploy the judicial power simply to address the concerns of a favored constituency or society at large.

These limitations outline the proper judicial role—as I have said, "to identify the meaning of the law based on a limited set of sources, with primacy given to the text; to make an earnest attempt to discern the intent behind the words used, where it is important or necessary to do so; to apply the law to the facts of a particular case, mindful always of the limited nature of the enterprise; and to ensure at every step that personal preferences do not infect the process."[9] This restrained role engenders respect for the authority of law, which, by the framers' design, is the source of the judiciary's power, legitimacy, and independence.[10] It is essential, then, that the people understand and appreciate these checks on the judicial power that so profoundly distinguishes that power from the exercise of political will.

A danger exists that Senate confirmation hearings, for lower-court judges especially, distort the judicial role in the public's eye. As legislators, interest groups, and the media increasingly question lower-court nominees on their agreement with Supreme Court precedent or their political views, it perpetuates the misconception that, as judges, those nominees can and will ignore or misapply precedents in furtherance of their personal policy preferences.[11] Likewise, questioning lower-court nominees about their political views erodes the public's faith in judicial impartiality by suggesting that judges reason backward by concocting legal reasoning to support a desired result.[12] Accordingly, I have called for a new partnership between a press that works hard to understand the difference between a judge's political views and the legal tools that he or she employs to decide a case, and politicians who not only recognize this difference but refrain from encouraging and capitalizing on the public perception that judging is just politics by another name.[13]

Nominees to the Supreme Court

With the spotlight on the confirmation hearings of John Roberts and Samuel Alito, I wish to augment my earlier observations with thoughts about how the hearings for Supreme Court nominees shape public perception of judicial legitimacy and, consequently, judicial independence. As an initial matter, it must be acknowledged that the role of a Supreme Court justice differs significantly from that of a lower-court judge. Justices, not strictly bound by Supreme Court precedent, may ignore or expressly overrule such precedent, and this lack of constraint introduces a political element into the Court's decisions and the nomination process generally. When asked to apply constitutional provisions written broadly for the ages to new situations not expressly contemplated by the text's authors, the justices are less constrained than lower-court judges. Nonetheless, limitations remain: The justices still must support their decisions with legal reasoning and must respect the institution of the Court as a court of law to maintain its legitimacy and authority.[14] The justices may overrule or alter precedent, but they must explain why.

This increased discretion casts a spotlight on a Supreme Court justice's "judicial philosophy"—his or her views about acceptable and preferable methods of dealing with legal sources. Therefore, it is entirely within bounds for legislators to probe a Supreme Court nominee's judicial philosophy directly and base their votes on it. Ascertaining these views justifies legislators' asking nominees about how they would go about deciding a particular case or how they would treat a particular legal source, for these questions shed light on a nominee's judicial philosophy. But this quest does not justify trying to pin a nominee down on a specific result. Too often, legislators use sought-after results as proxies for judicial philosophy and thereby contribute to a gross distortion of the concept of judicial independence.

Caving in to the pressures of interest groups who are greatly concerned with the prospect of a nominee's proclivity to rule in their favor, legislators often misrepresent the judicial role by painting the justices as results-driven jurists who side with or against parties or broad policies rather than basing their decisions on legal arguments. For example, a Planned Parenthood press release called Justice Alito's nomination "outrageous" in part because of his "callous disregard of battered women who would be affected" by the Pennsylvania law disputed in *Planned Parenthood v. Casey*.[15] This depiction of Justice Alito as disregarding parties rather than, say, disregarding arguments or applicable precedent impedes a proper understanding of the judicial role by suggesting that a judge's rulings are driven by his opinion for or against a party rather than his regard for neutral principles that each side advances. It may be too much to ask that legislators not cave in to the pressure brought by interest groups, or to the temptation to score political points, by depicting judicial decision making as turning on a jurist's sympathy for a party,[16] but I highlight this danger with the warning to conscientious legislators that such depictions foster a serious misperception of the judicial function and thereby undermine an independent judiciary.

In addition, legislators may engage in personal attacks against nominees as a proxy for their dislike of the nominee's judicial philosophy. With some exception, recent Supreme Court confirmation hearings have largely scored well on this point, remaining dignified and focusing on the nominee's qualifications and legal career rather than attacking the nominee personally. Noteworthy, however, were claims bordering on frivolous that then-Judge Alito should have recused himself in a mutual-fund case and remarks about his belonging to a college group decades ago, some of whose members evinced racial and gender bias without his knowledge. Thus, the danger of regression always lurks, and we still see moments in which legislators attack a nominee personally in what seems like pretext for disagreement with the nominee's judicial philosophy.

With the benefit of the recent hearings, we can conclude that the voice for protection of judicial independence and a proper public understanding of the judicial function is largely that of the nominee, assisted by supportive legislators. Although the canons of judicial ethics prevent judges from responding to some criticism,[17] confirmation hearings provide an opportunity for present and future jurists to educate the public about the judicial function and tactfully respond to criticisms that judges are result driven. One might reasonably expect that a few clear sentences from a nominee carry more weight than ten minutes of senatorial oration. In his hearing, Chief Justice Roberts did a commendable job of conveying the limited nature of the judicial role. He emphasized that judges "are constrained" when they apply the law: "They are constrained by the words that you choose to enact into a law—in interpreting the law. They are constrained by the words of the Constitution. They are constrained by the precedents of other judges that become part of the rule of law that they must apply."[18] He traced this "cabining of [judicial] discretion" to Alexander Hamilton, who in The Federalist No. 78 observed that the essence of the judicial function is being confined by the law. And when asked for his view of a judge's role in "advancing" freedom and progress, Roberts responded that "judges and justices . . . need to be on the side of the Constitution" rather than taking sides in a policy debate based on their personal understanding of "progress."[19]

Future nominees would do well to follow Chief Justice Roberts's example and take advantage of the opportunity in confirmation hearings to properly define the judicial role.[20] Nominees can temper the rhetoric of legislators and interest groups by explaining the cabined nature of judicial decision making and drawing attention to the distortions introduced in the confirmation process. This is not to lessen my request for a new partnership between legislators and the media in portraying the role of Supreme Court justices. Legislators must be mindful of the distortions of the judicial role communicated by their conduct in confirmation hearings and resist caving in to interest groups who base their advocacy and fund-raising on the political paradigm. Constructive lines of questioning exist that allow legislators to discern a nominee's judicial philosophy without distorting public opinion of the judicial function. For example, what is the nominee's understanding of stare decisis? To what legal sources does the nominee look for guidance? What weight does the nominee attach to those sources? Do the past opinions of nominees who have been judges shed light on the answer to these questions, and do they exhibit consistency in legal approach, internal coherence, and general competence?[21] Senators can ask useful questions and express their views without lambasting a nominee for his or her "insensitivity" to sympathetic parties and political movements or engaging in personal attacks.

At the same time, the media has an obligation to understand and communicate to the public the limited judicial role and the nonpolitical nature of the judicial process. I searched for such an understanding in the *New York Times* editorial pages in connection with the Alito hearing and found quite the opposite.[22] Indeed, the Maxwell Poll conducted in October 2005 shows that more than two-thirds of Americans agree that media coverage of the courts tends to pay more attention to a judge's partisan background than to the reasoning that judges use to justify their decisions.[23] My search of the *Wall Street Journal* editorial pages fared slightly better, turning up an editorial by law professor Jonathan Adler on the day following the Alito hearing. In *Not All Law is Politics in Robes*,[24] Adler pointed out the incorrect "assumption that judicial nominees are politicians with policy views that they will—and should—impose from the bench," an assumption that he attributed to the effect on politicians of various interest groups that "are now full participants in judicial nomination battles." Adler correctly noted that "[j]ournalists have also treated judicial nominees like political candidates," lamenting that "[v]iewing judges as life-tenured politicians who get to impose their own policy preferences furthers the downward spiral of judicial politicization."[25]

The confirmation hearings for Chief Justice Roberts and Justice Alito were for the large part dignified and conducted with respect for the judiciary and the nominee. They marked a departure from the hearings of Robert Bork and Clarence Thomas that I hope will become common practice. While the nominees themselves play a major role in promoting a proper conception of the judicial role, appropriate legislative questioning and media reporting is essential to foster public understanding of the constrained nature of judicial decision making and public respect for the rule of law.

Notes

1. Campbell Public Affairs Institute, Maxwell Poll on Civic Engagement and Inequality, at p. 5 (Oct. 2005) (margin of error ±5 percent), *available at* http://www. maxwell.syr.edu/campbell/Poll/CitizenshipPoll.htm (last visited Aug. 14, 2006).

2. *Id.*

3. John M. Walker, Jr., *Politics and the Confirmation Process: The Importance of Congressional Restraint in Safeguarding Judicial Independence*, 55 SYRACUSE L. REV. 1 (2004).

4. THE FEDERALIST NO. 81, at 484–85 (Alexander Hamilton) (Clinton Rossiter ed., 1961).

5. Walker, *supra* note 3, at 4–5.

6. *See* Richard H. Fallon, Jr., Daniel J. Meltzer, and David L. Shapiro, HART & WECHSLER'S THE FEDERAL COURTS AND THE FEDERAL SYSTEM 67 (5th ed. 2003).

7. *See generally id.* at 70–71.

8. *See generally* Erwin Chemerinsky, FEDERAL JURISDICTION 49–54 (4th ed. 2003).

9. Walker, *supra* note 3, at 5.

10. *Id.* at 3.

11. *Id.* at 7–8.

12. *Id.* at 8–9.

13. *Id.* at 11–13.

14. *Cf.* Peter M. Shane, *Rights, Remedies, and Restraint*, 64 CHI.-KENT L. REV. 531, 546 (1988).

15. *See* Press Release, Planned Parenthood, Bush Nominates Samuel Alito (Oct. 31, 2005), *available at* http://www.plannedparenthood.org/news-articles-press/politics-policy-issues/alito-nomination-10330.htm; *cf.* 947 F.2d 682 (3d Cir. 1991).

16. See, for example, Senator Kennedy's complaint in Justice Alito's hearing that Americans are "losing their jobs or working for less" and his reference to a study by Cass Sunstein to denounce Justice Alito for acting "in favor of government, large corporations and other powerful interests" and not "the claims of individual citizens." *Nomination of Samuel A. Alito, Jr. to be an Associate Justice of the Supreme Court of the United States*, Transcript Day 1 (remarks of Senator Kennedy).

17. *E.g.*, Code of Conduct for United States Judges, Canon 7(A).

18. *Nomination of John G. Roberts, Jr. to be Chief Justice of the United States*, Bound Transcript at 76 (response to Senator Grassley).

19. *Id.* at 104 (response to Senator Kyl).

20. Justice Alito also set a positive example, "explain[ing] the process he would go through to evaluate various types of cases without committing himself to a given outcome" and stressing "that the process of judging—the exercise of judgment rather than will—is more important than a specific result." Jonathan Adler, Op-Ed, *Not All*

Law Is Politics in Robes, WALL ST. J., Jan. 14, 2006, at A9. Adler highlighted a recent case in which Justices Stevens and Thomas joined in dissent on the basis that the text of an act should be followed, despite its wholly mistaken economic theory, as a "reminder that judges should apply the law irrespective of the policy result[,] . . . a lesson that the Senate, and the public, should take to heart." *Id.*

21. *See* Alper, "Selecting the Judiciary: Who Should Be the Judge?," this volume at 138–144 (noting Virginia's high marks for public perception of judicial competence and tying the high marks to Virginia's depoliticized legislative election of judges, in which the state legislature avoids questioning candidates about hot-button social or legal issues and instead is largely concerned about intellect, patience, ability to be fair, and performance as a judge).

22. *See, e.g.,* Editorial, *Judge Alito and Abortion*, N.Y. TIMES, Dec. 3, 2005, at A18 ("The Senate needs to look through the cloud of explanations and excuses and examine where Judge Alito really stands on abortion rights."); Editorial, *Another Lost Opportunity*, N.Y. TIMES, Nov. 1, 2005, at A26 (complaining about "Judge Alito's frequent rulings to undermine the federal government's authority to address momentous national problems.").

23. *See supra* note 1, at 4; *see also* Lithwick, "The Internet and the Judiciary: We Are all Experts Now," this volume at 181 ("The mass media in general and the Internet in particular have become so relentlessly focused on the holding of each case, that any meaningful explication of how the courts arrived at that decision is deemed irrelevant at worst, and boring but necessary at best.").

24. WALL ST. J., Jan. 14, 2006, at A9.

25. *Id.*

6 Selecting the Judiciary

Who Should Be the Judge?

Joanne F. Alper

*The very underlying principle that necessitates the election of the legislative
department by the people is that the Legislature shall reflect the views and
wishes of the people . . . while the whole theory of a judicial system is that
the men upon the bench shall respond to nothing except truth and justice;
that they shall simply declare the law as it is, and that they shall make no
law. . . . As I understand the function of a judge, it is to reflect nobody's views,
nobody's wishes, nobody's theories in his decisions. The fundamental principle
upon which our judicial system is founded is that there shall be absolute
independence of every consideration except to find out what is the truth and
to declare it.*[1]

Introduction

The U.S. Constitution created a system of government comprised of three
branches—executive, legislative, and judicial—with a system of checks and
balances to protect against tyranny by one branch. Of these three branches,
the judicial is structurally the weakest because it must rely on the legislature
and the executive to appropriate money and enforce its orders. Therefore, it
is paramount that the courts maintain the respect of the other branches and
the public that they serve. To earn such respect, the judiciary must be strong,

Judge, Circuit Court for the Seventeenth Judicial Circuit, Arlington, Virginia. The author
wishes to gratefully acknowledge the assistance of Vincent J. Gaiani, Esq., J.D., George Mason
University School of Law, *magna cum laude*, 2005, B.A., University of Virginia, 2002; Sarah M.
Haley, Esq., J.D., Washington College of Law, American University, 2005, A.B., Kenyon College,
cum laude, 2002; and Sean S. Kumar, Esq., J.D., University of Richmond, *cum laude*, 2005, B.A.,
University of Virginia, 2001, law clerks to the Circuit Court, for their invaluable assistance in the
research and preparation of this essay.

and to be strong it must be independent. The courts must be accepted by the public as fair and impartial arbiters of disputes whose decisions are not influenced by political or any other form of bias or prejudice. Therefore, a strong and independent judiciary at both the federal and state levels is essential to preserve American democracy.

There has been a heightened attack on judicial independence during the early years of the twenty-first century. Interest groups and the media blame judges at every level, from local courts to the U.S. Supreme Court, for many of America's social dilemmas. The judiciary is caught in the middle of a highly politicized and emotional atmosphere, caused in large part by the twenty-four-hour news cycle, advanced by politicians who are either ignorant of or choose to ignore the proper role of the courts, and accepted by a citizenry often uninformed about the role of the judge as impartial arbiter with the responsibility of enforcing the laws. The furor surrounding the Terry Schiavo case in 2005 and the increasingly partisan and invasive confirmation proceedings for Supreme Court justices are national examples of a crisis that is occurring at all levels of the judiciary. At the root of this crisis is the need for the American public to recognize the importance of judicial independence from politics and other branches of government. As noted by Justice Elizabeth B. Lacy of the Virginia Supreme Court: "Judicial independence does not mean that judges can or should resolve disputes without regard for statutory law, common law, or principles of stare decisis and precedent. Rather, it means that judges may make decisions in cases before them independent of external influences, such as a need to satisfy a particular constituency or to reflect a particular ideology."[2]

The framers of the Constitution had the foresight to provide that federal judges "[S]hall hold their Offices during good Behaviour...."[3] Providing lifetime appointments for federal judges allows them to make rulings on matters of law without fear of influence by politics or public opinion. Most state court judges do not have lifetime tenure;[4] rather, they have set terms with the option to run for reelection or reappointment. Hence, state judges do not have the same protection against politics and public opinion as federal trial and appellate judges. A state's method of judicial selection and the influence of partisan politics and interest groups on that selection are significant factors in determining public confidence in the judiciary.

The Commonwealth of Virginia is one of only two states in the United States that selects and retains its judges by legislative election,[5] which many view as preferable to popular elections: "This unique method of judicial selection and retention by the General Assembly for a term of years eliminates the offensive and distracting practices of campaigning and fundraising accompanying the popular election of judges in other jurisdictions. It also eliminates the pressure on a judicial candidate or sitting judge to tailor his or her behavior in a manner that will secure election or re-election by the voting public."[6]

Legislative election means, quite simply, the selection and election of judges by a majority vote of both houses of the Virginia General Assembly. The Constitution of Virginia specifically provides that the members of the Supreme Court of Virginia and the circuit courts "shall be chosen by the vote of a majority of the members elected to each house of the General Assembly."[7] The Virginia Code sets out an identical method of legislative election for the judges of the Court of Appeals of Virginia[8] and for the general district and juvenile and domestic relations district courts, which are the first tier of trial courts, designated as courts "not of record."[9] I will provide more detail on the mechanics of Virginia's method of legislative election in a later section of this chapter, but for all local judicial positions, the process generally involves the judicial candidate placing his or her credentials before a committee of the local bar and/or a citizens' advisory committee, enlisting the support of the local bar associations, sitting for an interview with the General Assembly members who represent the circuit or district, and ultimately obtaining the support of the local representatives whose choice is generally supported by the members in both houses. For positions on the Commonwealth's two highest courts, the Supreme Court and Court of Appeals, the process is similar but larger in scope; candidates are screened and evaluated by statewide bar associations, and supporters of the candidates try to persuade blocs of legislators from various regions to come together to support their candidate. For all judgeships in Virginia, the final selection is made by a majority vote of the House of Delegates and Senate.

As a Virginia circuit court judge who has had the opportunity to study and observe various methods of judicial selection, including partisan and nonpartisan popular elections, I firmly agree with Justice Lacy's conclusions about the superiority of legislative elections over any other form of judicial selection. This chapter will outline the history of judicial selection in Virginia, survey various methods of judicial selection in other states, and analyze the effect of nonpartisan legislative election on the quality of judges and on the public's confidence in the judiciary.

Judicial Selection in Virginia

History

From the earliest days of the Republic, Virginia has had a long history of pro-
ducing prominent lawyers and jurists, notably including Thomas Jefferson
and Chief Justice John Marshall. A hallmark of modern Virginia's legal and
governmental excellence is the quality of its judiciary. As one of only two
states where the legislature elects state judges,[10] Virginia has a rich history of
preferring a legislatively elected judiciary rather than one selected by popular
elections.[11] This method of judicial selection preserves judicial independence
and reduces the impact of politics and partisanship on judges' decisions, resulting in not only more qualified judges than would otherwise result from
popular elections but also increased public confidence in, and respect for, the
state judiciary.[12]

Selecting state judges by legislative election was widely accepted during
the early development of American judicial systems, in part as a reaction
to the British king's absolute control of the judiciary. The Declaration of
Independence articulated this sentiment by explicitly condemning the British monarch's domination over judicial posts.[13] Following the American
Revolution, eight states selected judges by legislative election,[14] but none
provided for a popularly elected judiciary. Alexander Hamilton advocated
legislative election and life tenure to ensure judicial independence, in part
because popularly electing judges would result in "too great a disposition
to consult popularity" instead of the "constitution and the laws."[15] But by
the early nineteenth century, Jacksonian democracy's emphasis on popular
sovereignty, coupled with widespread distrust of elitist control over the judiciary, led to the adoption of publicly elected judiciaries.[16] Consequently,
by the beginning of the Civil War, twenty-four of the thirty-four states had
established some form of popular election of state judges.[17]

In Virginia, the legislature has always been the strongest branch of government. In accordance with national trends, Virginia's first state constitution in
1776 established legislatively elected state judges.[18] Following the Reform Convention in 1850, Virginia briefly adopted a popularly elected judiciary "from
persons nominated by the governor," only to revert back to legislatively electing judges in 1870.[19] Under that constitution, which is similar to the current
method of judicial selection in Virginia, judges were elected by the General
Assembly to a term of years with the possibility of reelection.[20]

Although Virginia's method of selecting judges has remained largely unchanged since that time, the state court system has unquestionably evolved. Virginia's court structure initially consisted of "county courts" and a "supreme court of appeals," which had appellate jurisdiction over facts as well as law.[21] The county court judges had considerable power, including "recommend[ing] to the executive the persons whom they wish to admit into their own body," appointing sheriffs, and, surprisingly, "[t]hey may be at one and at the same time, members of the general assembly (or of congress), judges of the county courts, and militia officers of any rank."[22] In the early twentieth century, the General Assembly approved legislation whereby circuit court judges in counties with populations of 6,000 or more could appoint "trial justices," or lower court judges, to serve four-year terms.[23] The present-day circuit courts are "courts of record," the highest courts of trial jurisdiction in Virginia, and are the only trial courts specifically mentioned in the Virginia Constitution. By statute, lower trial courts "not of record" were created in 1950,[24] and the unified district court system was created in 1973, resulting in what are today known as the general district courts and juvenile and domestic relations district courts.

Following the surge of popularly elected state judges, as early as 1853, many states recognized that partisanship and campaigning had a negative impact on judicial elections. As a result, toward the late nineteenth century, judges began appearing on ballots for popular election without party labels in an attempt to diminish the influence of politics on judging.[25] In *Democracy in America*, Alexis de Tocqueville articulated common concerns surrounding popularly elected judges: "Certain constitutions make the members of courts [popularly] *elected* and submit them to frequent reelections . . . I dare to predict that sooner or later these innovations will have dire results and that one day it will be perceived that by so diminishing the independence of the magistrates, not only has the judicial power been attacked, but the democratic republic itself."[26]

Although many states continued to popularly elect judges, critics cited judicial dependence on public sentiment and the perception of judges as well within the political fray as reasons to question this method of judicial selection. The founding of the American Judicature Society in 1913 was largely inspired by such an aversion to popularly elected judges, described by its founder, Roscoe Pound: "Putting courts into politics, and compelling judges to become politicians, in many jurisdictions has almost destroyed the traditional respect for the bench."[27] Ironically, judicial reliance on public elections diminished the public's overall opinion of the bench. Inspired by this observation, the "merit plan" gained support, which promoted the creation of impartial committees to locate potential judicial candidates and make recommendations to the appointive body.[28]

Regardless of the method, it is impossible to fully remove politics from judicial selection, since the appointive bodies, whether they be the president, the governor, or the legislature, are politicians. For example, during the twentieth century, Democrats dominated both houses of Virginia's General Assembly, diminishing Republican influence on judicial selection. Throughout the 1980s, many perceived state judicial selection in Virginia as an overly partisan process because the minority party in the General Assembly had little, if any, influence over who was elected to the bench.[29] Then, in the mid-1990s, Republican gains in the Virginia legislature balanced party influence on judicial selection; instead of "rubber-stamping" judicial candidates, local legislative delegations recommended judicial nominees to the General Assembly.[30] In an attempt to downplay political influence on judicial selection, Republicans created the Joint Judicial Advisory Committee in the late 1990s. Its purpose was to screen judicial candidates and assist the legislature in selecting judges.[31] This plan, however, has not been used consistently statewide.

Virginia Today

The current Virginia Constitution was ratified in 1971 and Article VI defines the powers of the judiciary. As stated in Section 7, the justices of the Supreme Court and the judges of other courts of record[32] are chosen "by the vote of a majority of the members elected to each house of the General Assembly."[33] Justices of the Supreme Court of Virginia serve twelve-year terms while judges of all other courts of record serve eight-year terms.[34] Unlike the U.S. Constitution, which gives virtually no guidance on the qualifications for federal judges, the Virginia Constitution mandates that its justices and judges of courts of record "shall be residents of the Commonwealth and shall, at least five years prior to their appointment or election, have been admitted to the bar of the Commonwealth."[35] However, the Virginia Constitution does not contemplate the manner in which the General Assembly considers candidates for the bench.[36] It merely narrows the field by requiring judges to live in the jurisdiction over which they will preside.[37]

Because judges in Virginia are not selected by popular vote, they are not held directly accountable to the citizenry. This does not mean that they lack accountability. The Virginia Constitution provides for certain checks on the judiciary. After their legislative election, judges of all courts are commissioned by the governor. However, it is the General Assembly that has the authority to prescribe "salaries and allowances" of judges, to "enact such laws as it deems necessary for the retirement of justices and judges," and to provide for a mandatory retirement age for judges. These measures, along with the more obvious check of the election and reelection process itself, ensure a degree of accountability to the judicial system before starting a term on the bench.

There is also oversight regarding judges in the midst of their terms. From the enactment of the first Virginia Constitution in 1776 until the 1971 Constitution, the General Assembly had the power to impeach Virginia's judges. This power never resulted in removing any judge of the Supreme Court of Virginia or the Court of Appeals of Virginia.[38] Two lower court judges were removed in the early 1900s for improper behavior.[39]

The Virginia Constitution of 1971 provided for a new measure of judicial regulation. In the spirit of the self-governance of the legal profession and of judicial independence, the new constitution created the Judicial Inquiry and Review Commission (JIRC).[40] The General Assembly is charged with selecting members of JIRC from "the judiciary, the bar, and the public . . . to investigate charges which would be the basis for retirement, censure, or removal of a judge."[41] Charges against a judge that the JIRC finds to be well founded result in a formal complaint and subsequent hearing before the JIRC with an appeal to the Supreme Court of Virginia.[42] JIRC proceedings are confidential, but as recently demonstrated, the files are opened when a judge is considered for reelection by the General Assembly.[43] The system has been effective in enforcing and maintaining high standards for judicial ethics, but newer innovations are underway that may further increase the quality and accountability of the judiciary.

In 2005, the Virginia General Assembly adopted the Judicial Performance Evaluation Program in an effort to bring more uniformity to the way in which candidates for the bench are considered for election by the General Assembly and to give judges a method to receive feedback on their performance during their terms.[44] As one Virginia jurist remarked, "the qualifications of judicial candidates are often determined by evaluating a decision taken by the candidate in a specific case. Regardless of the legal merit of the candidate's position, it will inevitably conflict with the point of view of the losing litigant and his or her supporters."[45] It is likely that the use of this impartial evaluation system will further increase the integrity and fairness of Virginia's relatively de-politicized system.

A Comparative Analysis

As stated above, Virginia's system of legislatively electing judges is unique among the fifty states.[46] South Carolina is the only other state that selects its judges through a majority vote of the legislative body, but unlike Virginia, South Carolina's legislature votes on nominations that are first submitted by the state's Judicial Merit Selection Commission.[47] The Commonwealth does not require a merit selection committee to choose judicial nominees and, therefore, stands as the only purely legislative election of judges in the United States today.[48]

Maine, New Hampshire, and New Jersey provide for appointment of trial court judges by a system of gubernatorial appointment.[49] Sixteen states also involve the executive or legislative branches in appointing trial-level judges, but these states first provide for a nomination process of "merit selection," where a nonpartisan selection committee provides the governor or legislature with a roster of possible nominees whom it deems qualified to serve on the bench. States that provide for merit selection committees include Alaska, Arizona, Colorado, Connecticut, Delaware, Hawaii, Iowa, Kansas, Maryland, Massachusetts, Nebraska, New Mexico, Rhode Island, Utah, Vermont, and Wyoming.[50]

The majority of states continue to use public elections as the method of selecting judges for courts of general jurisdiction. Eighteen states provide for nonpartisan election of judges, including Arkansas, California, Florida, Georgia, Idaho, Kentucky, Michigan, Minnesota, Mississippi, Montana, Nevada, North Carolina, North Dakota, Oklahoma, Oregon, South Dakota, Washington, and Wisconsin.[51] Another eleven states elect their trial-level judges through a partisan election system. These states are Alabama, Illinois, Indiana, Louisiana, Missouri, New York, Ohio, Pennsylvania, Tennessee, Texas, and West Virginia.[52]

Virginia also stands among the minority of states where judges do not face public retention elections. Of the twenty-one states that do not use popular elections to select trial-level judges, more than half of those states still use some form of general election or retention system to determine whether a judge will continue to sit for an additional term.[53] In Virginia and ten other states, including Connecticut, Delaware, Hawaii, Maine, Massachusetts, New Hampshire, New Jersey, Rhode Island, South Carolina, and Vermont, judges are reappointed and confirmed by the executive and legislative branches, with no direct public involvement through a retention election.[54]

Virginia's unique method of judicial selection may, in part, be responsible for the public's satisfaction with its judges. A recent survey of Virginia residents who had experience with the Virginia court system in the previous five years revealed that 83.4 percent of respondents found the court process to be fair or very fair, and 79 percent stated that they had a positive or very positive impression of Virginia's court system.[55] These statistics compare favorably to the results of an American Bar Association (ABA) poll regarding perceptions of the American justice system.[56] In the nationwide ABA poll only 28 percent of respondents stated that they were very confident in their state and local courts, with an additional 47 percent stating that they were somewhat confident in their state court system.

As for the judges themselves, only 54 percent of the respondents in the ABA poll agreed that most judges were extremely well qualified for their jobs. It is noteworthy that the survey of Virginia residents regarding their impressions of Virginia's court system was a specific, targeted survey of those individuals who had *actual* experience with the courts at all levels and in all types of civil and criminal cases.

Moreover, a national poll of in-house general counsel and senior corporate attorneys indicated that Virginia ranked second in the nation in terms of overall judicial competence.[57] Virginia's high marks for judicial competence, when compared with other states' rankings in the poll, appear to have some correlation to the commonwealth's method for selecting judges. The average "judicial competence" ranking received by states that use gubernatorial or legislative appointment processes was 17.4 out of 50.[58] Those states using a "merit selection" approach for judicial nominations received an average ranking of 20.88. There is a notable drop-off for those states that use popular elections for selection of judges, with states using nonpartisan elections receiving an average ranking of 26.22, and states using partisan elections receiving an average ranking of 34.73.

Overall, the results of the survey indicate a striking difference in the legal community's perception of judicial competence based on whether judges are selected by popular elections. The twenty-one states that do not use popular elections for selection of judges received an average ranking of 20.05, while the twenty-nine states that use partisan and nonpartisan public elections received an average ranking of 29.45.

While the selection process used by any given state is only one of the many factors that may affect the public's perception of the competence and quality of its judiciary, the negative correlation between popularly elected judges and their relative "competence" may be too strong to ignore. Of the ten states that were ranked lowest in judicial competence, all of them were states that used partisan or nonpartisan elections for selecting their judges. There is an even stronger negative correlation for the eleven states that use partisan elections, as six of those states ranked in the lowest ten nationally.

Some argue that popular elections are preferable to legislative election of judges because the public is a better barometer of who should occupy the bench than an elected legislature.[59] In this volume, Justice Harold See argues that opponents of popular judicial elections incorrectly assume "that the public lacks the understanding of the judicial function needed to make wise selections of judges."[60] In fact, See states, "not only do the citizens know their judges, but the judges also know the voters and their concerns, and, thus, one would expect, know how to communicate with them."[61]

However, a recent California judicial election calls this "wisdom of the citizenry" into serious question. Lynn Diane Olson, a bagel shop owner with no judicial experience, unseated Dzintra Janavs, a Los Angeles Superior Court judge with over twenty years of experience.[62] When asked whether Olson challenged the incumbent judge because "she had a foreign sounding name which might meet with disfavor with the electorate," Olson had no response.[63] The fact that a popular judicial election left Janavs vulnerable because of her name is all the more shocking when combined with the fact that Janavs had substantial judicial experience while Olson had none. Olson was an active member of the bar during only six of the sixteen years in which she had been licensed to practice law, and many locals were unaware that she even had a legal background.[64] Not surprisingly, the Los Angeles County Bar Association rated Olson "not qualified" for the bench, and rated Janavs "exceptionally well qualified." Nevertheless, Olson defeated Janavs by 8 percentage points.[65]

The fact that an exceptionally well qualified judge with an odd or foreign-sounding name could be unseated by a person with no judicial experience and little legal experience raises serious questions about the public's ability to evaluate the best candidates to sit on the bench. One article speculated that "the voters' choice often comes down to the scant information in front of them in the voting booth: the candidates' names and job descriptions."[66]

Justice See forcefully argues that the popular election of judges is more democratic and more fair not only because it allows direct participation by the citizens in the choice of their judges but also because the very public nature of a political campaign allows for open discussion about the qualifications of particular judicial candidates. "The open process of judicial elections [by the public] makes more obvious the tone of the campaign."[67] He continues to criticize an appointed system of judicial selection, including legislative election, by noting that "the attacks on a candidate are focused on the decision maker and the public may be largely unaware of them."[68] See argues that a system of judicial selection that is not based on popular election essentially hides the workings of the system from the public and does not improve its legitimacy. "In the appointive process, because of its secrecy, it is hard for us to know whether the appointing authorities reject those on whose behalf an ugly campaign is launched, and it would be difficult for future candidates to learn of that fact."[69]

Recent experience in Virginia directly rebuts Justice See's conclusions. Arguments about a judicial candidate's qualifications are publicly reviewed and debated in bar association interviews and endorsements, in interviews before the Courts of Justice committees of the General Assembly and often in the news. This is true for candidates for initial election to the bench, and also those who are seeking reelection. The 2003 failed reelection of Virginia Circuit Judge Verbena Askew presents a clear example of the level of public information and involvement in the process. Judge Askew's reelection to a second, eight-year term was challenged in the legislature based on, inter alia, anonymous reports of poor demeanor on the bench, issues regarding her sexual orientation, and whether she had failed to report an out-of-court settlement of a sexual harassment claim on the standard questionnaire provided to candidates by the General Assembly.[70] The entire controversy was played out in public, heavily reported in the media, and culminated in a six and a half hour hearing before the General Assembly's Courts Committees in Richmond. Judge Askew's supporters and opponents had the opportunity to very publicly argue their positions on her qualification to remain on the bench. Ultimately, she was not reelected.[71] Contrary to See's conclusions, this was neither a secret proceeding nor one that excluded the public, but it was certainly more dignified and professional than it would have been had it become embroiled in a popular election. Virginia's legislators are informed about the judicial candidates' qualifications and act as the representatives of the people in our democracy; their actions in connection with judicial elections are among the many issues that the citizens consider when the delegates and senators stand for election in their local jurisdictions.

Americans are becoming increasingly sensitive to the effects of partisan politics on the selection and performance of the judiciary. The Maxwell School of Syracuse University recently released a national poll showing that an overwhelming majority of Americans believe that the partisan background of judges influences their court decisions. A large percentage of those surveyed, 36.6 percent, felt that the partisan background of judges affected their decisions "a lot," while another 45.4 percent believed that their partisan background has "some" affect on their rulings. More than half of those polled felt that in many cases, judges base their decisions on their own personal beliefs rather than legal precedent or the Constitution. Therefore, it is perhaps not surprising that nearly three-fourths of poll respondents believe judges should be shielded from outside pressures and allowed to make decisions based on their reading of the law.

An Illustration

I have been a trial court judge in Virginia since 1991. I was originally elected to serve on the Juvenile and Domestic Relations District Court for the Seventeenth District. The process by which I came to the bench was typical of the processes used by the jurisdictions around Northern Virginia and similar to those throughout the Commonwealth. When a judge of the court announced his impending retirement, eleven lawyers, including me, announced their intentions to seek the appointment.

The first step in the screening process involved the Judicial Selection Committee, a group of seven lawyers elected by members of the Arlington County Bar Association, who interviewed all the candidates, reviewed their qualifications, and published a written report recommending "highly qualified," "qualified," or "not qualified" for each candidate. After the report of the Judicial Selection Committee was made public, the members of the Bar Association were able to vote on the qualifications of each judicial candidate, utilizing the same categories as above with one additional category—"ability not known." The results of that vote, together with the report of the committee, were sent to the members of the legislative delegation representing the

Seventeenth District—the senators and delegates representing the County of Arlington and the City of Falls Church, Virginia. The legislative delegation met and interviewed each of the candidates and ultimately made their decision to recommend me to serve on the court.

The next step in the process required the completion of an extensive questionnaire about my background and experience that was submitted to the Courts of Justice committees for the Senate and the House. That was followed by in-person hearings in Richmond before the judiciary committees of both the House and the Senate. Subsequently, the committees recommended my nomination to the General Assembly, and I was elected to a six-year term. In 1997, I stood for reelection to the juvenile court. That process involved completing a similar background questionnaire and another interview before the house and senate courts committees.

Early in 1998, a vacancy occurred on the Circuit Court for the Seventeenth Judicial Circuit.[72] The nomination and election process was essentially similar to that which I experienced in 1991: recommendations by the Judicial Selection Committee of the bar, a vote by the members of the bar association, interviews by the local delegation followed by their recommendation, and a hearing before the Courts of Justice committees of the House and Senate resulting in election by a vote of both houses for a judicial term of eight years.[73] In January 2006 I was reelected to another eight-year term on the circuit court; the process was the same as that which occurred in 1997 for reelection to the juvenile and domestic relations district court.

In my opinion, this process is both fair and nonpolitical. I was never questioned about my political affiliations or opinions, nor was I asked my opinion on various "hot-button" legal or social issues. The legislators seemed most concerned about my intellect, patience, and ability to be fair to all who would appear before me, and not by how I would rule on any particular case. During my reelection process and when I ran for the circuit court, the members of the General Assembly were most interested in how I had performed as a judge on the juvenile court as a way to measure my qualifications to serve on the higher court. As a candidate for these judgeships, I was able to concern myself with the merits of my candidacy, rather than with pleasing any political constituency or party. Moreover, since I did not have to conduct a public campaign, I did not worry about fund-raising and the specter of bias that attends to any judge who must rely on the bar and other interest groups to raise money, only to have those same individuals and groups appear before him or her.[74]

It is this very freedom from political and financial pressure, and the ability to concentrate on the qualifications of judicial candidates, that makes the Virginia system of legislative election of judges the best method of selecting judges who will have the confidence and support of the public they serve. Certainly, this conclusion is supported by the survey of Virginia's citizens.[75]

Conclusion

The election of judges by Virginia's General Assembly allows for judicial independence while also providing a political check on the judiciary's power to review acts of the legislature.[76] As one scholar and observer noted, "[w]here both sides act with statesmanship, the system works extremely well."[77] Proponents of Virginia's system of legislatively electing judges emphasize that this process maintains judicial independence, ensures that judges rely solely on the law, not politics or popular views, and maintains the public's high regard for Virginia's judiciary. Virginia's system of legislative elections of judges has led to a strong and independent judiciary, a critically important cornerstone of a strong and vital democracy.

Appendix: State-by-State Comparison of Methods of Selection and Retention of Trial-Level Judges

State	Method of Selection	Method of Retention
Maine	Gubernatorial appointment	Reappointed, with legislative confirmation
New Hampshire	Gubernatorial appointment	Serve until age 70
New Jersey	Gubernatorial appointment	Reappointed, with legislative confirmation
South Carolina	Legislative election	Reappointment by legislature
Virginia	Legislative election	Reappointment by legislature
Alaska	Merit selection	Retention election
Colorado	Merit selection	Retention election
Connecticut	Merit selection	Reappointed, with legislative confirmation
Delaware	Merit selection	Reappointed, with legislative confirmation
Hawaii	Merit selection	Reappointed by judicial selection commission
Iowa	Merit selection	Retention election

Maryland	Merit selection	Nonpartisan retention election
Massachusetts	Merit selection	Serve until age 70
Nebraska	Merit selection	Retention election
New Mexico	Merit selection	Partisan election/Retention election
Rhode Island	Merit selection	Serve for life
Utah	Merit selection	Retention election
Vermont	Merit selection	Retained by General Assembly vote
Wyoming	Merit selection	Retention election
Arizona	Merit selection*	Retention election*
Kansas	Merit selection*	Retention election*
Arkansas	Nonpartisan election	Reelection
California	Nonpartisan election	Nonpartisan election
Florida	Nonpartisan election	Reelection
Georgia	Nonpartisan election	Reelection
Idaho	Nonpartisan election	Reelection
Kentucky	Nonpartisan election	Reelection
Michigan	Nonpartisan election	Reelection
Minnesota	Nonpartisan election	Reelection
Mississippi	Nonpartisan election	Reelection
Montana	Nonpartisan election	Reelection
Nevada	Nonpartisan election	Reelection
North Carolina	Nonpartisan election	Reelection
North Dakota	Nonpartisan election	Reelection
Oklahoma	Nonpartisan election	Reelection
Oregon	Nonpartisan election	Reelection
South Dakota	Nonpartisan election	Reelection
Washington	Nonpartisan election	Reelection
Wisconsin	Nonpartisan election	Reelection
Alabama	Partisan election	Reelection
Illinois	Partisan election	Retention election
Louisiana	Partisan election	Reelection
New York	Partisan election	Reelection
Pennsylvania	Partisan election	Retention election
Tennessee	Partisan election	Reelection
Texas	Partisan election	Reelection
West Virginia	Partisan election	Reelection
Ohio	Partisan election	Reelection
Indiana	Partisan election*	Reelection*
Missouri	Partisan election*	Reelection*

* Indicates the method of selection used by the majority of counties or districts in that state.
SOURCE: State statutes listed in notes 51–55.

Notes

1. Debates of the Virginia Constitutional Convention 1901–02 at 1399, Dec. 4, 1901. (statement of Hill Carter).

2. Elizabeth B. Lacy, *Annual Survey of Virginia Law: Foreword: The Challenges: Past is Prologue*, 38 U. RICH. L. REV. 5, 11 (2003).

3. U.S. CONST. art. III, §1.

4. Judges in Rhode Island have lifetime tenure; in New Hampshire and Massachusetts, judges serve an uninterrupted term until age 70.

5. Virginia elects its judges by majority vote of both houses of the General Assembly, a "legislative election." Because this chapter will discuss various methods of judicial selection, including gubernatorial appointments, legislative election, and popular election, I will refer to Virginia's system as *legislative election.*

6. Lacy, *supra* note 2.

7. VA. CONST, art. VI, §7.

8. VA. CODE ANN. §17.1-400.

9. VA. CODE ANN. §16.1-69.9(c).

10. In South Carolina, a commission assists the state legislature in appointing judges. This makes Virginia the only state in the nation where the legislature directly elects state court judges.

11. *See* VA. CONST. art. VI, §7 (1971) (establishing that the justices of the Supreme Court and judges of all other courts "shall be chosen by the vote of a majority of the members elected to each house of the General Assembly"). During a brief period in the 1850s, judges in Virginia were popularly elected. *See id.* at §6 (1853).

12. *See* Part II, *infra* (arguing that national surveys indicate that popularly elected state judges are less highly regarded than state judges appointed by legislative bodies or by merit selection).

13. THE DECLARATION OF INDEPENDENCE, para. 11 ("He George III has made judges dependent on his Will alone, for the Tenure of their Offices, and the Amount and Payment of their salaries"); *see also* Alex B. Long, *An Historical Perspective on Judicial Selection Methods in Virginia and West Virginia*, 18 J. L. & POL. 691, 711–12 (2002) (detailing judicial selection during the colonial period).

14. These states were Connecticut, Delaware, Georgia, New Jersey, North Carolina, Rhode Island, South Carolina, and Virginia. In the other five states, judges were appointed by the governor or his council. Larry C. Berkson, *Judicial Selection in the United States: A Special Report*, 64 JUDICATURE 176 (1980). Ten of the original thirteen states provided for life tenure. Long, *supra* note 13, at 712.

15. THE FEDERALIST NO. 78 (Hamilton).

16. In 1812, Georgia amended its constitution to provide for the popular election of inferior state court judges; in 1832, Mississippi became the first state to elect all its judges. Berkson, *supra* note 14.

17. ESCOVITZ, JUDICIAL SELECTION AND TENURE 6 (1975).

18. *See* W. Hamilton Bryson, *Judicial Independence in Virginia*, 38 U. RICH. L. REV. 705, 711 (2004) (adding that as a reaction to the British monarchy's domination over

judges' appointment and removal, Virginia's first state constitution provided that judges served "during good behavior," which was changed to a term of years in 1851).

19. VA. CONST. of 1851, art. VI, 6, 10, 27, 34; VA. CONST. of 1869, art. VI, 5, 11. Note that in the 1850s, the Virginia constitution provided for the popular election of circuit court judges: "[F]or each circuit a judge shall be elected by the voters thereof." Commonwealth v. Scott, 51 Va. 749, 752 (1853) (referring to VA. CONST. art. VI, §7). Although locating records evidencing Virginia's formal switch to legislative elections of all state court judges is a challenge, anecdotal evidence shows that judges in some of Virginia's lower courts were popularly elected in Virginia as late as the early 1950s.

20. Bryson, *supra* note 18, at 712.

21. *See id.* at 716. Virginia's highest appellate court was originally named the Court of Appeals of Virginia; the name was changed to the Supreme Court of Appeals of Virginia in 1830. VA. CONST., art. V, 1 (1830). It is presently known as the Virginia Supreme Court.

22. Bryson, *supra* note 18, at 717 (quoting 1 BLACKSTONE'S COMMENTARIES, Appendix, 115–16 [St. George Tucker, ed., 1803]).

23. Ch. 511, p. 862, §4988 (March 25, 1926); *see also* Quesinberry v. Hull, 159 Va. 270 (1932) (noting that two years later, an amendment to this legislation provided that the trial justice in Carroll County was to be popularly elected, not appointed by circuit court judges).

24. Title 16.1, VA. CODE ANN. (1950).

25. *See Note*, Nathan Richard Wilderman, *Bought Elections: Republican Party of Minnesota v. White*, 11 GEO. MASON L. REV. 765, 767 (2003).

26. ALEXIS DE TOCQUEVILLE, DEMOCRACY IN AMERICA 257 (Harvey C. Mansfield & Delba Wintrop, trans. and eds., 2000) (italics in original) (quoted in Long, *supra* note 13).

27. Roscoe Pound, *The Causes of Popular Dissatisfaction with the Administration of Justice*, 20 JUDICATURE 178 (1937).

28. This system is also referred to as the "Kales Plan" or the "Missouri Plan," as Missouri was the first state to implement it in 1940.

29. *See, e.g.*, Editorial, *Secret Judge-Makers*, WASH. POST, Jan. 30, 1980, at A22 (stating that the latest Virginia Supreme Court seat was filled "with the caucus-bound votes of all participating Democrats"); *Northern Virginia Democrats Agree on Judges for New Appeals Court*, WASH. POST, Feb. 10, 1984, at B4 (stating that the "process gives the minority party no role in judicial selections").

30. *See* Judicial Selection in Virginia, *at* http://www.ajs.org.

31. *E.g.*, Jeff E. Schapiro, *Split May Force Judge Selection to Go Bipartisan*, RICHMOND TIMES DISPATCH, Nov, 19, 2007, at G2 (noting that the House was slower to approve the commission than the Senate).

32. Courts of record in Virginia are the Supreme Court of Virginia, the Court of Appeals of Virginia, and the various Circuit Courts (*see generally* http://www.courts.state.va.us/main.htm).

33. VA. CONST. art. VI, §7.

34. *Id.*

35. *Id.*

36. This author is personally familiar with the modern process of judicial election in Virginia, having been elected and reelected to both the juvenile and domestic relations court and the circuit court.

37. VA. CONST. art. VI, §9.

38. *See* Bryson, *supra* note 18, at 713.

39. *See id.* at 713–14.

40. *Id.* at 716.

41. VA. CONST. art. VI, 10.

42. *Id.*

43. Tom Campbell, *Henrico Judge Was Disciplined,* RICHMOND TIMES DISPATCH, Dec. 13, 2005, at B3

44. VA. CODE ANN. §17.1-100 (2005).

45. Lacy, *supra* note 3, at 11.

46. VA. CONST. art. VI, §7.

47. S.C. CODE ANN. §2-19-90. While South Carolina does provide for a merit selection commission as part of its nomination process, this commission is still closely aligned with the legislative body. Nominating commissions in a number of states contain members appointed by the governor or legislature, but South Carolina is the only state where the legislators have final approval over a candidate as voting members of the nominating commission. The Judicial Merit Selection Commission in South Carolina contains six members of the General Assembly who are appointed by the speaker of the House of Representatives, the chairman of the Senate Judiciary Committee, and the president pro temp of the Senate. State legislators also choose the remaining four members of the commission, who are selected from the general public.

48. Attached hereto as Appendix: State-by-State Comparison of Methods of Selection and Retention of Trial-Level Judges is a chart demonstrating a state-by-state comparison of the methods of selection and retention of trial-level judges.

49. ME. CONST. art. V, pt. 1, §8; N.H. CONST ME. CONST. pt. 2, art. 46; N.J. CONST. art. VI, §6, para. 1.

50. ALASKA CONST. art. IV, §5; ARIZ. CONST. art. VI, §37; COLO. CONST. art. VI, §20; Conn. Gen. Stat. §51-44(a); HAW. CONST. art. VI, §3; IOWA CONST. art. V, §15; Kan. Stat. Ann. §20-2901; NEB. CONST. art. V, §21; N.M. CONST. art. VI, §36; R.I. CONST. art. X, §4; UTAH CONST. art. VIII, §8; VT. CONST. §32; WYO. CONST. art. 5, §4. In Delaware, Maryland, and Massachusetts, merit selection has been established by executive order.

51. ARK. CONST. amend. 80, §17; CAL. CONST. art. VI, §16; FLA. CONST. art. V, §20, GA. CONST. art. VI, §VII, para. I; IDAHO CONST. art. VI, §7; KY. CONST. §117; MICH. CONST. art. 6, §12; Minn. Stat. Ann. 204B.06; Miss. Code Ann. §23-15-976; Mont. Code Ann. §13-14-211; N.C. CONST. art. IV, §16; N.D. Cent. Code 16.1-11-08; OKLA. CONST. art. VII, §8; ORE. CONST. art. VII, §1; S.D. CONST. art. V, §7; Wash. Rev. Code Ann. 29A.52.231; WIS. CONST. art. VII, §9.

52. Ala. Code §17-2-2; ILL. CONST. art. VI, §12; Ind. Code Ann. §3-10-2-11; LA. CONST. art. V, §22; MO. CONST. art. V, §25(b); N.Y. CONST. art. VI, §6; OHIO CONST. art. IV,

§6; PA. CONST. art. V, §13; Tenn. Code Ann. 17-1-103; TEX. CONST. art. 5, §7; W. Va. Code Ann. 3-1-17.

53. ALASKA CONST. art. IV, §6; ARIZ. CONST. art. VI, §38; COLO. CONST. art. VI, §25; IOWA CONST. art. V, §17; Kan. Stat. Ann. §20-2901; MD. CONST. art. IV, §3; NEB. CONST. art. V, §21; N.M. CONST. art. VI, §33; UTAH CONST. art. VIII, §9; WYO. CONST. art. 5, §4.

54. VA. CONST. art. 6, §7; Conn. Gen. Stat. Ann. 51-44a; DEL. CONST. art. IV, §3; HAW. CONST. art. VI, §3; ME. CONST. art. 6, §4; MASS. CONST. pt. 2, ch. 3, art. I; N.H. CONST. pt. 2, art. 78; N.J. CONST. art. 6, §6, para. 3;R.I. Gen. Laws §8-16.1-7; S.C. Code Ann. 2-19-80; Vt. Stat. Ann. Tit 4, §71. Judges in New Hampshire and Massachusetts serve until the age of 70, while those in Rhode Island have lifetime appointments.

55. Jeannine B. Perry & Nanci A. Glassman, *Supreme Court of Virginia Telephone Survey of Virginia Residents*, at 19, 52 (Aug./Sept. 2005) (Continental Research; unpublished).

56. American Bar Association, *Symposium II: Public Understanding and Perceptions of the American Justice System* (February, 1999), *at* http://www.abanet.org/media/perception/perception.html.

57. *E.g.*, U.S. Chamber Institute for Legal Reform, *2005 State Liability Systems Ranking Study* (March 8, 2005), *at http://www.instituteforlegalreform.com/harris/pdf/HarrisPoll2005-Summary.pdf*. Last visited August 14, 2006.

58. Each of the states listed in the *2005 State Liability Systems Ranking Study* received a numerical rank measuring "judicial competence," between 1 (highest level of judicial competence) and 50 (lowest level of judicial competence).

59. Harold See, *An Essay on Judicial Selection*, this volume at 77.

60. *Id.* at 83.

61. *Id.* at 86.

62. *Voters Oust Veteran L.A. Judge, Replace Her With Bagel Shop Owner*, ASSOC. PRESS, Jun. 8, 2006, *available at* http://www.signonsandiego.com/news/state/20060608-1920-ca-judgeousted.html.

63. R.M.G., *20-year Incumbent With Foreign-Sounding Name Draws Challenge*, METROPOLITAN NEWS-ENTERPRISE (Los Angeles), Apr. 6, 2006, at 1.

64. *Id.*

65. Megan Garvey & Jessica Garrison, *Judge's Loss Stuns Experts*, L.A. TIMES, Jun. 8, 2006, at B1.

66. *Id.*

67. See, *supra* note 59, at 92.

68. *Id.*

69. *Id.*

70. Terry Scanlon and Jessie Halladay, *Sex Life May Be Used Against Judges*, DAILY PRESS, Jan. 15, 2003.

71. Jessie Halladay, *Askew Hangs Up Robe; Judge Ends Her Career After 8 Years on Bench*, DAILY PRESS, Mar. 15, 2003, at C1.

72. The circuit courts are courts of general jurisdiction and are the highest trial level courts in Virginia.

73. Juvenile and general district judges are elected for a term of six years; circuit judges and judges on the Court of Appeals serve eight-year terms, and Supreme Court justices have twelve-year terms. All are elected and reelected by the General Assembly in a manner similar to that which I have described herein.

74. Of course, since the members of the General Assembly are all politicians, it would be naive to believe that politics plays no role in the selection of judges; as discussed *infra*, there have been situations where raw partisan politics has been involved in decisions regarding who will serve on the bench. However, in my experience, that is the exception, rather than the rule, in modern Virginia.

75. *See generally* Perry & Glassman, *supra* note 55.

76. *See* Bryson, *supra* note 18, at 712.

77. *Id.*

III VIEWS FROM THE MEDIA

7   Winners and Losers

Mark Obbie

O N   T H E   A F T E R N O O N   of October 31, 2005, just hours after President George Bush nominated Samuel A. Alito, Jr., to the Supreme Court, CNN's Wolf Blitzer was flitting from one story to the next in typical cable-news fashion: fallout from the indictment three days earlier of the vice president's chief of staff; a news-free press briefing at the White House; the upcoming U.S. visit of Prince Charles and his new wife Camilla, Duchess of Cornwall; Rosa Parks' burial; and the first reactions to the Alito news. Bush had named the relatively obscure judge from the Third U.S. Circuit Court of Appeals while on the rebound from the embarrassment of the Harriet Miers nomination. Sandwiched between a commercial break and a handoff to CNN in Atlanta for the latest headlines, Blitzer turned to CNN producer/reporter Abbi Tatton for a quick tour of websites linking to Alito's opinions. Tatton started by noting that Alito's extensive paper trail would give the news media far more substantive grist than they had in Miers' case. As she clicked from one website to the next, she touched on just one piece of that record: Alito's best-known opinion, a concurrence and dissent in the Third Circuit's 1991 decision in *Planned Parenthood v. Casey*.[1] In Tatton's

Visiting Assistant Professor, S.I. Newhouse School of Public Communications, Syracuse University. The author thanks Brianne Betts for her valuable research assistance. Betts is a 2004 graduate of the Syracuse University College of Law and in 2006 received her master's degree in broadcast journalism from the S.I. Newhouse School of Public Communications.

quickie version of *Casey*, Alito "argued in favor of spousal notification in the case of abortion." After a few more mouse clicks, Tatton wrapped up: "So, all these opinions you can read online, Wolf." Blitzer responded, "All right, good. Thanks very much, Abbi. I'm sure a lot of our viewers will want to do that."[2]

Really? Blitzer's faith in the public's appetite for 45-page circuit court opinions is impressive, but it's wishful thinking. While he can be forgiven for this bit of anchorman ad lib, the brief exchange between Tatton and Blitzer leads to two key points: how heavily citizens depend on the news media for insight into a Supreme Court nominee's record, and one way in which that dependence can be betrayed. The nature of that betrayal, however, is not what is commonly asserted by critics on the right: a liberal bias that skews news judgment and intentionally misleads the reader or viewer. Instead, in this context of law and politics, it is one of sloppiness and ignorance: emphasizing each case's outcome—who won, who lost, with what result?—without explaining the law that arguably governed that outcome.

Putting *Casey*'s outcome in a legally correct perspective—as a dispute over whether the Supreme Court's constitutionally based guidelines on abortion regulations would prevent a state from legislating a particular restriction—is out of the question. It is presumed to be hopelessly technical for a mass audience. The preferred form is simpler: mandatory spousal notification, pro or con? In this journalistic fairy tale, we only want happy or sad endings. There are no precedents, no constitutional or statutory confines, nothing but judges' personal policy preferences that lead to a clear result.

This approach has grave public-policy consequences. When journalists boil all substance out of the law before serving it to the public, they distort the meaning of the rule of law. This, in turn, can undermine the people's faith in an independent judiciary, a concern that others in this volume also have noted.[3]

To examine this results-oriented sin of omission, I will view it in its most blatant forms, then discuss its likely effect on citizenship and democracy. Next is the focal point of this chapter: a more granular analysis of a nuanced form of results-oriented legal journalism, in the initial coverage of the Alito nomination by the *New York Times* and the *Washington Post* as the public formed opinions about the nominee. Finally, I will explore possible remedies—in hopes of inspiring more responsible legal journalism.

Illustrating the Mind-set

The media are not a monolith. When critics level a broadside at the nameless media blob, they obscure stark distinctions: between infotainment fluff and high-minded, policy-wonk journals; or between a lone blogger with opinions and time to spare and a professional journalist with decades of experience at enterprising, independent reporting, one whose pursuit of previously unreported facts is backed by seasoned, cautious editors and a hundreds-strong newsroom. The most difficult and interesting critical question, to me, concerns the behavior of the heavyweights, not of the lightweights and lone nuts. How high is the bar set, and can it be set higher? But before I parse the language of our most elite newspapers on a complicated story, I will illustrate the problem—and try to entertain a bit—by marveling at its cruder forms.

Among the most shameless examples of results-oriented treatment of a judge's record are attack commercials. Granted, this is propaganda, not journalism. But it is results-oriented demagoguery in its purest form. Alito is certainly not the first target of this tactic. Partisans of all stripes stand accused at various times. Most recently, a pro-choice group's commercial chastised John Roberts, as the nominee for chief justice, for filing "court briefs supporting violent fringe groups and a convicted clinic bomber" and "whose ideology leads him to excuse violence against other Americans."[4] In fact, what Roberts had done as a Reagan administration lawyer in the Solicitor General's office was argue *why*, in his view, a Reconstruction-era civil rights law could not be applied against abortion-clinic protestors.

When Alito entered the ring, People for the American Way threw one of the first punches. Its "Fool Me Once" commercial took Alito's dissent in a civil rights case[5]—and his disagreement with the circuit court panel's majority over Fourth Amendment case law and Supreme Court precedents for search warrants—and turned it into a morality play that all but cast Alito as a child molester. Backed by foreboding music, a narrator intoned:

> Ashland, Pennsylvania. 1998. A 10-year-old girl strip searched without a valid search warrant. The judge who voted to uphold the strip search of a child? Samuel Alito, George Bush and the right wing's pick for the Supreme Court. Alito's opinion was so extreme it was strongly rejected by a conservative judge, Michael Chertoff, now head of Bush's Homeland Security. The strip search decision is just one example of how far outside the mainstream Samuel Alito's judicial philosophy is.[6]

Pro-Alito forces answered in kind. In what one legal blogger likened to a *Saturday Night Live* ad parody,[7] the Judicial Confirmation Network's response to "Fool Me Once" was titled "Real America." Set to a comparably ominous soundtrack and accompanied by images of fleeing criminals and newspaper headlines about juvenile drug couriers, the script was extreme in its condemnation of extremism:

> Left-wing extremists opposing Judge Alito's nomination to the Supreme Court may have found new allies: drug dealers who hide their drugs on children. These extremist groups have even run TV ads attacking Judge Alito; ads siding with a convicted drug offender who sued police for searching his child during a raid at the suspected drug dealer's house. These liberal extremists oppose the search. They oppose Judge Alito. And they oppose his tough-on-crime positions. In *their* America drug dealers could freely use children to hide drugs. In *their* America honest police officers could be sued for doing their job. That's not the real America. Contact your senators. Ask them to support Judge Alito. Ask them whose side are they on?[8]

Reputable journalists could pull the same tricks. On December 23, 2005, the National Archives released a batch of memos that Alito wrote while in the Justice Department during the Reagan administration. In one memo for the Solicitor General's office, Alito had argued that the former attorney general, John Mitchell, should enjoy governmental immunity when sued for damages over illegal wiretapping.[9] In typical handling of the story that day, the Knight Ridder Newspapers article was headlined, "In 1984 memo, Alito defends domestic wiretaps."[10] It didn't help that the news broke amid a controversy over the Bush administration's post-9/11 wiretap policy. But one experienced legal journalist, Stuart Taylor, Jr., of *National Journal*, complained that the Bush-era echoes found in the long-ago Alito memo didn't excuse the "flat out false" error of confusing a defense of governmental immunity with advocacy of wiretapping—an error that he pointed out was commonplace in the hours and days following the release of the memo.[11]

The nightly war of words on cable television news provided a host of examples. The agenda from the start was influenced by partisans steeped in the art of "Borking"[12] an opponent early and often. In the words of the humorist Dave Barry, "Democrats immediately announce[d] that they strongly oppose Alito and intend[ed] to do some research to find out why."[13] The talking points were clear: Alito is "outside the mainstream." On October 31, the night of the nomination, CNN's Lou Dobbs interviewed former Bill Clinton aide Lanny Davis, who was in such a rush to slap a scary Halloween-night mask on Alito that he partially mangled the words, calling the nominee "a liberal activist radical conservative."[14] CNN's Paula Zahn could ask Nan Aron of the Alliance for Justice practically any question and she would get the same answer: Alito is a radical, Alito isn't the right replacement for the moderate Sandra Day O'Connor.[15] Democratic National Committee Chair Howard Dean told CNN's audience that Alito "has upheld all white juries trying African-American defendants . . . [and] made it harder for people with disabilities to avoid discrimination."[16] On MSNBC's *Hardball* show, host Chris Matthews—conducting a head count of reliably conservative and liberal votes on the Court—swatted away any explanatory detail offered by Ralph Neas of People for the American Way:

MATTHEWS: You've got Thomas, you've got Scalia, you've got Roberts, and now you've got this guy.

NEAS: As we said in our memo to you on July 1, Chris. . . .

MATTHEWS: Who's the fifth conservative?

NEAS: You have Sandra Day O'Connor being the fifth indecisive vote and about 20 decisions over the last five years protecting privacy, protecting reproductive rights. . . .

MATTHEWS: OK, but the numbers. Everybody wants the numbers.[17]

MSNBC's legal discourse continued in this mindless vein later that evening with program host Joe Scarborough, his political analyst Patrick Buchanan, and Court TV's Catherine Crier drawing the substance of *Casey* as a stick figure:

BUCHANAN: All right, here's what he decided—let me get in on this. You're right, it was a notification case. The Pennsylvania legislature. . . .

SCARBOROUGH: Hey, Pat, we've got a hard break.

BUCHANAN: OK. Are we going to come back?

SCARBOROUGH: No, I'm going to give you 10 seconds. Go.

BUCHANAN: OK. They said the husband had to be notified if the wife was going to kill his child. Pennsylvania decided that way, and Alito said . . .

CRIER: No other judges agreed.

BUCHANAN: . . . Alito said, "I'm not going to overturn the people's decision."

SCARBOROUGH: OK, thank you so much. All right, we'll see you another night. We'll be right back.

(COMMERCIAL BREAK)[18]

After one day and evening of this drive-by "analysis," most cable news shows dropped Alito as quickly as they'd found him. Natalee Holloway's disappearance in Aruba, after all, demanded nightly attention.[19]

Defining the Problem

These and other examples of slapdash, results-oriented reporting on the Alito nomination should not obscure the many laudatory examples of enterprising, legally sophisticated journalism—in that first week, and beyond.[20] Nor is it fair to accuse the news media as a whole of being anti-Alito. In fact, the overall tone was positive, routinely portraying the nominee as eminently qualified, safely restrained, and admirably humble[21]—"more methodical technician than theoretical firebrand," in the *Post*'s pre-confirmation profile,[22] and "a shyer, blander version" of the widely praised new chief justice, John Roberts, as veteran Supreme Court reporter Tony Mauro put it.[23] Many stories that portrayed Alito as Roberts' less polished twin ultimately painted Alito in sympathetic, everyman tones.[24] The point here is not ideological balance in the coverage, and not whether Alito was correct on the legal questions of search and seizure or governmental immunity or abortion restrictions; nor is it about his general fitness to serve on the Court; nor whether he is a nice man or a nerd or both. Reasonable minds—legal, sartorial, and otherwise— will make their judgments in the proper forums. The point here, instead, is to show how journalists—even the very best ones—sometimes omit one of journalism's "five W's" in reporting on legal substance, focusing on "who, what, where and when" to the exclusion of "why."

To make that analysis, I must define these terms. Complaints about legal reporting are as old as the republic.[25] Despite all manner of academic critiques—on the quantity and quality of legal news coverage, news judgments about which cases warrant coverage, qualifications of the reporters, interactions between courts and journalists, and effects of legal journalism on public opinion[26]—relatively little has been written specifically about results-oriented legal journalism. When scholars have noted the problem, some have explained it as a by-product of a long-term decline in space and time devoted to court news, and reporting resources devoted to covering the courts.[27]

Others considered it the nature of the media beast. Slotnick and Segal called it "scholarly orthodoxy" for at least forty years that the media focus more on reactions to decisions and conjecture about the likely fallout from decisions, rather than on the decisions themselves.[28] The authors illustrated this by quoting TV reporters complaining about the kinds of stories that their networks' producers wanted—and the sorts of details that got in the way of a good TV story, such as a case's underlying facts and what the Court actually held.[29] Richard Davis has noted the relationship between the media's preferences in story-telling (brevity, simplicity, decision's impact, and reactions to a decision) and the failure in those stories to explain the underlying legal reasoning.[30]

So what exactly is it? Results-oriented legal journalism is *reporting on the outcome of a court case without acknowledging the legal authority that the court cited in reaching that outcome.* Its close relative is ideological labeling that implies a judge has fixed views leading to a predetermined outcome.

Articulating this standard risks entanglement with controversies that have no clear answers. Does every court decision rely faithfully and clearly on proper legal authority? Can we all agree on the correct interpretation of that authority in light of the facts? Do all judges rise above their ideological allegiances or partisan affiliations to apply the law honestly, regardless of the "correct" outcome? No, no, and no. The law is anything but pure—at least in appearance, if not reality.[31] Partisan hacks do indeed exist, off and on the bench. This chapter takes no stand on whether Alito fails some or all of these tests, and it opts out of the somewhat tired debate over judicial activism, which is as much a real issue for liberals and conservatives as it is a rhetorical weapon used against a disfavored outcome.

The point here is simpler, because none of these debates absolves journalists of their duty to tell the truth. Context matters, and when a judge reaches a result by interpreting the relevant law, the journalist should at least mention the judge's legal justification for that result. When legal journalism ignores the legal basis for an outcome—when it simply skips whether any authority was cited as justification for the outcome—and throws around vague catch-all labels, it engages in lazy shorthand that must lead citizens to the inevitable conclusion that their courts are an undemocratic legislative body.

Our political culture breeds simplistic labels and casual charges of results orientation. Journalists Bob Woodward and Scott Armstrong in *The Brethren* portrayed Chief Justice Warren Burger as resentful that he was routinely identified as a conservative—but sympathetic to the reality that a barely attentive public could understand the Court only through simple labels.[32] Besides the all-purpose ideological label, one of the most common debate tactics in judicial politics is to accuse the other side of being results oriented.[33]

Some find it easy to dismiss tributes to the rule of law as naiveté, or "empty platitudes."[34] But it's not naive to regret news coverage that makes a local judge fear headlines like "Court frees accused rapist" or "Judge's ruling means big increase in school taxes," when the story beneath the headline then makes no attempt to explain why the judge ruled this way. It's understandable for legal experts to avoid reporters out of fear that their explanations will be mangled by inexperienced or irresponsible interpreters who dismiss legal reasoning as "technicalities."

Some analysts see the problem differently. Political scientist Dean E. Alger acknowledged the paucity of legal substance in even elite newspapers, and the obsession with outcomes. But he attributed that to a journalistic faith in legal absolutes—a deference paid to courts that they don't deserve, because in fact they are politicized policy makers.[35] Even if we concede the point made by Alger and other political scientists—about the inherent political, results-oriented, policy-making nature of the courts—this does not change my point that it's poor journalism to ignore entirely whether a court cited any authority for its decision, and to accept without question any unsupported ideological or partisan label. If the authority is cited as a cover for activism, or it's misinterpreted, then a journalist can evaluate and expose that. To avoid all mention of legal bases for decisions, however, strips legal news of much of its meaning and likely leads citizens to the belief, fair or not, that their courts dictate policy.

Several panelists at the Syracuse University symposium "Bench Press: The Collision of Media, Politics, Public Pressure, and an Independent Judiciary" in October 2005 lamented this sort of journalism. Alabama Supreme Court Justice Harold See, for example, commented on reporters' tendency to reach for political explanations when they don't understand a case's substantive underpinnings. George Washington University law professor Jeffrey Rosen, a legal writer and commentator for the *New Republic*, the *New York Times Magazine*, and National Public Radio, spoke at the "Bench Press" symposium and later that week at the Syracuse University College of Law of "lazy generalizations" bred by a media culture of attention-getting, ideologically simple, and predictable commentary. NPR's Nina Totenberg told a "Bench Press" luncheon audience how easily journalists are manipulated by advocates' spin-filled summaries of court decisions because the journalists often fail to look at the decisions themselves. She cited in particular her experience in the Terri Schiavo right-to-die case, where advocates and activists flatly contradicted the extensive record of trial court findings and guardian reports—but rarely were called on it because journalists didn't consult the record.[36]

Does results-oriented journalism necessarily cause the public to believe its courts are governed by something other than the rule of law? I have not tested that, so I cannot prove it. But the public does hold those beliefs—paired with ignorance of the courts' role and the rule of law—and so we can at least conclude that results-oriented legal journalism certainly does nothing to counter this serious gap in civic health.

Public opinion polls consistently show large numbers of Americans believe that judges' personal beliefs govern their decisions.[37] In Syracuse University's national Maxwell Poll, announced in October 2005:

- Two-thirds of respondents believed the media pay more attention to judges' partisan backgrounds than to legal reasoning when reporting on a court decision.
- The vast majority believed that judges' partisan backgrounds influence their decisions some (45 percent) or a lot (37 percent).
- More than half agreed that judges, despite claims of relying on the law, often base decisions on personal beliefs.
- When asked their view of what role judges play, respondents were evenly divided—indicating widespread ignorance or confusion—on whether judges strictly apply detailed rules to the facts to resolve a dispute, interpret general principles with broad discretion, or both.[38]

The prospects for self-governance and political stability are bleak if citizens do not trust their courts to follow the law, or do not understand that is what courts do. Journalists must take seriously their responsibility to foster healthy public debate, based on facts, regarding the courts.

Methodology

I will attempt to illustrate the problem by examining news articles in the *New York Times* and the *Washington Post* in the first week following Alito's nomination. Why and how did I choose this focus?

First, to answer why: These two newspapers are generally perceived as the two most important newspapers covering the Supreme Court and Court nominations. With their extraordinarily deep reporting resources, in numbers of journalists and expertise, they help set the agenda for the debate. Thus, their susceptibility to results-oriented treatment of court decisions suggests how pervasive the problem likely is among lesser newspapers, broadcasters, and other media. I confined the discussion to news stories, not editorials or op-ed articles, because the central question is whether journalists charged with the responsibility of fact gathering do, indeed, gather the needed facts.

Supreme Court confirmation debates are often said to be a seminar on law. Such debates—and arguably the Alito nomination in particular, given the circumstances—made this story as high profile a legal story as one will find. What circumstances made the Alito confirmation so irresistible? One, the widespread perception that replacing O'Connor's swing vote with a more conservative vote would upset (or correct, depending on perspective) the delicate balance of the court, particularly in abortion-rights cases. Two, Alito was nominated in place of Miers, who dropped out while under fire for her lack of reassuring ideological credentials (in the opinion of conservatives) or relevant experience. After touting Miers as deserving of confirmation because she would come to the bench with a fresh perspective, having never been a judge,[39] Bush promoted her replacement for having "more prior judicial experience than any Supreme Court nominee in more than 70 years."[40] Thus, Alito's more than 300 written opinions from fifteen years on the bench, plus his extensive dealings with national legal policy in the Justice Department, put his record front and center in the debate.

I chose the first week's coverage for practical reasons—given the volume of news coverage, it was necessary to contain the scope of the examination—and because it is the period during which casual media consumers form first impressions of a nominee. The news coverage at first is intense, then it recedes, with occasional bursts of activity; and finally it spikes during the Senate's deliberations. Daily journalism faces its greatest test when important news is breaking. First impressions do matter, as Harriet Miers will attest. I believe it is valid to evaluate these two important newspapers' coverage of the issues at the critical introductory phase of the nominee's journey.

Now, to explain how the articles are studied. Multiple print editions and frequent Web updates make it difficult to isolate any major newspaper's single, official version of a daily story. Each day in the one week following Alito's nomination, from November 1 through November 7, 2005, I downloaded all news stories on the Alito nomination appearing on the websites of the *Times* and *Post*. The stories were downloaded in the early morning hours to capture the presumably most complete version of each story as it appeared in print, while avoiding any changes or updates in the Web version of the stories throughout the following day. My goal was to give each newspaper its best daily shot, but only one shot.

I evaluated each article on two primary axes: the subject matter (whether it discussed particular cases, broader issues, or the political process), and whether those discussions of cases or issues acknowledged in any way the underlying legal bases for the decision or opinion. Many stories covered a mixture of broad principles and specific findings in cases. References to legal authority (e.g., the Constitution, statutes, or precedent) could be explicit or oblique, and often could be separated by many paragraphs from the first reference to the case. I used my judgment to code sections of stories as either results oriented or law based, but the analysis is largely not quantitative because it does not pose a binary question. Some mentions of legal reasoning are clear and illuminating, and some are merely hints. My judgment of how well each reference met the test is somewhat subjective and impressionistic. It is based on my experience as a journalist and my comprehension of the plain meaning of the words. Articles are footnoted on first reference, then referred to only in the text.

Introducing and Explaining Judge Alito

Day One: November 1

Howell Raines, the former executive editor of the *Times*, spoke often of "flooding the zone": using his newspaper's immense resources to cover an important news story as no other journalism organization could.[41] He would have been proud of his troops' handiwork in the first edition of the *Times* after the October 31 Alito nomination. They had ample warning that Alito might be named. His name had been on many shortlists since O'Connor's retirement announcement on July 1, 2005,[42] and his odds went up—given his extensive paper trail and perceived political pluses to the president's conservative base—once Miers' nomination failed. The president timed the Alito announcement for 8:30 AM on a Monday, giving daily newspaper reporters all day to flood various zones.

The *Times* and *Post* hit the Alito story predictably hard the first day, with depth and sophistication rarely rivaled in other mainstream media (many of which resorted to the ultimate shorthand phrase, "Scalito," grasping for an easy definition of the newly introduced nominee as Justice Antonin Scalia's double).

The *Times* weighed in with eight separate bylined articles totaling more than 10,000 words in the aggregate: an overview[43] plus two stories on Alito's abortion views (one each by the paper's top legal writers, Linda Greenhouse and Adam Liptak),[44] a broader look at his paper trail (Liptak again),[45] and additional articles on his supporters' reactions,[46] predictions of a pitched ideological battle,[47] a biographical piece (the only reference in either paper that day to "Scalito," mentioned only to poke holes in its logic),[48] and recognition that Alito would be the Court's fifth Catholic justice.[49] The *Post* covered largely the same angles, albeit with fewer articles (five) and words (just under 5,600 total): besides the obligatory overview,[50] an analysis of a handful of Alito's most controversial opinions (by *Post* Supreme Court reporter Charles Lane),[51] two stories of political reaction,[52] and predictions of the battle to come.[53]

While neither paper truly scooped the other with important, exclusive insights—in fact, throughout this first week (and generally throughout the confirmation debate), neither paper would beat the other with a huge scoop on Alito—the *Times*' first-day coverage as a whole, legally speaking, was more precise and less results oriented than the *Post*'s. Both glibly tossed around the "conservative" label without qualification, often without attribution, and used similarly expansive characterizations of Alito's entire record as a judge and legal thinker (the *Times*' story on Alito supporters referred to his "clear record on abortion rights and other social issues," and the *Post* overview referred without sourcing to Alito's "extensive record of conservative rulings on abortion, federalism, discrimination and religion in public spaces"). Both overview stories dealt with *Casey* in almost purely results-oriented terms (except where the *Post*'s overview mentioned that the Supreme Court later found the Pennsylvania law unconstitutional, implying a legal basis for the decisions rather than just a debate over spousal notification).

The quality of the two papers' legal content started to diverge in the overviews, and came into much sharper relief in other stories. Take, for example, these excerpts from the overviews.

Post:
Alito wrote a ruling upholding a city-sponsored holiday display in Jersey City that included a creche and menorah as well as secular symbols such as Frosty the Snowman. He struck down a Newark Police Department policy forbidding officers to wear beards after two Muslims complained that it violated their religious rights. He argued that Congress did not have the power to ban the intra-

state sale of machine guns. In a variety of other cases, he showed skepticism of court intervention in discrimination claims.

Times:

[T]he rulings show that on the death penalty, employment discrimination and immigrants' rights, Judge Alito has often read the governing cases and statutes narrowly to limit the ability of the individuals involved to obtain relief from the courts. He has also taken a skeptical view of the scope of Congressional power to regulate guns and allow lawsuits against state governments. But his First Amendment rulings have interpreted free speech rights broadly.

The *Post* noted the effects—"upholding a city-sponsored holiday display," striking down a policy on beards—or hinted only vaguely at legal constraints ("religious rights," or Congress' "power to ban the intrastate sale of machine guns"). The *Times* explicitly attributes Alito's actions to "governing cases and statutes." True, the two come out roughly equally on references to congressional powers—begging the question of where those powers come from—but the *Times* more clearly tells readers that the law required this judge to do certain things, or that he had to interpret laws a certain way to reach his desired result.

The contrast between the two papers' first-day legal analysis sidebars began with the headlines:

Post:

Alito Leans Right Where O'Connor Swung Left

Times:

Rulings That Are Lucid and Methodically Based

Where the *Post* signaled that ideology dictates outcomes, the *Times* said the opposite: rulings that are based on something other than a whim. The articles themselves follow that pattern. Lane's analysis in the *Post* tracks O'Connor's and Alito's votes when Alito's cases were reviewed by the High Court. This article focused virtually exclusively on outcomes—which judge would strike down a statute or sentence or not. The Liptak and Glater analysis in the *Times* examined the arguments over precedent and the Fourteenth Amendment in a Family Medical Leave Act case and similar bases (except involving the Sixth Amendment) in an ineffective-assistance-of-counsel case; actually mentioned the "commerce clause" in a brief discussion of the infamous machine-gun case;[54] and likewise cited explicit grounds for rulings on religious liberty, speech, advertising regulation, and contempt. Throughout, the message in the *Times* is clearer: Alito is interpreting the law, not simply voting his conscience.

Greenhouse followed suit in her *Times* story on *Casey*. Where the *Post* barely touched on the phrase "undue burden," Greenhouse took the time to ground the issue in constitutional arguments, and to explain how the majority and dissenting opinions at the Third Circuit anticipated how the Supreme Court would apply a new and subjective test to these facts. To lawyers, the process is obvious; to laymen, it is a mystery. Without the explanation, a layman is left to assume that judges have unlimited discretion to vote thumbs up or down on abortion restrictions—at least until a higher court imposes its own policy preferences.

On one issue, however, the *Post* triumphed—or at least did not blunder as obviously as the *Times*. Two *Times* stories, the overview and the article on the Catholic angle, refer to *Roe v. Wade*[55] having "legalized abortion." The *Post*'s main story referred to *Roe* without explanation, while Lane's analysis called it "the Supreme Court's 1973 abortion rights ruling," at least implying that it is based on something (the Constitution, perhaps?) other than a preference for abortion.

Days Two through Seven: November 2–7

Through the remainder of this section analyzing the first week of the Alito coverage, I will be more selective in citing high and low points, while pointing to recurring themes.

Both newspapers occasionally distinguished themselves with sophisticated analyses of the law, or at least useful explanations of where court-made law comes from. And both, all too often, took results-oriented shortcuts—particularly in stories not penned by the papers' legal experts—or engaged in a more subtle form of distortion, where ostensibly the legal process was revealed, but in such a cursory way as to leave a layman in the dark.

Until Alito's Senate confirmation hearings in January 2006, the first-day coverage of his nomination would mark the two papers' high-water mark in bylined stories. Between October 31 and January 9, both papers typically ran one or two stories per day. Exceptions included November 1, when the *Times* published five stories, and November 3, when it published three. Counting bylines and words provides a rough quantitative comparison to other media, but it sheds little light on questions of substance. It is quite possible to say nothing of substance in many stories or to pack many pithy observations into a single report. The overall effect was clear, and predictable: a big bang at the outset, quickly receding to a steady flow of daily stories until the Senate hearing.

During the remainder of the first week, when the newspapers took inventory of Alito's opinions by type of case, or type of action (e.g., in his dissents), they largely focused on keeping score of the cases' outcomes, with much less mention of any controlling legal authority that Alito cited in order to reach a particular result. The *Times* did this in its analysis of Alito's dissents,[56] zeroing in on who won or lost rather than why, and his record in business cases, which it said showed "far more" kinship with big business than with consumers and employees.[57] The *Post* did it in an analysis of Alito's civil rights record,[58] with a series of statements about Alito's siding with employers or prosecutors in the outcome of their cases. This *Post* story, like many, refers to a "narrow reading" of statutes, which in one respect lends a substantive cast to the discussion—recognizing that a judge has had to wrestle with a law's application in a particular case. But when such a vague phrase is used as a blanket explanation for judicial action, it does little to instruct the lay reader on the workings of the law.

Remarkably, even when a story's topic was ostensibly substantive, the discussion could take a results-oriented turn. This was the case when the *Post* tackled Alito's respect for precedent.[59] It started laudably, with a mini-lesson in civics:

> For 15 years as a federal appeals court judge, Samuel A. Alito Jr.'s job has been to follow the precedent of the Supreme Court. But if he is approved for the nation's highest court, he would not have to.

The very next paragraph suffers from vast oversimplification:

> As one of the nine final arbiters of American law he could vote to overturn long-standing decisions on abortion, affirmative action and religion—with nothing to stop him except *stare decisis*. . . .

The story then descended into generalities about the conservative results that Alito supposedly may seek, with hardly any recognition that a Supreme Court justice's discretion might be curtailed by the Constitution or statutes. The same fate befell a *Times* story asking a similar question: what is a judicial activist, and is Alito likely to be one?[60]

When the *Times* tackled yet another similar story, on Alito's philosophy on federalism,[61] it veered into irresponsible territory, referring to the Supreme Court's views on state power, as though it were mere policy preference. But then the story righted itself, steering away from a results-oriented wreck by explaining lucidly what constitutional provisions and precedents Alito and his colleagues wrestled with in their disagreement in *Rybar*.

Both papers' November 2 abortion case-law analyses[62] expertly wove substantive law into a political (and highly politicized) discussion. The *Post*'s story, in particular, stands as an exemplar of a savvy, readable news story that can explore the politics of a stance—even speculating about future cases' outcomes—without ignoring what law might guide a judge's decision making.

The abortion stories, however, were not trouble-free. The most subtle but pervasive problem in the coverage persisted throughout explanations of Alito's dissent in *Casey*. When the papers bothered to go beyond the standard synopsis—how Alito favored requiring women to notify fathers of an impending abortion—they tended to throw around the phrase "undue burden" with abandon, rarely explaining the roots of this test: in Supreme Court precedent, based on an interpretation of the Constitution. Similarly, perhaps from fatigue over the number of times that *Casey* merited mention, many stories simply ignored the Third Circuit's function in the case—to decide whether a state statute passed constitutional muster—and treated the case as one in which the courts simply voted on the merits: What should the state's abortion policy be?

Meanwhile, articles focusing on politics and procedure in the confirmation process typically took a strict results-oriented tack[63] or were largely substance-free discussions of the process.[64]

Throughout this first week, then, these two newspapers' commitment to explaining Alito was admirable and ambitious; it was frequently inspired and thoughtful; and it all too often committed the very same sin of omission that buffoonish commentator/entertainers were committing on TV. How often in that first week? Keeping in mind the earlier caveat about the imprecision of any quantitative analysis on this topic, I can at least summarize this way: No story mentioning legal principles or specific cases was completely free of results-oriented language; many made no mention whatsoever of the legal bases for decisions. Weighed against the many examples of stories that did explain the rule of law, the scorecard is essentially a draw: Results-oriented discussions of the law prevailed in about half of the stories.

The days after this first week, up to and through Alito's hearing and confirmation, are outside of this chapter's scope. But the bulk of the coverage left the same impression. In one notable example, the *Post*'s intellectually valid story idea (analyzing the ways in which Alito's record should not be defined strictly by his abortion views) was derailed by a thoroughly outcome-oriented viewpoint.[65] Amid its vote-counting overview showing, for example, "a harder line on criminal and immigration cases than most federal appellate judges nationwide, including those who, like him, were selected by Republican presidents," the results-oriented icing on the cake is a chart accompanying the story. Its headline: "Which Side Was He On?"

Conclusion

So, which side were the *Times* and *Post* on? No rational analyst could accuse them of a politically motivated agenda to hurt Alito or the president. Even an anti-Bush zealot could read these stories and come away thinking that Alito is well qualified, honest, earnest, and responsible. And certainly these two newspapers dwarf many of their media brethren in the scope and heft of their reporting on the nomination. They took seriously the ideas (and ideals) at stake in the nomination, and devoted considerable energy to explain them to their readers without hyperbole or overt bias. In a culture quickly becoming enamored of a blogger-driven media, the real reporting of facts and open-minded inquiry in the news coverage of these newspapers is instructive (or maybe just destined to be nostalgic). They explained the law well, when they took the time to do so. They are, in short, dramatically better than Joe Scarborough and Pat Buchanan and Chris Matthews and their ilk, who rarely shed light in their rush to praise or condemn a nominee based on what they like or dislike about his perceived policy stances.

But we should demand more from our best newspapers on such an important story—because they set an example for every novice courthouse reporter who doesn't know his *Miranda* from a hole in the ground.[66] When the *New York Times* and the *Washington Post* ignore the reasoning behind judges' decisions, as they did so often in covering the Alito nomination, they further poison a political culture that is growing hoarse from all the shouting. And they keep citizens ignorant, though not blissfully so, of how their Third Branch performs.

Quality legal journalism explains, to the extent possible, how courts reason their way to controversial outcomes, whether that's in the disputed election of a president, the anguished debate over euthanizing a brain injury victim, or rulings on matters as socially important and disparate as online file sharing, "intelligent design," eminent domain, and the death penalty. Journalists need not be—should not be—apologists for the courts. Critical reporting on contentious issues often will anger judges, which is as it should be—so long as the criticism is based on legal realities, and not just reflexively on outcomes. When judges decide cases on a whim, ignoring the law or making it up, journalists should document that and report it. When justice demands that the proper authority—a higher court or a legislature, for example—change the law, that should be reported, too. Just because judges themselves may engage in results-oriented decision making does not mean that journalists should ignore the instances (predominant, I hope) when judges bother to explain the legal bases for their rulings.

Journalistic balance is not achieved simply by pointing out when a judge, such as Alito, sometimes reached "liberal" results, not just "conservative" ones. Balance comes from an honest evaluation of what really happened— how the result was arrived at, regardless of its qualities that will please or enrage the public. Usually when we hear a lament about results-oriented analyses, it's by partisans who hauled out their substantive-law virtues to suit their argument: countering results-oriented critics on the opposing team. Journalists should rise above such debate-club tactics, and always apply the most complete, legitimate analysis to the facts at hand, regardless of whose cause is helped or harmed. Legal journalism, in short, must tell the whole truth, always.

How do we improve? Many critiques over the years have prescribed any number of ways to improve legal journalism. From the Supreme Court down to countless media-relations committees of local bar associations, reformers have drafted many recommendations, and have had some good effects. I will not attempt to duplicate every such plan. Nor will I address the bench or bar with my hoped-for reforms, except to endorse the latest legislation concerning camera access in federal courts, which can only help encourage broadcast coverage of serious legal stories.

This is my narrower wish list for journalists and journalism educators:

Employ Specialists.   No amount of complaining will change the economics of the business. It will still depend on the energy and economy of the inexperienced. Either the networks will see ratings in legal coverage, or they won't. Appeals to the public interest go about as far as a chief financial officer can throw them. But when news organizations do cover court decisions, perhaps they will see it in their self-interest to make their stories more legally correct and complete. The fear of litigation costs, from libel suits and subpoenas, is one negative incentive. Getting the story right and being careful about facts and attribution lessen those risks (and are what responsible journalists aspire to provide anyway). If legal-reporting expertise does not exist among reporters, then at least the ranks of editors and producers—those who review language before it is published or aired—can ensure that stories do not wholly ignore what has actually just happened. Ideally, the reliance on specialists will go much further—employing seasoned legal reporters to cover legal affairs and the courts regularly.

Use the Web. Broadcasters have done a reasonably good job of creatively using their websites to provide additional material on stories they cover. Newspapers and magazines are improving. If all mainstream media simply published or linked to the decisions they're reporting on, and to the underlying briefs and prior decisions, interested readers and viewers could learn more. Of course I started this chapter by mocking the notion, so I consider this a reform with only marginal benefits. But it's so easy and inexpensive to accomplish, it should be done routinely.

Teach by Example. Journalism critics (the honest, open-minded kind, not the partisans with ulterior agendas) should cover legal reporting—both the inept and the adept—more often. Bloggers, schools of journalism and law, bar associations, and others could do much more to assist legal reporters with background on the cases that they cover, and useful, unbiased translations of the decisions as they are announced. What did the court say, and on what did it base its decision? What is the legal context—a brief history of this area of law? These questions and more could be answered by writers who know the field and can be trusted to analyze notable cases from a neutral perspective. Harried, inexperienced reporters might come to trust and use a central legal-briefing service, if it existed on the Web.

Increase Legal Literacy. The expertise of legal journalists, at least at the national level, has advanced immeasurably since the *Front Page* era. Law degrees are fairly common in today's newsrooms. But a law degree is neither essential nor plausible in most cases. The intelligent, talented layman who has no interest in incurring law-school-scale debt may still develop a sophisticated understanding of the law—at least an understanding of how to read a court decision and brief and ask experts the right questions. It takes years of experience to develop this skill. To help that process along, journalism schools could do much more to offer legal-reporting specialty education and training. Besides teaching the nuts-and-bolts practicalities of finding and translating legal information, journalism schools should take advantage of the legal, political, and historical curricula offered elsewhere in their universities. Legal studies and other law-for-laymen courses—a constitutional primer here, a procedural overview there—would work wonders in the ranks of beginning reporters. For midcareer reporters, training opportunities that now exist— for example, seminars offered by groups such as Investigative Reporters and Editors or the National Judicial College's National Center for Courts and the Media—could be expanded, and newsrooms could be encouraged to send their reporters to short seminars on legal reporting. Universities' executive-education arms could do the same.

Aim High.   The media and the courts are guilty of having low expectations of the reading and viewing public. Journalists' highest calling is to make the complexities of life interesting and understandable. When we make the sad and false assumption that there is no appetite for news about the law beyond tabloid-style "trials of the century," we shortchange society in profound ways. Even a legal journalist of Nina Totenberg's caliber can make this mistake. At the "Bench Press" conference, the NPR legal reporter told of her interview with Justice Stephen Breyer about his recently published book on his legal philosophy.[67] She feared the interview was too long, too boring, to be noticed much. In fact, Totenberg was surprised by her listeners' enthusiastic response. They were hungry for knowledge—for an understandable narrative about how the Court works and how its justices think.

Those listeners were lucky that some justices will explain such things and some journalists have the skill to bring that story to the public. We must strive for more such surprises.

Notes

1. Planned Parenthood of Southeastern Pennsylvania et al. v. Robert P. Casey et al., 947 F.2d 682, 719 (3d Cir. 1991).

2. *The Situation Room* (CNN, Oct. 31, 2005), *available at* http://transcripts.cnn.com/TRANSCRIPTS/0510/31/sitroom.01.html.

3. John M. Walker, Jr., *Politics and the Confirmation Process*, this volume at 123.

4. Linda Greenhouse, *TV Ad Attacking Court Nominee Provokes Furor*, N.Y. TIMES,

Aug. 11, 2005. The commercial's sponsor was NARAL Pro-Choice America. The Supreme Court ultimately agreed 6–3 with the Roberts' position in *Bray v. Alexandria Women's Health Clinic*, 506 U.S. 263 (1993).

5. *Doe v. Groody*, 361 F.3d 232 (3d Cir. 2004).

6. People for the American Way, *Fool Me Once,* Television advertisement, *available at* http://www.savethecourt.org/tv#FoolMeOnce.

7. Orin Kerr, *Pro-Alito Ad Goes Over the Top*, VOLOKH CONSPIRACY, Dec. 12, 2005, at http://volokh.com/archives/archive_2005_12_11-2005_12_17.shtml#1134419252.

8. Judicial Confirmation Network, *Real America*, Television advertisement, *available at* http://www.judicialnetwork.com/contents/alito/jcn_ad.shtml. Emphases in original transcript.

9. Memorandum from Roger Clegg, Associate Deputy Attorney General, Department of Justice to Carol E. Dinkins, Deputy Attorney General, Department of Justice (Aug. 1, 1984) (on file with the National Archives), *available at* http://www.archives.gov/news/samuel-alito/accession-060-88-258/Acc060-88-258-box5-memoCleggtoDinkins-Aug1984.pdf.

10. Jonathan S. Landay, *In 1984 Memo, Alito Defends Domestic Wiretaps*, MERCURY NEWS, Dec.23, 2005, *available at* http://www.mercurynews.com/mld/mercurynews/news/politics/13476545.htm. Last visited on August 14, 2006.

11. Stuart Taylor, Jr., *The NewsHour* (PBS, Dec. 28, 2005), *available at* http://www.pbs.org/newshour/bb/law/july-dec05/alito_12-28.html.

12. It almost goes without saying that the verb "to Bork" derives from the Supreme Court nomination battle over Robert Bork in 1987. The Democrat-controlled Senate rejected Bork's nomination by President Reagan based on what supporters of the president believed were relentlessly negative, personal attacks portraying the nominee as an extreme ideologue.

13. Dave Barry, *Year On the Verge of a Nervous Breakdown*, WASH. POST, Jan.1, 2006, at A-W08.

14. *Lou Dobbs Tonight* (CNN, Oct. 31, 2005), *available at* http://transcripts.cnn.com/TRANSCRIPTS/0510/31/ldt.01.html.

15. *Paula Zahn Now* (CNN, Oct. 31, 2005), *available at* http://transcripts.cnn.com/TRANSCRIPTS/0510/31/pzn.01.html.

16. *The Situation Room* (CNN, Oct. 31,2005), *available at* http://transcripts.cnn.com/TRANSCRIPTS/0510/31/sitroom.03.html.

17. *Hardball with Chris Matthews* (MSNBC, Oct. 31, 2005), *available at* http://www.msnbc.msn.com/id/9884432/.

18. *Scarborough Country* (MSNBC, Oct. 31, 2005), *available at* http://www.msnbc.msn.com/id/9884593/.

19. One notable exception in that first week was MSNBC's Dan Abrams, whose savvy discussion of the issues with legal analysts on November 1 included one with Crier about precedent and Alito's changed role if he moved from the Third Circuit to the Supreme Court. On the same show, however, Abrams updated his viewers on developments in the Holloway disappearance. *The Abrams Report* (MSNBC, Nov. 1, 2005), *available at* http://www.msnbc.msn.com/id/9896554/.

20. For example, Jess Bravin, *Alito Prefers Scalpel to Sledgehammer: Allies Hope Less Combative Style Makes Judge More Effective in Moving Court to the Right*, WALL ST. J., Nov.16, 2005, at A4; David G. Savage, *Alito Dissent Draws Scrutiny; Liberal Groups Say the Supreme Court Nominee Supported the Strip Search of a 10-Year-Old, But Experts Say That's a Distortion*, L.A. TIMES, Nov. 24, 2005, at A38; Michael McGough, *Alito Critics Focus on 10 Appellate Opinions: Say He Would Shift Top Court to Right*, PITT. POST-GAZETTE, Nov. 25, 2005, at A20.

21. For example, Nancy Benac, *Alito Seen As Smart, Serious, Cautious*, ASSOC. PRESS (as published in WASH. POST), Jan. 3, 2006.

22. Jo Becker & Dale Russakoff, *Proving His Mettle in the Reagan Justice Dept.*, WASH. POST, Jan. 9, 2006, at A01.

23. Tony Mauro, *A Field Guide to the Alito Confirmation Hearings*, LEGAL TIMES, Jan. 9, 2006.

24. Scott Shane, *In Capital and at the Court, Baseball Rules*, N.Y. TIMES, Nov. 5, 2005, at A12; David D. Kirkpatrick, *Alito Team Says He Lacks Polish, but Grit Is a Plus*, N.Y. TIMES, Jan. 2, 2006, at A1.

25. DAVID L. GREY, THE SUPREME COURT AND THE NEWS MEDIA 50 (1968).

26. For an overview of the literature, *see* the reference list in ELLIOT E. SLOTNICK & JENNIFER A. SEGAL, TELEVISION NEWS AND THE SUPREME COURT: ALL THE NEWS THAT'S FIT TO AIR? 251 (1998).

27. Richard Davis & Vincent James Strickler, *The Invisible Dance: The Supreme Court and the Press*, PERSPECTIVES ON POL. SCI. 85 (Spring 2000).

28. SLOTNICK & SEGAL, TELEVISION NEWS AND THE SUPREME COURT 15 quoting Chester A. Newland, "Press Coverage of the United States Supreme Court," 17 W. POL. Q. 15 (1964).

29. *Id.*, at 67 and 235.

30. Richard Davis, *Lifting the Shroud: News Media Portrayal of the U.S. Supreme Court*, COMMUNICATIONS AND THE LAW 54 (October 1987).

31. For liberals, nothing may top Bush v. Gore, 531 U.S. 98 (2000), as a modern illustration. Conservatives see more to complain about, in the realms of civil liberties, religion, abortion, and the First Amendment, among others.

32. BOB WOODWARD & SCOTT ARMSTRONG, THE BRETHREN: INSIDE THE SUPREME COURT 140 (1979).

33. For example, this comment by Democratic Senator Charles Schumer: "In case after case, Judge Alito gives the impression of applying meticulous legal reasoning, but each time he happens to reach the most conservative result," quoted by David D. Kirkpatrick, *Debate in Senate on Alito Heats Up Over '85 Memo*, N.Y. TIMES, Nov. 17, 2005, at A26.

34. Schumer again, in his opening statement at the Alito confirmation hearings; Charles Babington & Amy Goldstein, *Alito on Day 1: A Judge Can't Have Any Agenda*, WASH. POST, Jan. 10, 2006, at A01.

35. DEAN E. ALGER, THE MEDIA AND POLITICS 177 (1989). See also, Michael Comiskey,

Not Guilty: The News Media in the Supreme Court Confirmation Process, J. L. & POL. (Winter 1999).

36. From the author's notes; "Bench Press: The Collision of Media, Politics, Public Pressure, and an Independent Judiciary," Washington, DC, October 17, 2005; and Jeffrey Rosen. University Lecture at Syracuse Univ. (Oct. 19, 2005) (notes available with the author).

37. Roper Center at University of Connecticut, Public Opinion Online, 2005 polls.

38. Maxwell Poll on Civic Engagement and Inequality, at 5 (Oct. 2005) (margin of error ±5 percent), *available at* http://www.maxwell.syr.edu/campbell/Poll/CitizenshipPoll.htm. Last visited on August 14, 2006.

39. President George W. Bush, Statement on the nomination of Harriet Miers to the Supreme Court (Oct. 3, 2005), *available at* http://www.whitehouse.gov/news/releases/2005/10/20051003.html.

40. President George W. Bush, Statement on the nomination of Samuel Alito to the Supreme Court (Oct. 31, 2005), *available at* http://www.whitehouse.gov/news/releases/2005/10/20051031.html.

41. Ken Auletta, *The Howell Doctrine*, NEW YORKER, June 10, 2002, at 48.

42. William Branigin, Fred Barbash & Daniela Deane, *Supreme Court Justice O'Connor Resigns*, WASH. POST, July 1, 2005, *available at* http://www.washingtonpost.com/wp-dyn/content/article/2005/07/01/AR2005070100653.html.

43. Elisabeth Bumiller & Carl Hulse, *Bush Picks U.S. Appeals Judge to Take O'Connor's Court Seat*, N.Y. TIMES, Nov. 1, 2005, at A1.

44. Linda Greenhouse, *Court in Transition: A Major Decision; Abortion Case May Be Central in Confirmation*, N.Y. TIMES, Nov. 1, 2005, at A1; Robin Toner & Adam Liptak, *2 Camps, Playing Down Nuances, Stake Out Firm Stands*, N.Y. TIMES, Nov. 1, 2005, at A25.

45. Adam Liptak & Jonathan Glater, *Lucid Rulings Tackling Many of Biggest Issues*, N.Y. TIMES, Nov. 1, 2005, at A25.

46. David D. Kirkpatrick, *Conservatives Scrambling to Prepare for a Tough Fight*, N.Y. TIMES, Nov. 1, 2005, at A23.

47. Todd S. Purdham, *Potentially, the First Shot in All-Out Ideological War*, N.Y. TIMES, Nov. 1, 2005, at A22.

48. Neil A. Lewis & Scott Shane, *The Methodical Jurist*, N.Y. TIMES, Nov. 1, 2005, at A1.

49. Lynette Clemetson, *Alito Could Be 5th Catholic on Current Supreme Court*, N.Y. TIMES, Nov. 1, 2005, at A23.

50. Peter Baker, *Alito Nomination Sets Stage for Ideological Battle*, WASH. POST, Nov. 1, 2005, at A01.

51. Charles Lane, *Alito Leans Right Where O'Connor Swung Left*, WASH. POST, Nov. 1, 2005, at A01.

52. Michael A. Fletcher, *A Rapid Response on All Sides*, WASH. POST, Nov. 1, 2005, at A10; Mark Leibovich, *A Very Tight Grip-and-Grin*, WASH. POST, Nov. 1, 2005, at C01.

53. Dan Balz, *With a Pick From the Right, Bush Looks to Rally GOP in Tough Times*, WASH. POST, Nov. 1, 2005, at A06.

54. U.S. v. Rybar, 103 F.3d 273 (3d Cir. 1996).

55. 410 U.S. 113 (1973).

56. Adam Liptak & Jonathan D. Glater, *Alito's Dissents Show Deference to Lower Courts*, N.Y. TIMES, Nov. 3, 2005, at A1.

57. Stephen Labaton, *Court Nominee Has Paper Trail Businesses Like*, N.Y. TIMES, Nov. 5, 2005, at A1.

58. Amy Goldstein & Jo Becker, *Critics See Ammunition in Alito's Rights Record*, WASH. POST, Nov. 3, 2005, at A01.

59. Charles Lane, *Alito Respectful of Precedent, Associates Say*, WASH. POST, Nov. 6, 2005, at A13.

60. Scott Shane, *Ideology Serves as a Wild Card on Court Pick*, N.Y. TIMES, Nov. 4, 2005, at A1.

61. Neil A. Lewis, *In Cases Involving Federal Government, Nominee Is Seen as Favoring Authority of the States*, N.Y. TIMES, Nov. 6, 2005, at A28.

62. Adam Liptak, *In Abortion Rulings, Idea of Marriage Is Pivotal*, N.Y. TIMES, Nov. 2, 2005, at A1; Charles Lane, *Nominee's Reasoning Points to a Likely Vote Against Roe v. Wade*, WASH. POST, Nov. 2, 2005, at A06.

63. David D. Kirkpatrick & Carl Hulse, *G.O.P. Reaches to Other Party on Court Pick*, N.Y. TIMES Nov. 2, 2005, at A1; Peter Baker & Charles Babington, *Moderates' Support Sought for Alito*, WASH. POST, Nov. 2, 2005, at A06; Kirkpatrick, *Judge Said He Struggled on '91 Abortion Opinion*, N.Y. TIMES, Nov. 3, 2005, at A24; Babington, *Senators Praise Nominee's Candor; Alito Shows Willingness to Discuss Controversial Issues Facing Supreme Court*, WASH. POST, Nov. 5, 2005, at A07.

64. Charles Babington & Amy Goldstein, *"Specter Bucks White House on Alito; Judiciary Panel Hearing on Supreme Court Nominee Is Set for January,"* WASH. POST, Nov. 4, 2005, at A07.

65. Amy Goldstein & Sarah Cohen, *Alito, In and Out of the Mainstream: Nominee's Record Defies Stereotyping*, WASH. POST, Jan. 1, 2006, at A01.

66. No undue disrespect is intended, as I was once one of those courthouse reporters learning law on the fly.

67. STEPHEN BREYER, ACTIVE LIBERTY: INTERPRETING OUR DEMOCRATIC CONSTITUTION (2005).

8   The Internet and the Judiciary

We Are All Experts Now

Dahlia Lithwick

THE INTERNET AND THE JUDICIARY: On the face of it they pull in opposing directions. The Internet looks forward while courts face backward. The Internet celebrates "edginess" and opinion, courts reify wisdom. The Internet is informal, open, and democratic; the courts operate under the most rigid rules and hierarchical constraints. The Internet works at lightning speeds—yesterday is too long ago to even be of interest—whereas the progress of the law is glacial—*Roe v. Wade*[1] is still unsettled. The Internet has been quick to embrace law—legal bloggers and websites grow exponentially. And while the courts have been slower to join the Information Age, even they have come to recognize some of the benefits of instant and comprehensive information, conveyed at light speeds.

Courts once devoted exclusively to paper communications have slowly developed websites that clarify and disseminate opinions, rules, and procedures. Judges who once hid from technology have—with help from savvy law clerks—come to understand the benefits of electronic databases, and the myriad joys of late-night Googling. And the proliferation of online journalism and legal blogging has helped lay readers access primary sources—opinions and statutes that were once largely inaccessible to them.

In many ways this direct access to sources points toward a more informed

Senior Editor and Legal Correspondent, *Slate.com*.

audience. As Mark Obbie suggests in his chapter, the widespread assumption is that since actual cases, like *Brown v. Board of Education,*[2] are now as easy to find online as your local movie listings, instead of subjectively summarizing the case, an online reporter or blogger can simply link to it.[3] Gone are the days when I, as a reporter, must tell you what a case means; today I can urge you to read it, start to finish, and decide for yourself. This is a form of democracy never imagined by the framers.

At least that was the promise. That was the argument I once gave for why the Internet would inevitably render the judicial project more open and, ultimately, I believed, more sympathetic. Having covered the courts for eight years for an online publication, I have always believed that reader access to primary texts, law review articles, and to instant and frequently brilliant explication by legal bloggers, would make for a better informed and more sophisticated citizen.

But that has been only half the story. Because while the Internet has opened up the potential for a better-educated polity with a greater, more nuanced appreciation for what judges do, it's also ushered in an unprecedented new era of crabbed and narrow-minded readership. As Cass Sunstein predicted in 2001 in his book, *Republic.com,*[4] the Internet does not necessarily deepen or broaden our intellectual scope. By enabling each of us to create what Sunstein termed "The Daily Me" (the phrase was coined by MIT technology specialist Nicholas Negroponte) the Internet allows citizens to believe themselves well-informed and well-educated, even while they read hundreds, even thousands, of sources that merely reflect back their own, ferociously held views.[5] Sunstein feared that without regulation of the Internet, we were doomed to live in a world wholly lacking "unplanned, unanticipated encounters" with new ideas; and that absent such encounters we could not, as a society, have a "range of common experiences."[6]

I once described this phenomenon in a speech, suggesting that by going through our days confronting only dozens of opinions that mirror back our own, we run the risk of becoming "the most widely read, well-informed, and ignorant generation in history."[7]

And, as Obbie suggests while it's true that the Internet certainly offers the public the possibility of reading primary sources—all of Judge Samuel Alito's appellate opinions and dissents are suddenly just a mouse-click away—it also offers this more tantalizing option: Of visiting twenty websites that will summarize and critique those opinions in the most blatantly political terms.[8] If even some legal reporters cannot be bothered to read those opinions in their entirety, can we really expect our readers to do so?

Like all new media before it, therefore, the Internet carries both the promise of opening and democratizing the national conversation about the law, but also the threat of dismally lowering it. The open question—and I believe it is still open—is whether we will use the Web's potential to better understand what courts and judges do, or to render it as trivial, polarized, and ideological as the rest of our national political conversation.

My suspicion is that the recent political attacks on the judiciary—including the airing of nationwide television spectaculars—so-called Justice Sunday broadcasts, involving political assaults on "judicial activism" and judges who "make up the law"—have been profoundly aided and abetted by the Internet. And it was largely political and ideological websites that repeatedly trumpeted the message that a tragically comatose Terri Schiavo was alert and alive and in imminent peril from an abusive husband and a bloodthirsty judiciary. Those websites brushed aside years of judicial findings and legal processes, focusing only on the results they sought. "Ignore the trial court/appeals court/the medical experts/the statutes! See for yourself as she blinks at the floating balloon! We need to keep Terri alive now!" Millions of watchers suddenly became medical experts; hundreds of pages court findings were reduced to legal wallpaper.

And when a "bounty" was announced—again on the Internet—a monetary reward offered for the trial court judge in that case, the power of the Web to mobilize and radicalize the public reached its zenith. And all this happened just as public understanding of what judges do was at its lowest ebb in history.

At its core, the relationship between the Internet and the judiciary is both confounded and enriched by the possibility for precision: On the one hand the Internet makes more raw legal data publicly available than ever before. On the other, it's a medium that—not unlike the tabloids—still thrives on speed, on "page views," on "voiceyness" and sensationalism. And just as newspapers run the gamut from the *New York Times* to the *National Enquirer,* websites run the gamut from the brilliant and meticulous *Sentencing Law and Policy* blog, to "legal" blogs run by hysterical gun-wielding conspiracy nuts, powered by servers in their underground bunkers. And not all readers are sufficiently sophisticated yet to sort out the difference.

Moreover, as I suggested earlier—websites, too, have begun to recognize the value in "The Daily Me." Cable news has lit the way toward a media that merely echoes back one's own political viewpoint, sometimes at the expense of accuracy, often at the expense of balance. Whereas the print media still struggles to present viewpoints that counterbalance each other on the op-ed page, the Internet has sometimes followed the *Fox News* model and created communities of increasingly angry, like-minded thinkers.

Like *Fox News*, the Internet can blur the distinction between fact and opinion, opinion and bombast. And sometimes, before you, as a reader, know it, you have tumbled down the rabbit hole from legal news to legal Jeremiad.

All of these forces pull in the opposite direction from the formal legal project—which focuses on accuracy and precision, frequently at the expense of enthusiasm or excitement. As Obbie observes in his chapter, there is little about the methodical process of layering existing precedent over statutory interpretation that strikes readers as stimulating.[9] Judges strive hard to separate fact from opinion, and law from ideology, and while some do so more successfully than others, the nature of the Internet, indeed of much media coverage of the law, is to blur those lines. And this tug-of-war leads readers to focus on legal outcomes, rather than processes. It leads to the perpetuation and endless repetition of the most basic and damaging errors about what courts do every day.

Two years ago, the Supreme Court decided in *Kelo v. New London*[10] that the use of eminent domain for economic development, for a depressed—but not blighted—region, did not violate the takings clauses of the state and federal constitutions. The High Court arrived at that 5–4 decision by first carefully parsing the state eminent domain statute, then examining the prior case law and weighing the relevant constitutional provisions. The court's decision was close, but neither side was rooted in illogic, ideology, or whim. Yet somehow, and I'd add unexpectedly, *Kelo* unleashed a national war of wildly inaccurate headlines, including such whoppers as "Ruling Allows Governments To Wrest Property From Citizens,"[11] "Supreme Court Rules Cities May Seize Homes,"[12] and "Is Your Home Still Your Castle?"[13]

Media criticism—particularly on the Internet—of the court's holding was so overheated that few of us noticed, amid all the screaming, that the public was being given the impression that the Supreme Court was itself grabbing private land for redevelopment—perhaps for Justice Souter's summer home. Lost amid all this bluster was any recognition of the nuanced dance of legislative interpretation, statutory construction, and the application of precedent.

Months later, members of the United States Senate were still parroting these sloppy sound bytes at the Supreme Court confirmation hearings for John Roberts and Samuel Alito and angry citizens were organized to turn Justice David Souter's home into a hotel. The whole episode left the American public with a woefully inaccurate sense of what the court had done and—more critically—why it had done so.

Similarly, when the Massachusetts Supreme Court read its own laws and constitution to permit gay marriage,[14] relying largely on unremarkable precepts of statutory interpretation and Supreme Court precedent, commentators—particularly on the Internet—disregarded that process in favor of hysterical conclusions about activist judges who merely fabricate the law from spun sugar and rampant ideology. The mass media in general and the Internet in particular have become so relentlessly focused on the holding of each case, that any meaningful explication of how the courts arrived at that decision is deemed irrelevant at worst, and boring but necessary at best. Reporting on a holding without explaining the rationale behind it is like reviewing a film by merely describing what happens in the last ten minutes. Certainly you spoil the ending. But you have also explained nothing.

Having been raised exclusively on Lexis and Westlaw, it might seem hypocritical of me to long for a time when, before writing about a case, you had to shuffle up to the law library, locate the correct federal reporter, then tuck your feet under you and read the opinion (and the dissents) in their entirety. But I do long for that time. Because all that shuffling and tucking and reading offered the reporter the benefit of context.

What the Internet does—with its nested links and flashing, tempting incentives to hop from website to website—is to strip out random sentences and phrases, and leave them to stand alone, like so many stolen hubcaps. It is never wise to read the dissent without reading the majority opinion. But that seems to be all we do anymore.

The law is slow and tedious. Reading old case law and distinguishing it from new facts can be mind-numbing. That's why we entrust it to people who have studied this process, rather than to the pundits on cable news—who will spend more time in the makeup chair than they will reading the case; or some partisan bloggers—who are legal experts today, and auto-repair experts tomorrow. Most cases—particularly those on appeal to the nation's highest courts—have meritorious claims on both sides. The difference between authoring a concurrence and a dissent has little to do with "making up the law" and everything to do with tiny shadings of facts and analysis. Most judges are well aware of this truth. But most of the American public is not.

As Thomas Goldstein notes in his contribution, judges and reporters have been struggling to bridge the gap between their worlds for decades.[15] Indeed in some sense, both parties have found themselves in a hostage situation much of the time: Judges depend on the media to speak for them when they cannot speak from themselves. And reporters depend on recalcitrant judges for the behind-the-scenes insight that might liven up a dull story. But the Internet has created a vast class of legal "reporters" who expect no personal access to judges, and thus treat them without the kid gloves Goldstein describes. An anonymous Internet website called *Underneath Their Robes* took the legal world by storm in 2004 with gossipy tidbits about the dating habits of judicial law clerks and a "Superhotties of the Federal Judiciary" vote-in contest.[16] (The winners, for the curious, were Judge Alex Kozinski of the Ninth Circuit and Judge Kimba Wood, SDNY.)

To the extent that the mainstream media has tended to treat the judiciary with kid gloves, most legal bloggers tend to go at them with boxing gloves. Whether this serves as necessary "demystification" of the bench, or merely as overt disrespect, is also an open question.

Add to all these pernicious factors this new one: The Internet is uniquely able to conflate instant misinformation with immediate action. "Don't like what Judge X did? Click here to sign a petition/contribute to his opponent/ initiate impeachment proceedings!" Armed with less information than they need, armies of polarized citizens are instantly mobilized for a battle on the judiciary they don't really want. Believing that any idiot can do what judges do, they are willing to substitute their own judgment for that of the judiciary, and—with the help of some demagogues in Congress—they are uniquely positioned to threaten, court-strip, or browbeat judges into complying with their demands.

To paraphrase Dickens, then, this is—when it comes to public understanding of the judicial project—the best of times, and also the worst of times. The number of law professors who have taken to the Internet with a constitutional law textbook in one hand, and a hard copy of the *Wall Street Journal* in the other, is phenomenal. That they have left the ivory tower and joined the national fray is a benefit for everyone. Their efforts, combined with the ready availability of case law, statutes, journal articles, truly great legal reporting, and precedent, make it possible for lay readers to recognize and celebrate the complexity of what judges do.

We can use the Web to peel the oak paneling off the courthouses and show the public that this isn't just politics in black robes. Hopefully this offers some comfort to Cass Sunstein and Mark Obbie: The very best legal sites on the Internet either aggregate vast amounts of legal information brilliantly (see, for instance Howard Bashman's wonderful blog *How Appealing*) or comment thoughtfully and carefully on legal matters (see Ann Althouse or Eugene Volokh). These things could never have happened in the print media. They are largely better than anything the print media can do.

But at the same time, the sheer number of websites, the stark polarization of the national political dialogue, and the premium placed on volume and outrage over accuracy, and outcomes over processes, still imperils the judiciary as never before.

Americans wrongly believe they can read a line or two of an opinion, and fully comprehend what a judge really does with her time. Whereas the flow of information was once mediated (possibly badly, but mediated nonetheless) by editors, the Internet allows each of us to be our own editor, every day. It shifts the burden entirely to us as the consumers, to seek balance and accuracy. And there is simply no mechanism to force that impulse; it must come from fair-minded, moderate people who wish to make their own decisions.

My suspicion is that this is not a utopian fantasy: With the advent of fact-checking and watchdog sites, much of the public increasingly uses the Internet to dial down the partisan bluster. Consider how many viewers of the televised presidential debates in 2004 were simultaneously logging onto websites like FactCheck.Org to figure out whether President Bush was mischaracterizing the *Dred Scott*[17] decision.

Of course these truths, too, are only as self-evident as their purveyors, but—as is the case with any wide open market—the general trend is toward good legal websites gaining prominence and silly ones disappearing. It's also worth recalling that we have had this debate about every emerging form of media, from the printing press to television.

Ultimately, I believe that judges have for too long mystified and obscured what they do, and I know for certain that lay readers are capable of understanding their work, even without the benefit of a law degree. The high quality of most print legal journalism has proven that. But at the same time it provides the public with the tools to better understand the law, the Internet offers every incentive to deliberately misunderstand it—to distort and demean and politicize it in ways that may have irreparable consequences.

As is so often true in a democracy, the choice is ours to make.

Notes

1. 410 U.S. 113 (1973).
2. 347 U.S. 483 (1954).
3. See Mark Obbie, *Winners and Losers*, in this volume.
4. CASS SUNSTEIN, REPUBLIC.COM (2001).
5. *Id.*
6. *Id.* at 9.
7. Dahlia Lithwick, Address at the dedication of the Charlottesville monument to Free Speech (Apr. 20, 2006), *at* http://loper.org/george/trends/2006/Apr/926.html.
8. Obbie, *supra* note 3.
9. *Id.*
10. 545 U.S.469 (2005).
11. Josh Gerstein, *Ruling Allows Governments To Wrest Property From Citizens*, N.Y. SUN, June 24, 2005, at 1.
12. Matt Apuzzo, *Supreme Court Rules Cities May Seize Homes*, ASSOC. PRESS, June 24, 2005, *available at* http://www.sfgate.com/cgi-bin/article.cgi?f=/n/a/2005/06/23/national/w073747D75.DTL.
13. Michelle Malkin, *Your Home Is Not Your Castle*, MICHELLEMALKIN.COM, June 23, 2005, *at* http://michellemalkin.com/archives/002830.htm.
14. Goodridge v. Dept. of Public Health, 798 N.E.2d 941 (Mass. 2003).
15. Tom Goldstein, *The Distance between Judges and Journalists*, this volume.
16. Article III Groupie (David Lat), *Too Sexy For Their Robes: The Nominees for Superhotties of the Federal Judiciary!*, UNDERNEATH THEIR ROBES, July 7, 2004, *at* http://underneaththeirrobes.blogs.com/main/2004/07/_general_commen.html.
17. 60 U.S.393 (1856).

9 The Distance between Judges and Journalists

Tom Goldstein

I HAVE VIVID RECOLLECTIONS of covering legal issues for the *New York Times* in the 1970s—recollections that might be helpful in untangling urgent questions still unanswered about the relation between the press and the legal system in general and the judiciary in particular. These questions, evident in the 1970s and in many instances long before then, are unanswered largely because judges and journalists still do not sufficiently understand each other.

As a starting point, it is important to postulate that judicial business is the public business. It has yet to be fully agreed on, however, just *how much* disclosure is compatible with the public interest. And this question is inextricably tied to how differently journalists and judges see the world. Each operates with a set of important limitations. Reporters, by and large, experience the world secondhand, through the prism of others' interpretations. The very structure of the news business limits the time, the space, and the resources that can be allocated to any single story or a single beat. Conventions of journalism suggest that news must be novel. News of conflict almost automatically crowds out news of cooperation. Judges, on the other hand, operate with their own restrictions. They are reluctant to respond when attacked. A judge's work speaks for itself. Judges do not discuss their deliberations. Conventions

Director of Mass Communications, University of California at Berkeley.

of jurisprudence are built on an adherence to precedent—not novelty. Moreover, we live increasingly in a culture of disclosure, which has been facilitated by journalists and discouraged by judges. I think it is impossible to develop a unitary explanation of why the bench and press are so often speaking different languages. Guided by experience, though, small steps should be taken to bridge the gap between the bench and the press.

I started reporting on legal issues for the *New York Times* in 1973 when I was 28 years old and when 250,000 or so lawyers practiced, about a quarter of the number who practice today. When I started, I had a law degree and a journalism degree from Columbia (the law degree was much more important in my getting hired to a dream job) and modest experience as a reporter at the *Buffalo Evening News*, the Associated Press in New York and the *Wall Street Journal*. I also had been the founding editor of *Juris Doctor* magazine—a magazine for young lawyers named after the degree that had just replaced the LLB degree in most schools. The name of the degree was so unfamiliar that many people whom I called quizzically asked: "Jewish doctor magazine?"

The *New York Times* was a vastly different paper then than now. It was only two sections, one of which consisted largely of metropolitan area news. The newspaper still clung to the view that it was a paper of record (living up to its motto: "All the News That is Fit to Print"), a conceit that has been largely abandoned today, when there is a recognition that it is utter hubris to think one paper publication could capture all the news that is worthy of dissemination.

At first, I was assigned to the metropolitan desk, but my specific duties were ill-defined. Unlike most beat reporters, I did not cover a specific building. I was given great latitude in coming up with trend and issue stories, and I occasionally covered spot stories. As my job evolved, the state Court of Appeals, based in Albany, came under my jurisdiction.

This represented a relatively small portion of my beat, so I was able to devote only a limited amount of time to it. During the period I covered the court, it converted from a bench of elected judges to one of judges appointed by the governor. That represented a seismic shift for the court, but I found it very hard to write stories on this shift that were compelling enough to attract broad attention.

Most of the stories I wrote about the court involved opinions it rendered. Logistical problems presented themselves in days of older technologies. These obstacles were largely overcome by a spokesman the court hired early in my tenure, a genial Albany veteran named Walter Mordaunt. Mordaunt never in my memory discussed the substance of any opinion, but he was kind enough to call me the night before an opinion was being issued to give me a heads up. Sometimes, he told me it would be worth my while to get up to Albany early the next day. Decoded, that meant a very important decision was about to be decided and that I probably needed a full day to absorb it and write about it. Other times, for less pressing opinions, he would place a packet on a Greyhound bus, and three hours later, I would walk over the bus station near the *New York Times* to fetch the package. On rare occasions, he would fax decisions, but facsimile technology of that era was so crude and slow that it usually was faster to send an opinion by bus than it was to fax it.

Over time, I developed a good relationship with the chief judge of the court, Charles Breitel. I think we liked and respected each other, but I also tried to maintain a professional distance. We took to seeing each other occasionally in his New York office so that he could give me background briefings on the court. I found these very useful, and his insights, I think, helped my reporting. One day when I visited his downtown chambers, I noted a tape recorder sitting prominently on his desk. I asked him what that was all about, and he responded that he wished to tape our conversation so that he could listen before he went to sleep to see how well he answered my questions. On my next visit, I felt it prudent for me to bring my own tape recorder, and from there on, the quality of our private conversations deteriorated.

I also gained the trust of the other judges on the court, which I thought was a positive development, but once my very closeness put me in an unacceptable quandary. A new judge had joined the court. He was considered brash by many, so after several months, I decided to do a story on what his colleagues thought of him as a judge. I pledged everyone to confidentiality, and every colleague—to a person—had something negative to say about their newest colleague. The pledge of confidentiality was tantamount to no pledge at all if I were to write a story saying that Judge X's colleagues *all* felt he was not up to the job. And so, duty bound, I wrote no story at all.

I had a more complicated relationship with another chief judge, who was also sitting that time in New York, Irving Kaufman, chief judge of the Second Circuit Court of Appeals, thought by its judges to be the second most important court in the country. Someone else was assigned to cover that building full time (as if all the newsworthy trials in the Southern District and all the newsworthy appeals that were decided by the Second Circuit could be tracked by one person!).

But Kaufman, a small man physically, had outsized energy and a healthy ego, and it fell to me to cover much of what he did. I was designated the person in the newsroom who would take calls from the judge, and these calls were plentiful. This was more than awkward. He had a very special relationship with the *New York Times*. Any reader could see that. At a time when news values were changing and fewer and fewer speeches of any kind were covered, the *Times* routinely carried articles about Judge Kaufman's speeches and it even ran news stories on law review articles he had written. In addition, he became one of the most frequent outside contributors to the paper, writing often for the *New York Times Magazine* (in one six-year period, he was the most prolific outside contributor to the magazine) and to the newspaper's op-ed page. In exercising his full-throated freedom of speech, Kaufman was untroubled by the kinds of inhibitions that Charles Gardner Geyh enumerates in his lead-off essay in this volume.

But there was much more to the relationship between the judge and the paper, some of which I related in a book I wrote many years ago, called *The News at Any Cost*.

In the pages of the *Times*, Judge Kaufman received special, uncritical treatment, sometimes to the point of sycophancy. Coincidentally, he would champion freedom of the press, including the *New York Times*, in his opinions. Often, he would be the one to connect the two, calling me to wonder why his continued advocacy of a free press did not merit greater coverage than he had already received.

For many, Judge Kaufman behaved like a man obsessed, trying to erase the past. Years earlier, in 1951, in a watershed case, Judge Kaufman, then a trial judge, presided over the espionage trial of Julius and Ethel Rosenberg, who were charged with conspiring to steal and deliver atomic secrets to the Soviet Union. A jury convicted the couple, and Kaufman imposed the death sentence. It was a sentence that ignited controversy for the rest of his career, and it was a sentence that prompted leaders of the New York bar, notably Simon Rifkind, to come to his defense. Sometimes Rifkind, but more frequently Judge Kaufman, would call *Times* executives, editors, and reporters to complain about stories dealing with the Rosenbergs and to encourage the paper to write about the judge's activities on behalf of the First Amendment.

In death, Kaufman could not escape his past. In the obituary, the *Times's* reporter wrote: "It was Judge Kaufman's hope that he would be remembered for his role not in the Rosenberg case, the espionage trial of the century, but as the judge . . . whose rulings expanded the freedom of the press." His wish was not to be. The headline to his obituary in the *New York Times* read: "Judge Irving Kaufman, of Rosenberg Spy Trial and Free-Press Rulings, Dies at 81."

Judge Kaufman had a prickly personality, as did his colleague and sometimes antagonist on the bench, Chief Justice Warren Burger. The two often sparred, with Justice Burger on occasion going to great, almost gleeful lengths to reverse an opinion written by Judge Kaufman. The Supreme Court received extraordinary coverage from the *Times*. (In those days, unlike now, the three television networks and two newsweeklies also had reporters assigned largely full-time to cover the highest court.) In my beat, I occasionally got to cover the outside activities of the justices, particularly at meetings of the American Bar Association, which unlike now were staples of legal coverage. Justice Burger enjoyed coming to these meetings, but he intensely disapproved of television coverage of his appearances.

He disliked bright lights. His eyes were quite sensitive, and he said he could not see his notes when lighting was intense. Moreover, he came off surprisingly poorly as a public speaker. And it was therefore not shocking that with few exceptions, the chief justice refused to let television cameras cover his outside appearances. In the spring of 1979, the chief justice, in a particularly shrill statement released by the Supreme Court's public information office, reiterated his policy toward television. Citing the "long tradition of isolation of judges from day-to-day controversy," the statement expressed dismay at the behavior of television reporters who at American Bar Association meetings "as well as elsewhere accosted the Chief Justice in hotel lobbies, on streets, and in other public places, thrusting microphones at him for impromptu press conferences with questions on subjects wholly inappropriate for comment by any judge."

This antipathy to cameras filming him in public places extended to cameras in the courtroom. Placing television in courtrooms, a movement that was gaining momentum those years, received no encouragement from the Supreme Court. This anti-press position was especially regrettable because the Burger Court was far more sympathetic to the press in its opinions than was generally understood. This aversion to television seemed out of step with the rest of the culture, particularly in appellate courtrooms where the only participants are judges and lawyers.

Importantly, as the three chief judges—Charles Breitel, Irving Kaufman, and Warren Burger—engaged with the press (and public) in very different ways, a much larger trend had begun washing over the legal profession. As Victor Navasky, the writer (who was trained as a lawyer) put it to me, a welcome demystification of the law was gaining momentum.

This official date of this demystification can roughly be traced to 1977, when barriers to lawyers' promoting themselves dissolved after the Supreme Court, in *Bates v. State Bar of Arizona*,[1] gave its permission for lawyers to advertise in limited circumstances. (A year earlier, I had done a long profile on the firm of Paul, Weiss, Rifkind, Wharton & Garrison, much in the news for its high-profile clients, including many state and municipal agencies at a time of the highly uncertain economic condition of New York. Not unimportantly, a senior partner in the firm was Simon Rifkind, the same man that had on many occasions come to the defense of Judge Kaufman when he was criticized. I thought my article was tough, but the headline, which I did not write, was anything but tough: "The Law Firm that Stars in Court." Shortly after the article appeared, several complaints were filed with the grievance committee of the Association of the Bar of the City of New York accusing the firm, which had pointedly not cooperated with me, of unethical self-promotion.)

With the ban on self-promotion and advertising lifted, the dark ages for lawyers ended. Coverage of law became a staple in the popular press. An ancillary business of providing public relations advice to law firms flourished. The emergence of the *American Lawyer* and the *National Law Journal* helped turn on its head the traditional reticence of many lawyers to speak to reporters. Lawyers, like many others, actually enjoyed seeing their names in print.

However, the winds of change blowing over the legal profession and other parts of society have not had a corresponding effect on the judiciary—a point underscored from a different angle by Professor Jeffrey Rosen in an intriguing essay in the *New York Times Book Review* in January 2006 on the unlikely subject of books by justices of the Supreme Court.

"In an unbuttoned, confessional age, the judiciary has remained the last institution of American government to resist the public's relentless demands for personal exposure," Rosen wrote. "But the norms about what's appropriate for judges to reveal about themselves are in the middle of a sea change."[2]

On one hand, "defenders of the new judicial openness say that the more the public knows about judges' political views and personal habits, the better informed we will be about the basis for their decisions."[3] For Rosen, it remains to be seen whether judges "by revealing too much about themselves in books and blogs, will squander the sense of impersonal respect on which their legitimacy depends."[4] If there is any doubt where Rosen comes down on this, his words at the "Bench Press" conference in October 2005 were revealing. He said it would be dangerous if the "veil of mystery" were to be removed from the judiciary.[5] How long this "veil of mystery" will endure is an open question, given the recent decisions trending to judicial openings that Charles Gardner Geyh describes.[6]

Arguing from anecdote surely has its pitfalls. The reason for going into the early part of my career at such length is to show how convoluted the relationship between the judiciary and journalism can be. Sometimes simple informal solutions, such as Walter Mordaunt's giving me early notice of a Court of Appeals decision, work best. Other problems have resisted solution. While I firmly believe that the worst mistake in discussing the press is to view it as a monolith, it is easy to slip into generalizations. I shall try not to overgeneralize, but my sense then—and now—is that many judges are unhappy with coverage of the judiciary because they misunderstand the nature of news and the role of reporters.

News involves novelty, conflict, and finding out what others wish to keep secret. As Jeffrey Toobin noted at the "Bench Press" conference, it is natural for a journalist to look for something to catch readers' attention.[7] Moreover, journalists are not stenographers. As Toobin noted, the "business of journalism is the business of condensation."[8] By its very nature, journalism violates context. When someone complains about a story being "out of context," this is, in some sense, always correct.

Most assuredly, reporters do not see their job as promoting the interests of those whom they cover. I am not sure that judges—or university administrators or athletes or actors or politicians—always understand that. The classic role of reporters was captured by Finley Peter Dunne, who lived from 1867 to 1936 and wrote satirical "Mr. Dooley" columns that were nationally syndicated. The fictional Dooley was an opinionated, first-generation, Irish-American bar owner who skewered powerful people. It was Dunne who thought that the duty of a newspaper was to "afflict the comfortable and comfort the afflicted." That sentiment remains strong among some journalists, although it is a rare newspaper today that feels a mission to afflict the comfortable. More often, journalists feel that their goal is to keep those in power accountable, and this alone can make those in power feel uncomfortable.

The most recent sustained stories in which the judiciary played a leading role were the confirmation hearings of justices John Roberts Jr. and Samuel Alito Jr. In a book review, Judge Richard Posner, the influential federal appeals judge based in Chicago, complained in an article in the *New York Times*:

> News coverage of a political campaign is oriented to a public that enjoys competitive sports, not to one that is civic-minded. We saw this in coverage of the selection of Justice Sandra Day O'Connor's successor. It was played as an election campaign; one article even described the jockeying for the nomination by President Bush as the "primary election" and the fight to get the nominee confirmed by the Senate the "general election" campaign. With only a few exceptions, no attention was paid to the ability of the people being considered for the job or the actual consequences that the appointment was likely to have for the nation.[9]

In all deference, I do not think Judge Posner, usually an astute observer of current events, was reading the same publications that I was—or the same publications that Mark Obbie so astutely analyzes in his chapter of this volume. The amount of space devoted to succession was extraordinary, and it did not seem that any stories were missing. The coverage was so comprehensive that no one could possibly have read all of it.

This fits in with the mission of the highly regarded daily newspapers and the national daily broadcast news. According to Robert Entman, a professor at North Carolina State University, the prestige media claim roughly the same core mission: reporting on important events, people, and issues in ways that are accurate and balanced. It is certain that the gavel-to-gavel coverage of Justice Alito's confirmation were neither the most watched nor most read stories. But serious journalists have reached the consensus that such coverage is important.

Moreover, the confirmation hearings *did* have the whiff of a political campaign, and covering them that way was far from inappropriate, as Judge Posner suggests. In a revealing postmortem of the Alito confirmation, David Kirkpatrick of the *Times*, who once had the unusual beat of covering conservative issues, wrote about just how stage-managed the Alito confirmation was. Kirkpatrick's article began:

> The week before his Supreme Court confirmation hearings, Judge Samuel A. Alito Jr. e-mailed the text of his opening statement to the White House. It included very little about his legal thinking, dwelled at length on his family and opened with a tired and rambling joke about courtroom banter between a lawyer and a judge.

The response from the White House: "Perfect, don't change a word," according to an administration official who was granted anonymity because Judge Alito's preparation sessions were confidential.[10]

In other words, the reporters covering the hearings were justified in treating them as political theater, sometimes devoid of substance.

In describing the tensions between the press and judiciary, it would be wrong to read too much into the coverage of the nomination hearings. They are rare events—the first in a dozen years—and the rarity itself may help account for the generous coverage they received. Analyzing coverage of these nomination hearings offers only the barest help in trying to unpack the tangled relationship between the press and the judiciary.

Writ large, the judiciary may be the least well understood branch of government—or surely the most poorly covered. It would smack of self-interest if we were to dismiss out of hand judges who complain about press coverage. They are not the only ones to complain. The public itself seems to be saying that it feels poorly served. In the national survey conducted during October by the Maxwell School at Syracuse University, less than 30 percent of those polled agreed that "media coverage of the courts provides a good explanation of why judges make decision they do."[11] Nearly half of those polled described themselves as very well informed; that is, they read a newspaper every day.[12] But even in this group, only 35 percent agreed with that media coverage provides a good explanation.[13] As a next step, those results beg for amplification. Are we talking federal or state courts, trial or appellate courts?

The demystification of the courts has a long way to go, and from one angle little progress has been made since the 1970s. I do not have numbers to prove this, but my sense is that in many ways, attention to law and the judiciary among journalists has withered. With a determinedly less active Supreme Court (and by and large that is the only appellate court that has ever received substantial coverage), many news organizations have paid less attention to courts in general.

Trials continue to capture the attention of large swaths of the public. In some states, cameras are permitted in courtrooms. Court TV and some other cable channels have helped to whet the public appetite for coverage of trials, many of which are devoid of traditional news content but full of entertaining plot twists and turns. A very small percentage of disputes ever get to the trial stage, and fewer still of those can sustain a narrative. But those that do mesh nicely with television's perceived needs of structural drama.

Certain people on cable television revel in going after judges. In January 2006, for example, Bill O'Reilly of Fox News was unrelenting in his attacks on Judge Edward Cashman, a Vermont judge, who had sentenced a rapist of a six-year-old girl to a relatively light sentence because he believed the perpetrator could be rehabilitated better outside prison. Ultimately, under pressure, he raised the sentence.

But just as we cannot extrapolate from the coverage of the Supreme Court nominations, we cannot extrapolate from Bill O'Reilly's rants or from wall-to-wall coverage of soap opera–like fact situations that find their way to television. Remember: The press is not monolithic.

Given all these caveats, I believe that there are specific ways that the bench and press can learn from each other to resolve problems that have been affecting the relationship for decades. First steps are important. We need to know much more:

- We need to know more about what actually gets covered. How much coverage does the Supreme Court receive? Is it up or down? Is this related in any way to other coverage of the bench? How many reporters are assigned to circuit courts of appeal? What kinds of decisions get reported at the state level? Are these the important decisions?

- We need to know much more about who actually covers courts and how they are trained. At the lunch meeting of the "Bench Press" conference, Nina Totenberg of NPR suggested that covering a courthouse is not necessarily a prestige job. Can that impression be quantified? Is there, in fact, high turnover on such beats? If reporters who cover courts are inexperienced, can this be corrected?

- A repository of past journalistic practices needs to be developed. For instance, covering long trials under deadline and with limited space can be daunting to the point of impossibility. What are examples of excellent coverage? How can such coverage be recognized?

- In covering who gets to sit as a judge, we need to know more of which confirmation hearings—beyond the Supreme Court—get covered. In jurisdictions where judges get elected, we need to understand better the role of television commercials and whether these differ in style and tone from other political advertisements.

- We need to know more about informal contacts between bench and press. When I started, I went to literally dozens of conferences bringing reporters and judges together. I thought those were helpful to me. My sense now is that such meetings have atrophied. In a related question, can we determine how often judges or law clerks or people designated by judges speak to reporters to help them understand what a decision really means?

- Better training for everyone needs to be encouraged. Reporters—not just beat reporters—but all reporters and their editors need to know about how the judiciary works, and judges surely need to know about journalism. Short courses should be developed. Model curricula for journalism students should be created, and compelling refresher courses should also be instituted. In doing this, recognition must be given to the sad fact that most media organizations stint on devoting resources to training.

- We need to understand larger issues, such as whatever happened to the presumption of innocence. It seems to have been lost, especially when it comes to teenagers, whom we used to think should be treated differently.

. . .

No judge or journalist should be against either formal or informal attempts at mutual understanding. Without question, judges need to learn about journalism, and journalists need to learn about judges. At the "Bench Press" conference, several judges commented how they wanted to see more coverage. "More" does not necessarily mean "better" for judges. For instance, in 2006, the *San Jose Mercury News* ran an in-depth series, three years in preparation, on how local judges made mistakes at criminal trials and how appeals court did little to correct these mistakes.

I think that judges want more *positive* coverage—better public relations, if you will, not necessarily *better* coverage. And journalists unequivocally feel that their job descriptions do not include public relations.

Bridging the wide gap between the bench and the press will not be simple.

Notes

1. 433 U.S. 350 (1977).
2. Jeffrey Rosen, *Judicial Exposure*, N.Y. TIMES BOOK REVIEW, Jan. 29, 2006, at 27.
3. *Id.*
4. *Id.*
5. *Id.*

6. Charles G. Geyh, *Preserving Public Confidence in the Courts in an Age of Individual Rights and Public Skepticism*, this volume at 21.

7. Jeffrey Toobin, Comments at "Bench Press," Panel 2, Impartial Judging in a Results Oriented World (Oct. 17, 2005).

8. *Id.*

9. Richard A. Posner, *Bad News*, N.Y. TIMES BOOK REVIEW, July 31, 2005.

10. David Kirkpatrick, *Two Nominee Strategies. One Worked*, N.Y. TIMES, Jan. 31, 2006 at A19.

11. Maxwell Poll on Civic Engagement and Inequality, at p.5 (Oct. 2005) (margin of error ±5 percent), available at http://www.maxwell.syr.edu/campbell/Poll/CitizenshipPoll.htm. Last visited on August 14, 2006.

12. *Id.*

13. *Id.*

Afterword

The State of Judicial Independence

Anthony Lewis

J USTICE SANDRA DAY O'CONNOR said it: "The present climate is such that I worry about the future of the federal judiciary. . . . In our country today we're seeing efforts to prevent an independent judiciary."[1]

Justice O'Connor's comment, made in July 2005, summed up the concern underlying the "Bench Press" conference that produced the essays in this book. Her words were if anything an understated response to vitriolic verbal attacks on judges, state and federal, and not only verbal. In 2005 Congress intervened aggressively in the work of the federal courts, trampling on the idea of the separation of powers.

Congress's lack of respect for the third branch of the federal government was dramatically demonstrated by the case of Terri Schiavo, the woman who had spent years on life support in a Florida hospital after an accident that left her brain-dead. Her husband, reflecting what he said were her views, wanted to end the artificial measures that kept her alive. Her parents strongly objected. The issue was put to the state courts in Florida. In hearing after hearing they dismissed the parents' objections. The Supreme Court of the United States declined to hear their case. Then Congress intervened. Under the pressure of a campaign by right-to-life groups, both houses passed a bill directing the federal courts to take jurisdiction of issues that had been fully litigated by

James Madison Visiting Professor, Graduate School of Journalism, Columbia University.

the Florida courts in the Schiavo case.² President Bush rushed back to Washington from vacation to sign the bill. Federal judges, trial and appellate, duly considered the Schiavo parents' arguments—and rejected them. The Supreme Court again denied review.

Some members of Congress, who evidently thought they had given the federal judges implicit orders to overthrow the Florida decisions, were furious. The House majority leader, Rep. Tom DeLay, Republican of Texas, threatened impeachment. "The time will come," he says, "for the men responsible for this to answer for their behavior."³

What is striking about that scenario is that the representatives and senators involved paid no attention to themes they have often sounded. One is the rights of states in the federal system; the right of Florida courts to decide questions of Florida law was simply ignored. Another is the often-voiced demand that federal judges follow established precedents, not make new law. All that mattered, plainly, was the result that politics demanded. Congress had no hesitation in trying to make the judicial system reach that result.

Another example: The chairman of the House Judiciary Committee, James Sensenbrenner of Wisconsin, ran a campaign of personal attack on a federal district judge who he said had given excessively light criminal sentences. (The statistics show no such thing.) A staff aide to Sensenbrenner wrote a letter of complaint about a particular sentence to the Court of Appeals that had the case before it. Again, the threat of impeachment was in the air—as well as the reality that the chairman of the judiciary committee has influence on many matters of concern to the federal courts.

Sensenbrenner in 2005 proposed a new device to "punish" federal judges "for behavior that does not rise to the level of impeachable conduct": a judicial inspector general.⁴ His idea was a direct attack on the independence the framers of the Constitution sought to secure for federal judges by making impeachment the sole means to punish misconduct.

It was not only members of Congress who tried to put pressure on judges. The Reverend Pat Robertson of television fame charged in a broadcast that unnamed judges were "destroying the fabric that holds our nation together. Over 100 years, I think the gradual erosion of the consensus that's held our country together is probably more serious than a few bearded terrorists who fly into buildings."⁵

The year 2005 saw an extraordinary political intervention in the judicial process. The Senate adopted a proposal by Senator Lindsey Graham, Republican of South Carolina, to strip the federal courts of jurisdiction to hear habeas corpus petitions by detainees in the Guantanamo Bay, Cuba, prison. The measure eerily paralleled the notorious 1868 law that stripped the Supreme Court of jurisdiction to hear a case challenging the constitutionality of military governments in the South after the Civil War.[6] The House agreed to the Graham proposal, and President Bush signed the bill that included it. In deciding the Hamdan[7] case in June 2006, a 5–4 majority of the Supreme Court held that the court-stripping provision applied only to cases brought by Guantanamo prisoners after the provision became law.

Those who attack the courts and press legislation to make them conform with political wishes do not usually come out and say candidly that they want to do away with judicial independence. As Nina Totenberg explained at the "Bench Press" conference, the attackers try to achieve their ends in any way they can—by smearing judges, threatening impeachment, stripping courts of jurisdiction.

Why is this happening? There are no doubt a number of reasons. One is the growing partisan division in society. We live in a time when broadcast discussions are shouting matches, when the old sense of mutual respect between the parties in Congress is just about gone, when the only thing that matters to the politicians is winning. In that atmosphere, judges are not as likely to be respected for their vital role as simply to be scored as with us or against us.

Another reason, brought out by G. Alan Tarr at the "Bench Press" conference, is that the dockets of both state and federal courts are full of agitated issues that touch the emotions of Americans: abortion, the death penalty, same-sex marriage, tort reform, and the like. On issues like these, people may well care only about the results judges reach rather than the quality of their reasoning.

The agitated issues of today feed directly into another important phenomenon: the increasing politicization of state judicial elections. Most state judges are subject to election in the first place, at later elections to confirm their place on the bench, or both. In the past, judicial elections were almost all low-key affairs, with modest campaign spending. But in recent years interest groups have perceived the potential importance of judicial decisions—notably on such matters as punitive damages in tort cases—and have vastly increased the spending in judicial races and the hard-edged quality of the campaigns.

Millions are now spent in the judicial elections: $4.9 million in Alabama[8] and $9.3 million in Illinois.[9] And spending works. In 2003 and 2004, 35 of 43 races for state supreme court seats were won by the biggest spenders.[10]

As judicial elections have become more like political races in money terms, so they have mimicked the sleazy broadsides that have long been part of the latter. Advertisements describe sitting judges as "anti-family," "soft on crime," or in the case of a judge who presided at trials that produced big damage judgments against corporations, in the pocket of trial lawyers. Candidates even run against courts as institutions. An Alabama lawyer ran successfully for a seat on that state's supreme court in 2004 by attacking "liberal judges" who he said were "trying to take God out of public life."[11] It should be added that Justice Harold See of the Alabama Supreme Court, who was portrayed in his opponent's television ads as a skunk, nevertheless told the "Bench Press" conference that he believed in judicial elections as giving judges legitimacy.

The hope of focusing state judicial elections on issues of character, wisdom, and temperament rather than political views was dealt a severe blow by a Supreme Court decision in 2002, *Republican Party of Minnesota v. White*.[12] Minnesota's code of Judicial Conduct forbade candidates for judgeships from announcing their views on issues. A 5–4 majority held that the rule violated the right of judicial candidates, under the First Amendment, to say what they wished. The decision has exacerbated the trend of judicial races to become more like political campaigns.

Arguments about judges and politics are seldom elegant. The need for judicial independence is hardly mentioned in slanging matches about, for example, what conservatives like to denounce as "activist judges." "Activism" implies a readiness to decide cases not in terms of precedent or legal reasoning but in a way that satisfies the judge's personal preference. But those who use the term advocated interference in the Florida courts' Schiavo decisions—without a thought for the demands of precedent or legal rules. And they do not mention what must be the most "activist" decision of this or perhaps any age, *Bush v. Gore*.[13]

The odd thing is that Americans still believe in judicial independence. Or so they say. In the survey done by Syracuse's Maxwell School in 2005, 73 percent of those surveyed said judges should be shielded from outside pressures.[14] Yet when asked whether judges should be more accountable to elected officials, the same respondents were divided: 34 percent said yes, 56 percent no.[15]

Judicial independence is one of the most profound features of the American polity. John Adams made it a fundamental part of the constitution he wrote for Massachusetts in 1780, and the idea was taken up in the federal Constitution. If Americans come to know what is at stake, I cannot believe they will choose a system like that in China, where political officials tell judges how to decide cases. I cannot believe that we will give up the independent courts that guarantee our rights.

Notes

1. Jim Camden, *Justice Says Independent Courts at Risk*, SPOKESMAN REV., July 22, 2005 at A1.

2. Act for the relief of the parents of Theresa Marie Schiavo, Pub. L. No. 109-3 (Mar. 21, 2005).

3. Charles Babington, *Senator Links Violence to 'Political' Decisions*, WASH. POST, Apr. 5, 2005, at A05.

4. David Kirkpatrick, *Republicans Suggest a Judicial Inspector General*, N.Y. TIMES, May 10, 2005 at 12.

5. Interview with Pat Robertson on *This Week* (ABC, May 1, 2005).

6. Act of March 27, 1868, 15 Stat. at Large, 44. as cited in Ex parte McCardle, 74 U.S. 506 (1868).

7. 126 S.Ct. 2749 (2006).

8. DEBORAH GOLDBERG ET AL., THE NEW POLITICS OF JUDICIAL ELECTIONS 2004 1–12 (2004), *at* http://www.justiceatstake.org/files/NewPoliticsReport2004.pdf.

9. *Id.*

10. *Id.*

11. Tom Parker, candidate for the Supreme Court of Alabama as quoted by Heidi Beirich & Mark Potok, *Honoring the Confederacy*, Intelligence Report, Fall 2004, *at* http://www.splcenter.org/intel/intelreport/article.jsp?aid=491.

12. 536 U.S. 765 (2002).

13. 531 U.S. 98 (2000).

14. Campbell Public Affairs Institute, Maxwell Poll on Civic Engagement and Inequality, at p. 5 (Oct. 2005) (margin of error ±5 percent), http://www.maxwell.syr.edu/campbell/Poll/CitizenshipPoll.htm. Last visited on August 14, 2006.

15. *Id.*

Contributors

The Honorable Joanne F. Alper. Judge, Circuit Court for the Seventeenth Judicial Circuit, Arlington, Virginia. Judge Alper received a B.A., *magna cum laude* from Syracuse University in 1972 and a J.D., with honors, from the George Washington University Law School in 1975. She has been a trial judge in Virginia since 1991 and has been a frequent lecturer at state and national continuing education programs for both judges and lawyers. Judge Alper also serves as a member of the Board of Trustees of Syracuse University.

Keith J. Bybee. Associate Professor of Political Science and Michael O. Sawyer Chair of Constitutional Law and Politics at Syracuse University's Maxwell School of Citizenship and Public Affairs. Bybee directs the Sawyer Law and Politics Program at Maxwell and the Institute for the Study of Judiciary, Politics, and the Media at Syracuse University. He is author of *Mistaken Identity: The Supreme Court and the Politics of Minority Representation* (Princeton University Press, 1998; second printing, 2002). His current research examines the role of courtesy and hypocrisy in the judicial process, and he is in the process of completing a book manuscript entitled, *Legal Courtesy: A Study of Courts, Politics and Hypocrisy* (under contract with Stanford University Press). Before he began teaching at Maxwell in 2002, he was a faculty member in the Department of Government at Harvard University.

Charles Gardner Geyh. The John F. Kimberling Chair in Law, Indiana University at Bloomington. Geyh is the author of *When Courts and Congress Collide: The Struggle for Control of America's Judicial System* (University of Michigan Press, 2006), and coauthor of *Judicial Conduct and Ethics* (4th ed., Lexis Law, forthcoming). He has served as reporter to four American Bar Association Commissions: the Joint Commission to Evaluate the Model Code of Judicial Conduct; the Commission on the 21st Century Judiciary; the Commission on Public Financing of Judicial Campaigns; and the Commission on the Separation of Powers and Judicial Independence. He has also served as reporter to the Constitution Project Task Force on the Distinction between Intimidation and Legitimate Criticism of Judges, as director of the American Judicature Society's Center for Judicial Independence, as consultant to the Parliamentary Development Project on Judicial Independence and Administration for the Supreme Rada of Ukraine, as consultant to the Pennsylvania House of Representatives on the impeachment and removal of Pennsylvania Supreme Court Justice Rolf Larsen, as consultant to the National Commission on Judicial Discipline and Removal, and as legislative liaison to the Federal Courts Study Committee. He currently serves on the Board of Directors of Justice at Stake and on the Steering Committee of the Constitution Project's Courts Initiative.

Tom Goldstein. Former reporter, the *New York Times*, and other publications, and is director of the Mass Communications program at the University of California at Berkeley. He served as the dean of the Graduate School of Journalism at Berkeley and was dean of the school at Columbia University as well.

The Honorable James E. Graves, Jr. Justice, Supreme Court of Mississippi. Prior to joining the supreme court in 2001, Justice Graves served as a circuit court judge for ten years. He has taught trial advocacy at Harvard Law School and has been a jurist-in-residence at the Syracuse University College of Law. He has also been adjunct professor at Jackson State University, Tougaloo College, and Millsaps College where he taught media law, civil rights law, and sociology of law. In 2005, the 100 Black Men of America named him the recipient of its Equal Justice Award; and in 2006, the National Conference of Black Mayors gave him the President's Award. He received his undergraduate degree from Millsaps College, and is a graduate of Syracuse University's College of Law and Maxwell School of Citizenship and Public Affairs.

Anthony Lewis. Former *New York Times* columnist and James Madison Visiting Professor, Graduate School of Journalism, Columbia University. Lewis is author of *Gideon's Trumpet* and *Make No Law: The Sullivan Case and the First Amendment*, both published by Vintage.

Dahlia Lithwick. Senior Editor and Legal Correspondent, *Slate.com*. Lithwick's work has appeared in the *New Republic, Commentary*, the *New York Times*, the *Washington Post*, and the *Los Angeles Times*, among other places. She is a weekly legal commentator for the NPR show *Day to Day*, and her work appears in the *Washington Post's Outlook* section every other week. She cowrote *"Me v. Everybody: Absurd Contracts for an Absurd World"* (Workman, 2003), a legal humor book. She is also author of *"I Will Sing Life: Voices from the Hole in the Wall Gang Camp"* (Little, Brown, 1992), a book about seven children from Paul Newman's camp who have life-threatening illnesses. Lithwick has received several awards from the Online News Association and in 2005 she was voted by the readers of *Legal Affairs* magazine as one of the twenty most influential legal thinkers in America.

Mark Obbie. Visiting Assistant Professor, S.I. Newhouse School of Public Communications, Syracuse University. Obbie teaches newspaper and magazine journalism and media law, and he is developing a legal reporting program with a grant from the Carnegie Corporation of New York. He is the former executive editor of *The American Lawyer* magazine and in his twenty-five years as a legal journalist has been a reporter or editor for the *Houston Post, Texas Lawyer* weekly newspaper, and *Counsel Connect*, a first-generation online service for lawyers.

The Honorable Harold See. Justice, Supreme Court of Alabama. His publications include *The Commercial Law of Intellectual Property* (with P. Alces, Aspen Publishers, 2004); *Justice and Equity* (translation, MIT Press, 2002); "The Separation of Powers and the Public Policy Role of a State Court in a Routine Case," 8 *Texas Review of Law & Politics* 345 (2004); and "An Essay on Legal Ethics and the Search for Truth," 3 *Georgetown Journal of Legal Ethics* 323 (1989).

G. Alan Tarr. Distinguished Professor of Political Science and Director, Center for State Constitutional Studies, Rutgers University-Camden. He is the author of *Understanding State Constitutions* (Princeton University Press, 1998) and *Judicial Processes and Judicial Policymaking* (4th ed., Wadsworth, 2006), and the coeditor of *State Constitutions for the Twenty-first Century* (3 vols. SUNY Press, 2006), *Constitutional Origins, Structure, and Change in Federal Countries* (McGill-Queen's University Press, 2005), and *Federalism, Subnational Constitutions, and Minority Rights* (Praeger Paperback, 2004).

The Honorable John M. Walker, Jr. Chief Circuit Judge on the United States Court of Appeals for the Second Circuit. Formerly, he was a district judge for the Southern District of New York, an assistant secretary of the Treasury for Enforcement and Operations, a partner at Carter, Ledyard & Milburn in New York City, where he specialized in commercial litigation, and an assistant United States attorney for the Southern District of New York in the criminal division. Judge Walker is an adjunct professor at New York University Law School, a visiting lecturer at Yale Law School, and on the teaching faculty of the Institute of Judicial Administration's Appellate Judges Seminar. He is a graduate of Yale College and the University of Michigan Law School.

Cited Authorities

Cases

Bates v. State Bar of Arizona, 433 U.S. 350 (1977).

Bray v. Alexandria Women's Health Clinic, 506 U.S. 263 (1993).

Briggs v. Ohio Elections Com'n, 61 F.3d 487, 492 (6th Cir. 1995).

Brown v. Board of Education, 347 U.S. 483 (1954).

Bush v. Gore, 531 U.S. 98 (2000).

Cheney v. United States District Court, 541 U.S. 913 (2004).

Clinton v. New York, 524 U.S. 417, 450–51 (1998) (Kennedy, J., concurring).

Commonwealth v. Scott, 51 Va. 749, 752 (1853).

Dimes v. Grand Junction Canal, 10 Eng. Rep. 301, 315 (H.L. 1852).

Doe v. Groody, 361 F.3d 232 (3d Cir. 2004).

Dred Scott v. Sandford, 60 U.S. 393 (1856).

Duplantier v. United States, 606 F.2d 654 (5th Cir. 1979), cert. denied, 449 U.S. 1076 (1981).

Estate of Lynde, 250 N.Y.S. 2d 358 (N.Y. App. Div. 1964).

In re Antonio, 612 A. 2d 650, 654 (R.I. 1992).

In re Filipiak, 113 N.E.2d 282, 284 (Ind. 1953) (Emmert, concurring).

In re Gorsuch, 75 N.W. 2d 644 (S.D. 1956).

In re Heggerty, 241 So. 2d 469 (La. 1969).

In re McCutcheon, No. 3 JD 03 (Pa. Ct. of Jud. Discipline, April 15 2004).

In re Somers, 182 N.W. 341 (Mich. 1971).

In re Stanley Greenburg, 280 A.2d. 370 (Pa. 1971).

Kelo v. City of New London, 545 U.S. 469 (2005).

La Rue v. Township of East Brunswick, 172 A. 2d 691 (N.J. App. Div. 1961).

Lochner v. New York, 198 U.S. 45 (1905).

Mississippi Commission on Judicial Performance v. Wilkerson, 867 So. 2d 1006 (Miss. 2004).

Olson v. Cory, 26 Cal. 3d 672 (Cal. 1980).

Planned Parenthood v. Casey, 947 F.2d 682 (3d Cir. 1991).

Plessy v. Ferguson, 163 U.S. 537 (1896).

Quesinberry v. Hull, 159 Va. 270 (1932).

Republican Party of Minnesota v. White, 536 U.S. 765 (2002).

Republican Party of Minnesota v. White, 416 F.3d 738, 754 (8th Cir. 2005).

Roe v. Wade, 410 U.S. 113 (1973).

State v. Lawrence, 123 N.E. 2d. 271 (Oh. 1954).

Tharp v.Massengill, 28 P.2d 502 (Wa. 1933).

United States v. Rybar, 103 F.3d 273 (3d Cir. 1996).

United States v. Will, 449 U.S. 200 (1980).

Woods v. Covington County Bank, 537 F.2d 804, 813 (5th Cir. 1976).

Constitutions

ALASKA CONST. art. IV, § 5.

ALASKA CONST. art. IV, § 6.

ARIZ. CONST. art. VI, § 37.

ARIZ. CONST. art. VI, § 38.

ARK. CONST. amend. 80, § 17.

CAL. CONST. art. VI, § 16.

CAL. CONST., art. 1, §. 27.

COLO. CONST. art. VI, § 20.

COLO. CONST. art. VI, § 25.

CONSTITUTION OF THE REPUBLIC OF BULGARIA, art. 129, 130 (2005).

DEL. CONST. art. IV, § 3.

FLA. CONST. art. V, § 20.

GA. CONST. art. VI, § VII, para. I.

HAW. CONST. art. VI, § 3.

IDAHO CONST. art. VI, § 7.

IOWA CONST. art. V, § 15.

IOWA CONST. art. V, § 17.

ILL. CONST. art. VI, § 12.

KY. CONST. § 117.

LA. CONST. art. V, § 22.

MASS. CONST., Declaration of Rights, art. 26, amendment 1116.

MASS. CONST. pt. 2, ch. 3, art. I.

MD. CONST. art. IV, § 3.

ME. CONST. art. V, pt. 1, § 8.

ME. CONST. art. VI, § 4.

MICH. CONST. art. 6, § 12.

MO. CONST. art. V, § 25(b).

N.C. CONST. art. IV, § 16.

NEB. CONST. art. V, § 21.

N.H. CONST. pt. 2, art. 46.

N.H. CONST. pt. 2, art. 78.

N.J. CONST. art. 6, § 6.

N.M. CONST. art. VI, § 33.

N.M. CONST. art. VI, § 36.

N.Y. CONST. art. VI, § 6.

OKLA. CONST. art. VII, § 8.

OHIO CONST. art. IV, § 6.

ORE. CONST. art. VII, § 1.

PA. CONST. art. V, § 13.

R.I. CONST. art. X, § 4.

S.D. CONST. art. V, § 7.

TEX. CONST. art. 5, § 7.

U.S. CONST. art. I, § 2.

U.S. CONST. art. I, § 3.

U.S. CONST. art. II, § 2.

U.S. CONST. art. II, § 1.

U.S. CONST. art. II, § 9, cl. 7.

U.S. CONST. art. III, § 1.

U.S. CONST. amend. XVII.

UTAH CONST. art. VIII, § 8.

UTAH CONST. art. VIII, § 9.

VA. CONST., art. V, 1 (1830).

VA. CONST. of 1869, art. VI, 5, 11.

VA. CONST. of 1851, art. VI, 6, 10, 27, 34.

VA. CONST. art. VI, § 7 (1971).

VA. CONST. art. VI, § 7.

VA. CONST. art. VI, § 9.

VA. CONST. art. VI, 10.

VT. CONST. § 32.

WYO. CONST. art. V, § 4.

WIS. CONST. art. VII, § 9.

Statutes

Ala. Code § 17-2-2.

Conn. Gen. Stat. Ann. 51-44a.

Ind. Code Ann. § 3-10-2-11.

Kan. Stat. Ann. § 20-2901.

Va. Code Ann. §17.1-400.

Va. Code Ann. §16.1-69.9(c).
Va. Code Ann. § 17.1-100 (2005).
Title 16.1, Va. Code Ann. (1950).
S.C. Code Ann. § 2-19-90.
Minn. Stat. Ann. 204B.06.
Miss. Code Ann. § 23-15-976.
Mont. Code Ann. § 13-14-211.
N.D. Cent. Code 16.1-11-08.
R.I. Gen. Laws § 8-16.1-7.
S.C. Code Ann. 2-19-80.
Tenn. Code Ann. 17-1-103.
Vt. Stat. Ann. Tit 4, § 71.
W. Va. Code Ann. 3-1-17.
Wash. Rev. Code Ann. 29A.52.231.

Legislative materials

Impeachment Charges Against Judge Kenesaw Mountain Landis, House Rep. No. 1407, 66th Cong. 3d Sess., March 2, 1921.

Restatement (Third) of the Law Governing Lawyers § 5(c) (2000).

Non-judicial activities of Supreme Court Justices: Hearing on S. 1097 Before the Subcomm. On Separation of Powers of the Senate Comm. On the Judiciary, 91st Cong. 1st Sess. (1969).

Bibliography

Owen G. Abbe & Paul S. Hernson, How Judicial Election Campaigns Have Changed, 85 JUDICATURE 286 (2002).

The Abrams Report (MSNBC, Nov. 1, 2005), available at http://www.msnbc.msn.com/id/9896554/.

Leslie Abramson, Canon 2 of the Code of Judicial Conduct, 79 MARQ. L. REV. 949, 955 (1996).

Jonathan Adler, Op-Ed, Not All Law Is Politics in Robes, WALL ST. J., Jan. 14, 2006, at A9.

Administrative Office of the U.S. Courts, News Release: Judicial Conference Opposes Sweeping Restrictions on Educational Programs, Sept. 19, 2000.

Alabama State Supreme Court Elections Data 2004, available at http://www.justiceatstake.org/contentViewer.asp>breadcrumb=4,124,47,489. Last visited on August 14, 2006.

JAMES ALFINI, CHARLES GARDNER GEYH & STEVEN LUBET, JUDICIAL CONDUCT AND ETHICS §4.02 (3d Ed. 2004 Supp).

DEAN E. ALGER, THE MEDIA AND POLITICS 177 (1989).

Akhil Reed Amar, A Neo-Federalist View of Article III: Separating the Two Tiers of Federal Jurisdiction, 65 B. U. L. REV. 205, 227 n. 81 (1985).

AMERICAN BAR ASSOCIATION, CANONS OF JUDICIAL ETHICS (1924).

American Bar Association Comm. On Evaluation of Model Rules of Prof'l Conduct 53 (Prop. Final Draft 1981).

AMERICAN BAR ASSOCIATION, Formal Op. 342, n. 17 (1975).

AMERICAN BAR ASSOCIATION, JUSTICE IN JEOPARDY: REPORT OF THE COMMISSION ON THE 21ST CENTURY JUDICIARY 10 (2003) (JUSTICE IN JEOPARDY).

AMERICAN BAR ASSOCIATION, JUSTICE IN JEOPARDY: REPORT OF THE COMMISSION ON THE 21ST CENTURY JUDICIARY 29 (2002) (JUSTICE IN JEOPARDY).

AMERICAN BAR ASSOCIATION, MODEL CODE OF JUDICIAL CONDUCT, Canon 2.E.(1)(e).

AMERICAN BAR ASSOCIATION, MODEL CODE OF PROFESSIONAL RESPONSIBILITY, Canon 9 (1969).

AMERICAN BAR ASSOCIATION, PERCEPTIONS OF THE U.S. JUSTICE SYSTEM 1 (1999), available at http://www.abanet.org/media/perception/perception6.html. Last visited on August 14, 2006.

AMERICAN BAR ASSOCIATION, REPORT OF THE COMMISSION ON PUBLIC FINANCING OF JUDICIAL CAMPAIGNS 1–2 (2002).

AMERICAN BAR ASSOCIATION, REPORT OF THE COMMISSION ON PUBLIC FINANCING OF JUDICIAL CAMPAIGNS 34–37 (2002).

Address of the President, 33 REPORT OF THE 31ST ANNUAL MEETING OF THE AMERICAN BAR ASSOCIATION 341 (1908).

AMERICAN BAR ASSOCIATION, SECTION OF LITIGATION, PUBLIC PERCEPTIONS OF LAWYERS: CONSUMER RESEARCH FINDINGS 6, 29 (2002).

American Bar Association, Symposium II: Public Understanding and Perceptions of the American Justice System (Feb. 1999), available at http://www.abanet.org/media/perception/perception.html. Last visited on August 14, 2006.

American Judicature Society, Merit Selection: The Best Way to Choose the Best Judges, available at http://www.ajs.org/js/ms_descrip.pdf.

AMERICAN JUDICATURE SOCIETY, JUDICIAL SELECTION IN THE STATES: APPELLATE AND GENERAL JURISDICTION COURTS (2004), available at http://www.ajs.org/js/JudicialSelectionCharts.pdf.

AMERICAN JUDICATURE SOCIETY, JUDICIAL MERIT SELECTION: CURRENT STATUS (2003).

Seth Andersen, Examining the Decline in Support for Merit Selection in the States, 67 ALB. L. REV. 793 (2004).

Matt Apuzzo, Supreme Court Rules Cities May Seize Homes, ASSOC. PRESS, June 24, 2005, available at http://www.sfgate.com/cgi-bin/article.cgi?f=/n/a/2005/06/23/national/w073747D75.DTL.

Article III Groupie (David Lat), Too Sexy For Their Robes: The Nominees for Super-hotties of the Federal Judiciary!, UNDERNEATH THEIR ROBES, July 7, 2004, available at http://underneaththeirrobes.blogs.com/main/2004/07/_general_commen.html.

Larry T. Aspin, Trends in Judicial Retention Elections, 1964–1998, 83 JUDICATURE 79 (1999).

Larry T. Aspin et al., Thirty Years of Judicial Retention Elections: An Update, 37 SOC. SCI. J. 1 (2000).

Larry T. Aspin & William K. Hall, Retention Elections and Judicial Behavior, 77 JUDICATURE 306, table 4 (1994).

Ken Auletta, The Howell Doctrine, NEW YORKER, June 10, 2002, at 48.

Charles Babington, *Senators Praise Nominee's Candor; Alito Shows Willingness to Discuss Controversial Issues Facing Supreme Court*, WASH. POST, Nov. 5, 2005, at A07.

Charles Babington & Amy Goldstein, Alito on Day 1: A Judge Can't Have Any Agenda, WASH. POST, Jan. 10, 2006, at A01.

Charles Babington & Amy Goldstein, Specter Bucks White House on Alito; Judiciary

Panel Hearing on Supreme Court Nominee Is Set for January, WASH. POST, Nov. 4, 2005, at A07.

Peter Baker, Alito Nomination Sets Stage for Ideological Battle, WASH. POST, Nov. 1, 2005, at A01.

Peter Baker & Charles Babington, Moderates' Support Sought for Alito, WASH. POST, Nov. 2, 2005, at A06.

Dan Balz, With a Pick From the Right, Bush Looks to Rally GOP in Tough Times, WASH. POST, Nov. 1, 2005, at A06.

David Barnhizer, "On the Make": Campaign Funding and the Corrupting of the American Judiciary, 50 CATH. U. L. REV. 361, 365 n. 10 (2001).

Dave Barry, Year On the Verge of a Nervous Breakdown, WASH. POST, Jan. 1, 2006, at A-W08.

Brian Basinger, Perdue Looks at Partisan Judicial Races, AUGUSTA CHRON., May 23, 2005, available at http://chronicle.augusta.com/stories/052405/met_4227612.shtml.

William C. Bayne, Lynchard's Candidacy, Ads Putting Spice into Judicial Race, COMMERCIAL APPEAL, Oct. 29, 2000, at DS1.

Jo Becker & Dale Russakoff, Proving His Mettle in the Reagan Justice Dept., WASH. POST, Jan. 9, 2006, at A01.

Robert Becker, Convicted Judge Seeks $113,222: Shields Contends State Owes Pension Payout, CHI. TRIB., Apr. 26, 2000, at 1.

Nancy Benac, Alito Seen As Smart, Serious, Cautious, ASSOC. PRESS (as published in WASH. POST), Jan. 3, 2006.

Larry C. Berkson, Judicial Selection in the United States: A Special Report, 64 JUDICATURE 176 (1980).

Luke Bierman, Beyond Merit Selection, 29 FORDHAM URB. L. J. 851 (2002).

EARL BLACK & MERLE BLACK, THE RISE OF THE SOUTHERN REPUBLICANS (2002).

1 BLACKSTONE'S COMMENTARIES, Appendix, 115–16 (St. George Tucker, ed., 1803).

Chris Bonneau, Patterns of Campaign Spending and Electoral Competition in State Supreme Court Elections, 25 JUST. SYS. J. 21 (2004).

Chris Bonneau & Melinda Gann Hall, Predicting Challengers in State Supreme Court Elections: Context and the Politics of Institutional Design, 56 POL. RES. Q. 337–49 (2003).

DANIEL BOORSTIN, THE IMAGE: A GUIDE TO PSEUDO-EVENTS IN AMERICA (1961).

MATTHEW H. BOSWORTH, COURTS AS CATALYSTS: STATE SUPREME COURTS AND PUBLIC SCHOOL FINANCE EQUITY (2001).

Paul Brace & Melinda Gann Hall, Studying Courts Comparatively: The View from the American States, 48 POL. RES. Q. 13–24 (1995).

William Branigin, Fred Barbash, & Daniela Deane, Supreme Court Justice O'Connor Resigns, WASH. POST, July 1, 2005, available at http://www.washingtonpost.com/wp-dyn/content/article/2005/07/01/AR2005070100653.html.

Jess Bravin, Alito Prefers Scalpel to Sledgehammer: Allies Hope Less Combative Style Makes Judge More Effective in Moving Court to the Right, WALL ST. J., Nov. 16, 2005, at A4.

Stephen B. Bright, Can Judicial Independence Be Attained in the South: Overcoming History, Elections, and Misperceptions about the Role of the Judiciary, 14 GA. ST. U. L. REV. 817, 859 (1998).

STEPHEN BREYER, ACTIVE LIBERTY: INTERPRETING OUR DEMOCRATIC CONSTITUTION (2005).

"Essays of Brutus" in THE ANTI-FEDERALIST 183 (Herbert Storing, ed., University of Chicago Press, 1985).

W. Hamilton Bryson, Judicial Independence in Virginia, 38 U. RICH. L. REV. 705, 711 (2004).

Brian Buescher, Out with the Code and in With the Rules: The Disastrous Nebraska "Bright Line" Rule for Conflict of Interest: A Direct Consequence of the Shortcomings in the Model Code, 12 GEO. J. LEGAL ETHICS 717 (1999).

Elisabeth Bumiller & Carl Hulse, Bush Picks U.S. Appeals Judge to Take O'Connor's Court Seat, N.Y. TIMES, Nov. 1, 2005, at A1.

Stephen B. Burbank & Barry Friedman, Reconsidering Judicial Independence, in JUDICIAL INDEPENDENCE AT THE CROSSROADS: AN INTERDISCIPLINARY APPROACH 37 (Burbank & Friedman, eds., 2002).

BUREAU OF JUSTICE STATISTICS, U.S. DEPARTMENT OF JUSTICE, STATE COURT ORGANIZATION 1998, available at http://www.ojp.usdoj.gov/bjs/abstract/sco98.htm.

President George W. Bush, Statement on the nomination of Harriet Miers to the Supreme Court (Oct. 3, 2005), available at http://www.whitehouse.gov/news/releases/2005/10/20051003.html.

President George W. Bush, Statement on the nomination of Samuel Alito to the Supreme Court (Oct. 31, 2005), available at http://www.whitehouse.gov/news/releases/2005/10/20051031.html.

Jim Camden, Justice Says Independent Courts at Risk, SPOKESMAN REV. (Spokane), July 22, 2005, at A1.

J. CAMPBELL, LIVES OF THE CHIEF JUSTICES OF ENGLAND 208 (1873).

Tom Campbell, Henrico Judge Was Disciplined, RICHMOND TIMES DISPATCH, Dec. 13, 2005, at B3.

Campbell Public Affairs Institute, The Maxwell Poll on Civic Engagement and Inequality, (Oct. 2005) (margin of error ± 5%), available at http://www.maxwell.syr.edu/campbell/Poll/2005Poll/MaxwellPoll.pdf. Last visited on August 14, 2006.

Paul D. Carrington, Butterfly Effects: the Possibilities of Law Teaching in a Democracy, 41 DUKE L. J. 741, 780 n. 206 (1992).

Paul D. Carrington, Judicial Independence and Democratic Accountability in Highest State Courts, 61 LAW & CONTEMP. PROBS. 79, 111 (1998).

PAUL D. CARRINGTON, DANIEL J. MEADOR, & MAURICE ROSENBERG, JUSTICE ON APPEAL 150 (1976).

Statement of Hill Carter, Debates of the Virginia Constitutional Convention 1901–02 at 1399, Dec. 4, 1901.

Anthony Champagne & Kyle Cheek, The Cycle of Judicial Elections: Texas as a Case Study, 29 FORDHAM URB. L. J. 907, 929 (2002).

Anthony Champagne, National Summit on Improving Judicial Selection: Interest Groups and Judicial Elections, 34 LOY. L.A. L. REV. 1391, 1402 (2001).

Kyle Cheek & Anthony Champagne, Money in Texas Supreme Court Elections, 1980–1998, 84 JUDICATURE 20, 22 (2000).

Erwin Chemerinsky, FEDERAL JURISDICTION 49–54 (4th ed. 2003).

ADDRESSES AND ORATIONS OF RUFUS CHOATE 360–63 (6th Ed. 1891).

Memorandum from Roger Clegg, Associate Deputy Attorney General, Department of Justice to Carol E. Dinkins, Deputy Attorney General, Department of Justice (Aug. 1, 1984) (on file with the National Archives), available at http://www.archives.gov/news/samuel-alito/accession-060-88-258/Acc060-88-258-box5-memoCleggtoDinkins-Aug1984.pdf.

Lynette Clemetson, Alito Could Be 5th Catholic on Current Supreme Court, N.Y. TIMES, Nov. 1, 2005, at A23.

Michael Comiskey, Not Guilty: The News Media in the Supreme Court Confirmation Process, J. L. & POL. (Winter 1999).

Code of Conduct for United States Judges, Canon 7(A).

Steven P. Croley, The Majoritarian Difficulty: Elective Judiciaries and the Rule of Law, 62 U. CHI. L. REV. 689 (1995).

John H. Culver & John T. Wold, Judicial Reform in California, in JUDICIAL REFORM IN THE STATES 139, 154–55 (Anthony Champagne & Judith Haydel eds., 1993).

John H. Culver & John T. Wold, Rose Bird and the Politics of Judicial Accountability in California, 70 JUDICATURE 81 (1986).

Jay A. Daugherty, The Missouri Non-Partisan Court Plan: A Dinosaur on the Edge of Extinction or a Survivor in a Changing Socio-Legal Environment, 62 MO. L. REV. 315, 319 (1997).

Richard Davis, Lifting the Shroud: News Media Portrayal of the U.S. Supreme Court, COMMUNICATIONS AND THE LAW 54 (Oct. 1987).

Richard Davis & Vincent James Strickler, The Invisible Dance: The Supreme Court and the Press, PERSPECTIVES ON POL. SCI. 85 (Spring 2000).

THE DECLARATION OF INDEPENDENCE (U.S. 1776).

Joseph Deitch, New Jersey Q&A: Harold A. Ackerman; Seeking a Raise for Federal Judges, N.Y. TIMES, Aug. 20, 1989, at 12NJ3.

Paul J. De Muniz, Eroding the Public's Confidence in Judicial Impartiality: First Amendment Jurisprudence and Special Interest Financing of Judicial Campaigns, 67 ALB. L. REV. 763, 764 (2004).

Lyle Denniston & Arch Parsons, Rights Groups Await NAACP's Call on Thomas Nomination, BALT. SUN, July 31, 1991, at 3A.

Michael R. Dimino, The Futile Quest for a System of Judicial 'Merit' Selection, 67 ALB. L. REV. 803, 813 (2004).

Michael R. Dimino, Sr., The Worst Way of Selecting Judges—Except All the Others That Have Been Tried, 32 N. KY. L. REV. 267 (2005).

PHILIP L. DUBOIS, FROM BALLOT TO BENCH: JUDICIAL ELECTIONS AND THE QUEST FOR ACCOUNTABILITY (1980).

Editorial, Weakening the Rules for Judges, N.Y. TIMES, May 22, 2004, at A16.

Editorial, This Is No Way to Choose Who's on Appeals Courts, MOBILE REG., Nov. 8, 2000, at 12A.

Editorial, Judge Alito and Abortion, N.Y. TIMES, Dec. 3, 2005, at A18.

Editorial, Another Lost Opportunity, N.Y. TIMES, Nov. 1, 2005, at A26.

Editorial, Secret Judge-Makers, WASH. POST, Jan. 30, 1980, at A22.

James Eisenstein, Financing Pennsylvania's Supreme Court Candidates, 84 JUDICATURE 10, 12 (2000).

Richard E. Ellis, THE JEFFERSONIAN CRISIS: COURTS AND POLITICS IN THE YOUNG REPUBLIC (1971).

CHARLES R. EPP, THE RIGHTS REVOLUTION: LAWYERS, ACTIVISTS, AND SUPREME COURTS IN COMPARATIVE PERSPECTIVE (1998).

Lee Epstein et al., Selecting Selection Systems, in JUDICIAL INDEPENDENCE AT THE CROSSROADS: AN INTERDISCIPLINARY APPROACH 198 (Stephen B. Burbank & Barry Friedman, eds., 2002).

SARI S. ESCOVITZ ET AL., JUDICIAL SELECTION AND TENURE 6 (1975).

WILLIAM N. ESKRIDGE, DYNAMICS OF STATUTORY INTERPRETATION (1994).

PATRICIA EWICK & SUSAN SILBEY, THE COMMON PLACE OF LAW: STORIES FROM EVERYDAY LIFE (1998).

John D. Fabian, The Paradox of Elected Judges: Tension in the American Judicial System, 15 GEO. J. LEGAL ETHICS 155, 156–57 (2001).

Richard H. Fallon, Jr., Daniel J. Meltzer, and David L. Shapiro, HART & WECHSLER'S THE FEDERAL COURTS AND THE FEDERAL SYSTEM 67 (5th ed. 2003).

THE RECORDS OF THE FEDERAL CONVENTION OF 1787 app. A, at 85 (Max Farrand, ed., 1911).

THE FEDERALIST NO. 1.

THE FEDERALIST NO. 10 (Madison).

THE FEDERALIST NO. 47 (Madison).

THE FEDERALIST NO. 48 (Madison).

THE FEDERALIST NO. 49 (Madison).

THE FEDERALIST NO. 63 (Madison).

THE FEDERALIST NO. 68 (Hamilton).

THE FEDERALIST NO. 76 (Hamilton).

THE FEDERALIST NO. 78 (Hamilton).

THE FEDERALIST NO. 81 (Hamilton).

Federalist Society, White Paper Task Force, The Case for Partisan Judicial Elections, 33 U. TOL. L. REV. 393, 401 (2002).

Federalist Society, White Paper Task Force, The Case for Partisan Judicial Elections, 33 U. TOL. L. REV. 353, 363 (2002).

Bruce Fein, Squandering a Supreme Opportunity, WASH. TIMES, Sept. 30, 2005.

Victor Eugene Flango & Nora F. Blair, Creating an Intermediate Appellate Court: Does It Reduce the Caseload of a State's Highest Court? 64 JUDICATURE 74–84 (1980).

Michael A. Fletcher, A Rapid Response on All Sides, WASH. POST, Nov. 1, 2005, at A10.

Charles H. Franklin, Behavioral Factors Affecting Judicial Independence, in Burbank & Friedman, eds. (2002) at 152.

Barry Friedman, Mediated Popular Constitutionalism, 101 MICH. L. REV. 2596, 2609 (2003).

MICHAEL J. GERHARDT, CONSTITUTIONAL THEORY: ARGUMENTS AND PERSPECTIVES (1993).

Josh Gerstein, Ruling Allows Governments to Wrest Property from Citizens, N.Y. SUN, June 24, 2005, at 1.

CHARLES GARDNER GEYH, WHEN COURTS AND CONGRESS COLLIDE: THE STRUGGLE FOR CONTROL OF AMERICA'S JUDICIAL SYSTEM (2006).

Charles Garner Geyh, Why Judicial Elections Stink, 64 OH. ST. L. J. 43, 54–55 (2003).

Henry R. Glick, The Promise and Performance of the Missouri Plan: Judicial Selection in the Fifty States, 32 U. MIAMI L. REV. 509, 519 (1978).

Henry R. Glick & Craig F. Emmert, Selection Systems and Judicial Characteristics: The Recruitment of State Supreme Court Judges, 70 JUDICATURE 229–35 (1986).

Megan Garvey & Jessica Garrison, Judge's Loss Stuns Experts, L.A. TIMES, June 8, 2006, at B1.

STEPHEN GILLERS & ROY D. SIMON, REGULATION OF LAWYERS: STATUTES AND STANDARDS 4 (2005).

Mark Gillispie, 3 More Officials Face Charges: Corruption of Judiciary Probe Continues, THE PLAIN DEALER (Cleveland), Oct. 26, 1999, at 3B.

DEBORAH GOLDBERG ET AL., THE NEW POLITICS OF JUDICIAL ELECTIONS 2000 8 (2000), available at http://faircourts.org/files/JASMoneyReport.PDF.

DEBORAH GOLDBERG ET AL., THE NEW POLITICS OF JUDICIAL ELECTIONS 2004: HOW SPECIAL INTEREST PRESSURE ON OUR COURTS HAS REACHED A "TIPPING POINT"—AND HOW TO KEEP OUR COURTS FAIR AND IMPARTIAL, at 14, figure 9 (2004).

DEBORAH GOLDBERG ET AL., THE NEW POLITICS OF JUDICIAL ELECTIONS 2002: HOW THE THREAT TO FAIR AND IMPARTIAL COURTS SPREAD TO MORE STATES IN 2002, at 18, figure 9 (2002).

DEBORAH GOLDBERG ET AL., THE NEW POLITICS OF JUDICIAL ELECTIONS: HOW 2000 WAS A WATERSHED YEAR FOR BIG MONEY, SPECIAL INTEREST PRESSURE, AND TV ADVERTISING IN STATE SUPREME COURT CAMPAIGNS, at 11, figure 5 (2000).

Jonna Goldschmidt & Jeffrey Shaman, Judicial Disqualification: What Do Judges Think?, 80 JUDICATURE 68, 71 (1996).

Amy Goldstein & Jo Becker, Critics See Ammunition in Alito's Rights Record, WASH. POST, Nov. 3, 2005, at A01.

Amy Goldstein & Sarah Cohen, Alito, In and Out of the Mainstream: Nominee's Record Defies Stereotyping, WASH. POST, Jan. 1, 2006, at A01.

DORIS GRABER, MASS MEDIA AND AMERICAN POLITICS 93 (1989).

James E. Graves, Jr., A Look Back at Brown v. Board of Education, 43 JUDGES' J. 25 (Spring 2004).

Linda Greenhouse, Abortion Case from 1991 May Be Central in Confirmation, N.Y. TIMES, Nov. 1, 2005, at A1.

Linda Greenhouse, TV Ad Attacking Court Nominee Provokes Furor, N.Y. TIMES, Aug. 11, 2005.

Marla Greenstein, Ethical Relativity, 41 JUDGES J. 38, 38 (2002).

DAVID L. GREY, THE SUPREME COURT AND THE NEWS MEDIA 50 (1968).

Kenyon N. Griffin & Michael J. Horan, Patterns of Voter Behavior in Judicial Retention Elections for Supreme Court Justices in Wyoming, 67 JUDICATURE 68, 72 (1983).

Roger D. Groot, The Effects of an Intermediate Appellate Court on the Supreme Court Work Product: The North Carolina Experience, 7 WAKE FOREST L. REV. 548–72 (1971).

Kermit L. Hall, Progressive Reform and the Decline of Democratic Accountability: The Popular Election of State Supreme Court Justices, 1850–1920, AM. B. FOUND. RES. J. (1984).

Melinda Gann Hall, Electoral Politics and Strategic Voting in State Supreme Courts, 54 J. POL. 427, 428 (1992).

Melinda Gann Hall, State Supreme Courts in American Democracy: Probing the Myths of Judicial Reform, 95 AM. POL. SCI. REV. 324 (2001).

Jessie Halladay, Askew Hangs Up Robe; Judge Ends Her Career After 8 Years on Bench, DAILY PRESS, Mar. 15, 2003, at C1.

Hardball with Chris Matthews (MSNBC, Oct. 31, 2005), available at http://www. msnbc.msn.com/id/9884432/.

Nathan S. Heffernan, Judicial Responsibility, Judicial Independence and the Election of Judges, 80 MARQ. L. REV. 1031, 1048 (1997).

Emily Heller, Judicial Races Get Meaner, NAT'L L. J., Oct. 25, 2004, available at http:// www.law.com/jsp/article.jsp?id=1098217051328.

Neil Hicky, Money Lust: How Pressure for Profit Is Perverting Journalism, in THE POWER OF THE PRESS 36 (Beth Levy & Denise Bonilla, eds. 1999).

RAN HIRSCHL, TOWARD JURISTOCRACY: THE ORIGINS AND CONSEQUENCES OF THE NEW CONSTITUTIONALISM (2004).

MORTON HORWITZ, THE TRANSFORMATION OF AMERICAN LAW, 1870–1960: THE CRISIS OF LEGAL ORTHODOXY (1992).

Gregory A. Huber & Sanford C. Gordon, Accountability and Coercion: Is Justice Blind When It Runs for Office? 48 AM. J. POL. SCI. 247–63 (2004).

Cynthia Jacob, A Polemic Against R.P.C. 1.7(C)(2): The Appearance of Impropriety Rule, THE NEW JERSEY LAWYER 23 (June 1996).

Gary Jacobson, Party Polarization in National Politics: The Electoral Connection, in POLARIZED POLITICS: CONGRESS AND THE PRESIDENT IN A PARTISAN ERA 25 (Jon R. Bond & Richard Fleisher, eds., 2000).

Stewart Jay, Origins of Federal Common Law, 133 U. PA. L. REV. 1003, 1116 (1985).

Judicial Confirmation Network, Real America, Television advertisement, available at http://www.judicialnetwork.com/contents/alito/jcn_ad.shtml.

Justice at Stake, National Survey Results (2001), available at http://faircourts.org/files/JASNationalSurveyResults.pdf.

Robert A. Kagan, Bliss Cartwright, Lawrence M. Friedman & Stanton Wheeler, The Business of State Supreme Courts, 1870–1970, 30 STAN. L. REV. 121 (1977).

Robert A. Kagan, Bliss Cartwright, Lawrence M. Friedman & Stanton Wheeler, The Evolution of State Supreme Courts, 76 MICH. L. REV. 961 (1978).

LAURA KALMAN, THE STRANGE CAREER OF LEGAL LIBERALISM 13 (1996).

ROBERT E. KEETON, VENTURING TO DO JUSTICE: REFORMING PRIVATE LAW 3 (1969).

CECELIA KENYON, INTRODUCTION, THE ANTI-FEDERALISTS (Cecelia Kenyon, ed., Bobbs-Merrill, 1966).

Orin Kerr, Pro-Alito Ad Goes Over the Top, VOLOKH CONSPIRACY, Dec. 12, 2005, available at http://volokh.com/archives/archive_2005_12_11-2005_12_17.shtml#1134419252.

David D. Kirkpatrick, Alito Team Says He Lacks Polish, but Grit Is a Plus, N.Y. TIMES, Jan. 2, 2006, at A1.

David D. Kirkpatrick, *Conservatives Scrambling to Prepare for a Tough Fight*, N.Y. TIMES, Nov. 1, 2005, at A23.

David D. Kirkpatrick, Debate in Senate on Alito Heats Up Over '85 Memo, N.Y. TIMES, Nov. 17, 2005, at A26.

David D. Kirkpatrick, Judge Said He Struggled On '91 Abortion Opinion, N.Y. TIMES, Nov. 3, 2005, at A24.

David D. Kirkpatrick, *Two Nominee Strategies. One Worked*, N.Y. TIMES, Jan. 31, 2006, at A19.

David D. Kirkpatrick & Carl Hulse, G.O.P. Reaches to Other Party on Court Pick, N.Y. TIMES, Nov. 2, 2005, at A1.

Alan T. Klots, The Selection of Judges and the Short Ballot, 38 J. AM. JUD. SOC'Y. 134 (1955).

Alex Kozinski, The Appearance of Propriety, LEGAL AFFAIRS, Feb. 2005, at 19.

Nicholas D. Kristof, Drop the Judicial Activism, INT'L HERALD TRIB., Oct. 5, 2005, at 7.

Stephen Labaton, Court Nominee Has Paper Trail Businesses Like, N.Y. TIMES, Nov. 5, 2005, at A1.

Elizabeth B. Lacy, Annual Survey of Virginia Law: Foreword: The Challenges: Past Is Prologue, 38 U. RICH. L. REV. 5, 11 (2003).

Chief Justice Joseph E. Lambert of the Supreme Court of Kentucky, Contestable Judicial Elections: Maintaining Respectability in the Post-White Era, 94 KY. L. J. 1 (Apr. 14, 2005).

Jonathan S. Landay, In 1984 Memo, Alito Defends Domestic Wiretaps, MERCURY NEWS, Dec. 23, 2005, available at http://www.mercurynews.com/mld/mercurynews/news/politics/13476545.htm. Last visited on August 14, 2006.

Charles Lane, Alito Leans Right Where O'Connor Swung Left, WASH. POST, Nov. 1, 2005, at A01.

Charles Lane, Alito Respectful of Precedent, Associates Say, WASH. POST, Nov. 6, 2005, at A13.

Charles Lane, Nominee's Reasoning Points to a Likely Vote Against Roe v. Wade, WASH. POST, Nov. 2, 2005, at A06.

Elizabeth A. Larkin, Judicial Selection Methods: Judicial Independence and Popular Democracy, 79 DENV. U. L. REV. 65, 85 (2001).

BARRY LATZER, STATE CONSTITUTIONS AND CRIMINAL JUSTICE (1993).

Mark Leibovich, A Very Tight Grip-and-Grin, WASH. POST, Nov. 1, 2005, at C01.

Neil A. Lewis, *In Cases Involving Federal Government, Nominee Is Seen as Favoring Authority of the States*, N.Y. TIMES, Nov. 6, 2005, at A28.

Neil A. Lewis & Scott Shane, *The Methodical Jurist*, N.Y. TIMES, Nov. 1, 2005, at A1.

Hans A. Linde, The Judge as Political Candidate, 40 CLEV. ST. L. REV. 1, 7 (1992).

Adam Liptak & Jonathan D. Glater, Alito's Dissents Show Deference to Lower Courts, N.Y. TIMES, Nov. 3, 2005, at A1.

Adam Liptak, In Abortion Rulings, Idea of Marriage Is Pivotal, N.Y. TIMES, Nov. 2, 2005, at A1.

Adam Liptak & Jonathan Glater, *Lucid Rulings Tackling Many of Biggest Issues*, N.Y. TIMES, Nov. 1, 2005, at A25.

Dahlia Lithwick, Address at the dedication of the Charlottesville monument to Free Speech (Apr. 20, 2006), available at http://loper.org/~george/trends/2006/Apr/926.html.

Alex B. Long, An Historical Perspective on Judicial Selection Methods in Virginia and West Virginia, 18 J. L. & POL. 691, 711–12 (2002).

Lou Dobbs Tonight (CNN, Oct. 31, 2005), available at http://transcripts.cnn.com/TRANSCRIPTS/0510/31/ldt.01.html.

Nicholas P. Lovich, Citizen Knowledge and Voting in Judicial Elections, 73 JUDICATURE 28, 32–33 (1989).

DAVID LUBLIN, THE REPUBLICAN SOUTH: DEMOCRATIZATION AND PARTISAN CHANGE (2004).

JOHN P. MACKENZIE, THE APPEARANCE OF JUSTICE 182 (1974).

Michelle Malkin, Your Home Is Not Your Castle, MICHELLEMALKIN.COM, June 23, 2005, available at http://michellemalkin.com/archives/002830.htm

KENNETH A. MANASTER, ILLINOIS JUSTICE: THE SCANDAL OF 1969 AND THE RISE OF JOHN PAUL STEVENS (2001).

Paul Marcus & Vicki Waye, Australia and the United States: Two Common Criminal Justice Systems Uncommonly at Odds, 12 TUL. J. INT'L & COMP. L. 27, 109 (2004).

Robert Martineau, Enforcement of the Code of Judicial Conduct, 1972 UTAH L. REV. 410, 411.

Tony Mauro, A Field Guide to the Alito Confirmation Hearings, LEGAL TIMES, Jan. 9, 2006.

Tony Mauro, Breyer Consulted Ethics Expert Over Sentencing Case Recusal, LEGAL TIMES, Jan. 17, 2005.

Nolan McCarty et al., The Hunt for Party Discipline in Congress, 95 AM. POL. SCI. REV. 673–87 (2001).

Madison B. McClellan, Merit Appointment Versus Popular Election: A Reformer's Guide to Judicial Selection Method in Florida, 43 FLA. L. REV. 529, 548 (1991).

Michael McGough, Alito Critics Focus on 10 Appellate Opinions: Say He Would Shift Top Court to Right, PITT. POST-GAZETTE, Nov. 25, 2005, at A20.

Michael McGough, Roberts to Face Tough Questions, PITT. POST-GAZETTE, Sept. 12, 2005, at A1.

Aman McLeod, If at First You Don't Succeed: A Critical Analysis of Judicial Selection Reform Efforts, 107 W. VA. L. REV. 499 (2005).

Matthew Medina, Note, The Constitutionality of the 2003 Revisions to Canon 3(E) of the Model Code of Judicial Conduct, 104 COLUM. L. REV. 1072 (2004).

LISA MILORD, THE DEVELOPMENT OF THE ABA JUDICIAL CODE 8 (1992).

MINISTRY OF JUSTICE OF NEW ZEALAND, APPOINTING JUDGES: A JUDICIAL APPOINTMENT COMMISSION FOR NEW ZEALAND? (Apr. 2004), available at http://www.justice.govt.nz/pubs/reports/2004/judicial-appointment.

Letter from Ronald Minkoff, on behalf of the Association of Professional Responsibility Lawyers, to the ABA Joint Commission to Evaluate the Model Code of Judicial Conduct, June 30, 2004, at 6, 9.

LEE M. MITCHELL, WITH THE NATION WATCHING: REPORT OF THE TWENTIETH CENTURY FUND TASK FORCE ON TELEVISED PRESIDENTIAL DEBATES 44–45 (1979).

Peter Morgan, The Appearance of Propriety: Ethics Reform and the Blifil Paradoxes, 44 STAN. L. REV. 593 (1992).

Otto B. Mullinax, Judicial Revision—An Argument Against the Merit Plan for Judicial Selection and Tenure, 5 STAN. L. REV. 21, 25 (1973).

Edward R. Murrow. RTNDA Convention, Oct. 15, 1958.

NATIONAL CENTER FOR STATE COURTS, MEMORANDUM ON FOSTERING JUDICIAL INDEPENDENCE IN STATE AND FEDERAL COURTS 4 (Feb. 27, 1998), available at http://ncsconline.org/WC/Publications/KIS_JudInd_S98-0281_Pub.pdf.

Caleb Nelson, A Re-Evaluation of Scholarly Explanations for the Rise of the Elective Judiciary in Antebellum America, 37 AM. J. LEGAL HIST. 190, 190 (Apr. 1993).

Chester A. Newland, "Press Coverage of the United States Supreme Court," 17 W. POL. Q. 15 (1964).

Nomination of Samuel A. Alito, Jr. to be an Associate Justice of the Supreme Court of the United States, Transcript Day 1 (remarks of Senator Kennedy).

Nomination of John G. Roberts, Jr. to be Chief Justice of the United States, Bound Transcript at 76 (response to Senator Grassley).

Northern Virginia Democrats Agree on Judges for New Appeals Court, WASH. POST, Feb. 10, 1984, at B4.

Paula Zahn Now (CNN, Oct. 31, 2005), available at http://transcripts.cnn.com/TRANSCRIPTS/0510/31/pzn.01.html.

Robert S. Peck, In Defense of Fundamental Principles: The Unconstitutionality of Tort Reform, 31 SETON HALL L. REV. 672 (2002).

People for the American Way, Fool Me Once, Television advertisement, available at http://www.savethecourt.org/tv#FoolMeOnce.

Jeannine B. Perry & Nanci A. Glassman, Supreme Court of Virginia Telephone Survey of Virginia Residents, at 19, 52 (Aug./Sept. 2005) (Continental Research; unpublished).

DANIEL R. PINELLO, IMPACT OF JUDICIAL-SELECTION METHOD ON STATE SUPREME COURT POL-ICY: INNOVATION, REACTION, AND ATROPHY 130 (1995).

KEITH T. POOLE & HOWARD ROSENTHAL, CONGRESS: A POLITICAL-ECONOMIC HISTORY OF ROLL-CALL VOTING (1997).

Richard A. Posner, Bad News, N.Y. TIMES BOOK REVIEW, July 31, 2005.

Roscoe Pound, The Causes of Popular Dissatisfaction with the Courts, reprinted in 20, JUDICATURE 178 (1936).

Roscoe Pound, The Causes of Popular Dissatisfaction with the Administration of Justice, 8 BAYLOR L. REV. 1, 23 (1956).

Todd S. Purdham, Potentially, the First Shot in All-Out Ideological War, N.Y. TIMES, Nov. 1, 2005, at A22.

DOUGLAS REED, ON EQUAL TERMS: THE CONSTITUTIONAL POLITICS OF EDUCATIONAL OPPOR-TUNITY (2001).

Chief Justice William Rehnquist, Remarks at the Symposium on Judicial Independence, University of Richmond T.C. Williams School of Law (Mar. 21, 2003) available at *http://www.supremecourtus.gov/public*info/speeches/sp_03-21-03.html.

TRACIEL V. REID, THE POLITICIZATION OF JUDICIAL RETENTION ELECTIONS: THE DEFEAT OF JUSTICES LANPHIER AND WHITE, RESEARCH ON JUDICIAL SELECTION 1999 (2000).

R.M.G., 20-year Incumbent With Foreign-Sounding Name Draws Challenge, METRO-POLITAN NEWS-ENTERPRISE (Los Angeles), April 6, 2006, at 1.

Roper Center at University of Connecticut, Public Opinion Online, 2005 polls.

Jeffrey Rosen, Judicial Exposure, N.Y. TIMES BOOK REVIEW, Jan. 29, 2006, at 27.

WILLIAM G. ROSS, A MUTED FURY: POPULISTS, PROGRESSIVES, AND LABOR UNIONS CONFRONT THE COURTS, 1890–1937 (1994).

William Ross: The Resilience of Marbury v. Madison: Why Judicial Review Has Survived so Many Attacks, 38 WAKE FOREST L. REV. 733, 741–42 (2003).

Alex Roth, Judges Gain Little on Appeal: 2 Ex-jurists, Disbarred Attorney Are Resentenced, SAN DIEGO UNION-TRIB., June 13, 2000, at A1.

Roundtable, Judicial Elections and Free Speech: Ethics and a Judge's Campaign Rhetoric, 33 U. TOL. L. REV. 315, 318 (2002).

Theodore W. Ruger, 'A Question Which Convulses the Nation': The Early Republic's Greatest Debate about the Judicial Review Power, 117 HARV. L. REV. 826 (2004).

Rebecca Mae Salokar & Kimberly A. Shaw, The Impact of National Politics on State Courts: Florida After Election 2000, 23 JUST. SYS. J. 57, 59–60 (2002).

David G. Savage, Alito Dissent Draws Scrutiny; Liberal Groups Say the Supreme Court Nominee Supported the Strip Search of a 10-Year-Old, But Experts Say That's a Distortion, L.A. TIMES, Nov. 24, 2005, at A38.

ANTONIN SCALIA, A MATTER OF INTERPRETATION: FEDERAL COURTS AND THE LAW: AN ESSAY (1997).

Terry Scanlon and Jessie Halladay, Sex Life May Be Used Against Judges, DAILY PRESS, Jan. 15, 2003.

Scarborough Country (MSNBC, Oct. 31, 2005), available at http://www.msnbc.msn.com/id/9884593/.

Jeff E. Schapiro, Split May Force Judge Selection to Go Bipartisan, RICHMOND TIMES DISPATCH, Nov. 19, 2007, at G2.

John M. Scheb & John M. Scheb II, Making Intermediate Appellate Courts Final: Assessing Jurisdictional Changes in Florida's Appellate Courts, 67 JUDICATURE 474 (1984).

NANCY SCHERER, SCORING POINTS: POLITICIANS, ACTIVISTS, AND THE LOWER FEDERAL COURT NOMINATION PROCESS (2005).

JOHN SCHLEGEL, AMERICAN LEGAL REALISM AND EMPIRICAL SOCIAL SCIENCE (1995).

Edward Schoenbaum, A Historical Look at Judicial Discipline, 54 CHI.-KENT L. REV. 1, 13–15 (1977).

Roy A. Schotland, Comment, 61 LAW & CONTEMP. PROBS. 149, 154–55 (Summer 1998).

Roy A. Schotland, Financing Judicial Elections, in FINANCING THE 2000 ELECTION 220–22 (David B. Magleby, ed., 2002).

Roy A. Schotland, Financing Judicial Elections, 2000: Change and Challenge, 2001 L. REV. MICH. ST. U. DET. C. L. 849, 890.

Roy A. Schotland, To the Endangered Species List, Add: Nonpartisan Judicial Elections, 39 WILLAMETTE L. REV. 1397, 1405, n. 34 (2003).

Victor E. Schwartz & Leah Lorber, Judicial Nullification of Civil Justice Reform Violates the Fundamental Federal Constitutional Principle of Separation of Powers: How to Restore the Right Balance, 32 RUTGERS L. J. appendix (2002).

Harold See, Comment: Judicial Selection and Decisional Independence, 61 LAW & CONTEMP. PROBS. 141, 143 (1998).

Harold See, When Free Speech and Ethical Standards Collide, 3 ENGAGE: J. FEDERALIST SOC'Y PRACTICE GROUPS, 224 (Aug. 2002).

Whitney North Seymour, The Code of Judicial Conduct from the Point of View of a Member of the Bar, 1972 UTAH L. REV. 352, 352.

JEFFREY SHAMAN, STEVEN LUBET & JAMES ALFINI, JUDICIAL CONDUCT AND ETHICS §1.12 (3rd Ed. 2000).

Peter M. Shane, Interbranch Accountability in State Government and the Constitutional Requirement of Judicial Independence, 61 LAW & CONTEMP. PROBS. 21 (Summer 1998).

Peter M. Shane, Rights, Remedies, and Restraint, 64 CHI.-KENT L. REV. 531, 546 (1988).

Scott Shane, Ideology Serves as a Wild Card on Court Pick, N.Y. TIMES, Nov. 4, 2005, at A1.

Scott Shane, In Capital and at the Court, Baseball Rules, N.Y. TIMES, Nov. 5, 2005, at A12.

CHARLES H. SHELDON & LINDA S. MAULE, CHOOSING JUSTICE: THE RECRUITMENT OF STATE AND FEDERAL JUDGES 76 (1998).

JUDITH N. SHKLAR, LEGALISM: LAW, MORALS, AND POLITICAL TRIALS (1964).

Daniel W. Shuman & Anthony Champagne, Removing the People from the Legal Process: The Rhetoric and Research on Judicial Selection and Juries, 3 PSYCHOL. PUB. POL'Y & L. 242, 243 (1997).

The Situation Room (CNN, Oct. 31, 2005), available at http://transcripts.cnn.com/TRANSCRIPTS/0510/31/sitroom.01.html.

The Situation Room (CNN, Oct. 31, 2005), available at http://transcripts.cnn.com/TRANSCRIPTS/0510/31/sitroom.03.html.

ELLIOT E. SLOTNICK & JENNIFER A. SEGAL, TELEVISION NEWS AND THE SUPREME COURT: ALL THE NEWS THAT'S FIT TO AIR 251 (1998).

James M. Snyder, Jr. & Tim Groseclose, Estimating Party Influence in Congressional Roll Call Voting, 44 AM. J. POL. SCI. 193–211 (2000).

Leslie Southwick, The Least of Evils for Judicial Selection, 21 MISS. C. L. REV. 209, 220 (2002).

HERBERT J. STORING (with the editorial assistance of Murray Dry), WHAT THE ANTI-FEDERALISTS WERE FOR: THE POLITICAL THOUGHT OF THE OPPONENTS OF THE CONSTITUTION (1981).

HARRY P. STUMPF, AMERICAN JUDICIAL POLITICS 171 (1988).

CASS SUNSTEIN, REPUBLIC.COM (2001).

G. Alan Tarr, Rethinking the Selection of State Supreme Court Justices, 39 WILLAMETTE L. REV. 1445, 1446–47 (2003).

G. ALAN TARR, UNDERSTANDING STATE CONSTITUTIONS 161–170 (1998).

G. ALAN TARR & MARY CORNELIA ALDIS PORTER, CHAPTER 3, STATE SUPREME COURTS IN STATE AND NATION (1988).

HANNIS TAYLOR, THE ORIGIN AND GROWTH OF THE ENGLISH CONSTITUTION: AN HISTORICAL TREATISE (1898).

Stuart Taylor, Jr., The NewsHour (PBS, Dec. 28, 2005), available at http://www.pbs.org/newshour/bb/law/july-dec05/alito_12-28.html.

THE GLOBAL EXPANSION OF JUDICIAL POWER (C. Neal Tate & Torbjorn Vallinder, eds., 1995).

Texas State Supreme Court Elections Data 2004, available at http://www.justiceatstake.org/contentViewer.asp>breadcrumb=4,126,111,462. Last visited on August 14, 2006.

Clive S. Thomas et al., Interest Groups and State Court Elections: A New Era and Its Challenges, 87 JUDICATURE 135, 138 (2003).

ALEXIS DE TOCQUEVILLE, DEMOCRACY IN AMERICA 257 (Harvey C. Mansfield & Delba Wintrop, trans. and eds., 2000).

Robin Toner & Adam Liptak, 2 Camps, Playing Down Nuances, Stake Out Firm Stands, N.Y. TIMES, Nov. 1, 2005, at A25.

Jeffrey Toobin, Comments at Bench Press, Panel 2, Impartial Judging in a Results Oriented World (Oct. 17, 2005).

Carol Ann Traut & Craig F. Emmert, Expanding the Integrated Model of Judicial Decision Making: The California Justices and Capital Punishment, 60 J. POL. 1177 (1998).

Nicole Tsong, Anti-Abortion Group Wants Judges' Views, ANCHORAGE DAILY NEWS, November 20, 2004, at A1.

Gerald F. Uelman, Otto Kaus and the Crocodile, 30 LOY. L.A. L. REV. 971 (1997).

U.S. Chamber Institute for Legal Reform, 2005 State Liability Systems Ranking Study (Mar. 8, 2005), available at http://www.instituteforlegalreform.com/harris/pdf/HarrisPoll2005-Summary.pdf. Last visited on August 14, 2006.

MARY VOLCANSEK, JUDICIAL MISCONDUCT: A CROSS-NATIONAL COMPARISON 68–74 (1996).

Voters Oust Veteran L.A. Judge, Replace Her With Bagel Shop Owner, ASSOC. PRESS, June 8, 2006, available at http://www.signonsandiego.com/news/state/20060608-1920-ca-judgeousted.html.

John M. Walker, Jr., Politics and the Confirmation Process: The Importance of Congressional Restraint in Safeguarding Judicial Independence, 55 SYRACUSE L. REV. 1 (2004).

RICHARD A. WATSON & RONDAL G. DOWNING, THE POLITICS OF THE BENCH AND BAR: JUDICIAL SELECTION UNDER THE MISSOURI NONPARTISAN COURT PLAN (1969).

Peter D. Webster, Selection and Retention of Judges: Is There One "Best" Method?, 23 FLA. ST. U. L. REV. 1, 36 (1995).

Nathan Richard Wilderman, Bought Elections: Republican Party of Minnesota v. White, 11 GEO. MASON L. REV. 765, 767 (2003).

DEREK WILSON, IN THE LION'S COURT: POWER, AMBITION, AND SUDDEN DEATH IN THE REIGN OF HENRY VIII (2003).

Glenn R. Winters, How Much Do Voters Know or Care About Judicial Candidates?, 38 J. AM. JUD. SOC'Y. 141 (1955).

John T. Wold & John H. Culver, The Defeat of the California Justices: The Campaign, the Electorate, and the Issue of Judicial Accountability, 70 JUDICATURE 348 (1986).

GORDON S. WOOD, THE CREATION OF THE AMERICAN REPUBLIC, 1776–1787 (1972).

BOB WOODWARD & SCOTT ARMSTRONG, THE BRETHREN: INSIDE THE SUPREME COURT 140 (1979).

Jim Wooten, Voters in Dark on Judge Races, ATL. J. CONST., Nov. 28, 2004, available at http://www.ajc.com/opinion/content/opinion/wooten/2004/112804.html. Last visited on August 14, 2006.

Gerry Yandel, TV Watch, ATL. J. CONST., June 23, 1992; CMPA Election Watch, Oct. 30, 2000, available at http://cmpa.com/election2004/JournalistsMonopolize.htm.

Frances Kahn Zemans, The Accountable Judge: Guardian of Judicial Independence, 72 S. CAL. L. REV. 625, 640 (1999).

Index

abortion: anti-abortion groups, 58, 65, 155; parental consent, 64; press coverage of cases, 168; restrictions on, 64, 154, 166; spousal notification, 154, 164. *See also Planned Parenthood v. Casey; Roe v. Wade*

Abrams, Dan, 173

Abramson, Leslie, 34

activist judges. *See* judicial activism

Adams, John, 200

advertising: campaign, 54–56, 94, 135, 200; by lawyers, 44, 190

Alger, Dean E., 160

Alito, Samuel A., Jr.: confirmation hearings, 123–28, 181, 192; media coverage of, 161–70, 192; nomination of, 153; opinions, 126, 153–58, 178

Alliance for Justice, 157

Althouse, Ann, 183

American Bar Association: Canons of Judicial Ethics (1924), 28–30; Canons of Professional Ethics, 26; Code of Judical Conduct (1990), 31, 34, 36; Code of Judicial Conduct (1972), 23, 27, 30; Commission on the 21st Century Judiciary, 22, 31; Joint Commission to Evaluate the Model Code of Judicial Conduct, 31–32, 35, 39; Model Code of Professional Responsibility (1969), 33; Model Rules of Judicial Conduct (1999), 39; Model Rules of Professional Conduct (1983), 34

American Judicature Society, 68, 77, 135

American Lawyer, 190

"And For the Sake of the Kids," 64

announce clause, 37, 65

anti-court sentiment, 21–22

Anti-federalists, 1

appearance of propriety: constitutional objections, 35–39; in contemporary culture, 22–23, 40–43; erosion of, 32–39; media influence on, 23; philosophical objections to, 32–33; practical objections to, 33–35; rules regulating, 5-6, 24–32; vagueness of, 33, 49n50

appointments, judicial: effect on judicial independence, 84–85; effect on judicial legitimacy, 89–90; effect on judicial quality, 93; gubernatorial, 84, 89, 100n15, 101n20, 138, 144–45; legislative, 84–85, 89; press coverage of, 84; selection committees, 85, 89–90, 93, 120; versus elections, 119–121

Armstrong, Scott, 159

Aron, Nan, 157

Askew, Verbena, 141

Association of Professional Responsibility Lawyers, 34

Bacon, Sir Francis, 25, 47n23

Barry, Dave, 156

Bashman, Howard, 183

Bates v. State Bar of Arizona, 190

"Bench Press: The Collision of Media, Politics, Public Pressure, and an Independent Judiciary" (symposium), 5, 160, 172, 191, 194, 195, 197, 199

Bennett Jr., Lerone, 116

Bird, Rose, 55

Black, Hugh, 115

Black Sox scandal, 27

Blitzer, Wolf, 153–54

Bork, Robert, 63

"Borking," 156

Boston, Charles, 27, 28

Breitel, Charles, 187, 189

The Brethren (Woodward & Armstrong), 159